# Observer of the Dance
## 1958–1982

Nigel and Maude Gosling–'Alexander Bland'
(*Photo:* Jane Bown)

# Observer
# of the Dance
# 1958–1982

ALEXANDER BLAND

In Memory

DANCE BOOKS LTD
9 Cecil Court, London

*First published in 1985 by Dance Books Ltd.,*
*9 Cecil Court, London WC2N 4EZ.*

*© 1985 by the estate of Nigel Gosling*

*Printed in Great Britain at The Bath Press, Avon*

*Designed by Peter L. Moldon*

*British Library Cataloguing in Publication Data*
Bland, Alexander
Observer of the dance: 1958–1982.
1. Ballet—History—20th century
Rn: Nigel Gosling and Maude Lloyd    I. Title
792.8'45        GV1787

ISBN 0–903102–91–9

When so many of Nigel's friends asked whether a book like this was going to be published, I thought that perhaps it should be, and was tremendously pleased when David Leonard of Dance Books said that he would help me in the venture.

It has been enormously difficult choosing the pieces, and although I would, of course, like to have included all the dancers, ballets and companies that Nigel ever wrote about, it was obviously impossible. My guide line has been not necessarily to be comprehensive, but rather to pick out the pieces either about events which themselves were of lasting interest, or pieces which seem to throw new light, or to reveal a particular truth about a subject.

I wish to thank Tristram Holland and Terence Kilmartin for their encouragement and practical help, without which this book would not have been possible. Also my thanks to Kathy Elgin for her part in bringing it to fruition.

MAUDE LLOYD

Most of the review pieces in this book originally appeared in the *Observer* between 1958 and 1982 and we are grateful to the editors for allowing us to reproduce them.

# Contents

Nigel Gosling was one of the most gifted and versatile journalist-critics of his time. He was art critic of the *Observer* from 1962 to 1975, and dance critic (under the pseudonym Alexander Bland) from 1955 until three months before his death on 22 May 1982.

He joined the paper in 1950 as features editor and general arts reporter when he was already over forty. A member of a distinguished, well-to-do East Anglian family, he had spent his early adult years, after Eton and Cambridge, first in the diplomatic service in Berlin, then painting, writing experimental fiction and generally cultivating the arts. He was a convinced pacifist, and when war came declared himself a conscientious objector; but he served throughout, with great distinction, in the Red Cross.

Such a background of high-born and high-brow dilettantism sounds an unpromising basis for the more practical and down to earth demands of newspaper work. But Nigel Gosling showed an immediate natural flair both as an editor and a writer, and played a major part in the paper as the post-war restrictions on its size were gradually lifted.

He was capable of turning his hand to anything – from laying out pages, scribbling elegant captions and inventing witty headlines, to book-reviewing, profile-writing and general reporting. He even went up to Aintree to report the Grand National (with his slight but wiry build and sharp features he had something of the look of an aristocratic jockey – and indeed had been a point-to-point rider in his youth) and telephoned an expert and vividly entertaining dispatch for the paper's front page.

But it was as art critic and dance critic that he made his name. For twelve years he combined the two roles, foot-slogging round the galleries in the daytime and ballet-going at night. He was not a didactic or prescriptive critic; he did not lumber himself with theoretical preconceptions; he was never snobbish or dismissive. His function, he felt, was to describe and interpret, to stimulate and enlighten.

Aesthetically, he was in tune with the age, with a natural feeling for modern art, but the fact that he was instinctively sympathetic to what was new did not blind him to the virtues of the old. Indeed, in the case of ballet, his assiduity in attending the umpteenth performance of *Swan Lake* or *Giselle* (because of some minor change of cast or production detail that might call for comment or encouragement) was a source of awed admiration among his colleagues.

One of the great strengths of Alexander Bland as a reviewer was that the pen-name covered a unique critical double act – for his deft descriptive talent and interpretive intelligence were under-pinned by the technical insight and expertise of his beautiful wife, the former dancer Maude Lloyd, who had been a leading ballerina with the Ballet Rambert and was one of the outstanding British dancers of her time.

The combination gave their work a rare authority, and their influence in the ballet world went far beyond the critic's normal purview. For instance it was Alexander Bland who played a crucial role in urging that Nureyev should be invited to Covent Garden after his defection in Paris in 1961. Nureyev remained a devoted friend, and he interrupted a crammed schedule of performances in America to fly over to London to see Nigel before he died.

After retiring as art critic in 1975, Nigel found time to add several more books to the number he had already written. Monographs on Gustave Doré and the photographer Nadar (nineteenth-century French art and culture held a special place in his affections) were followed by a lively study of the Belle Epoque in Paris and a delightful evocation of Leningrad, the birthplace of Russian ballet, where he and Maude felt instinctively at home. Other books, on various aspects of dance, included a history of the Royal Ballet.

Nigel Gosling was so innocent of the resentments, snobberies, aggressions and neuroses that most of us are prone to that one was tempted to regard him as a sort of saint. It was not a designation that he himself – with his Puckish irreverence – would have allowed, or even understood. His gentleness and serenity were innate and instinctual. He would not have been aware that he was a man of unusual virtue as well as unusual gifts; but he was.

TERENCE KILMARTIN
Literary editor of the *Observer*

Nigel Gosling was a highly civilised and sensitive writer, knowledgeable in all the arts but also modest and kindly. He never tried to make his readers feel small nor the artists insignificant. In short he was, I think, an ideal critic.

What more can I say? Only that his books and writings will be important to dance historians in the future and are now a source of great interest and pleasure as, with deceptive simplicity, he catches the fleeting moments of theatre art and pins them down like butterflies for our inspection.

This collection is taken from reviews that cover dance companies and artists, principally in London, between 1958 and 1982. It includes some intriguing observations and evaluations for any of us who saw those performances or were part of them, or anyone who wants to learn something about a period that is already past and gone forever.

*Margot Fonteyn.*

I really came to know and trust Nigel through his writing. He was completely without prejudice, and extraordinarily detached – I felt he was like the Greek philosophers he admired so much.

He and Maude had seen me dance with the Kirov in Paris in 1961. Then, when I went to London to dance in Margot Fonteyn's gala in 1962, she asked them to take me to Covent Garden where she was to dance *Giselle* that night. I dined with them afterwards, and so began our long friendship. As soon as my English was good enough to read with understanding, it became clear to me from Nigel's pieces in the *Observer* that here was a person I could trust. I could see, even then, that as a critic he was totally objective, and never became so closely involved that he could not be scrupulously fair. As I grew to know him better while he was working with me on my autobiography in 1962, I came to realise his fantastic ability to see both sides of a question.

It was with Nigel and Maude that I was first able to indulge my love of films, and to catch up on some of those things that I had left Russia to find. We called those film evenings 'Roxys'. They were fun as well as stimulating, with lots of talk over dinner with designers Nicholas Georgiadis and Barry Kay – who worked with me later on many productions – and many avant-garde film-makers, writers and others who excited me with their ideas. I saw the Eisenstein masterpieces, the early Hollywood greats, and films by Genet, Markopolous and Kenneth Anger. My first meeting with the French film-maker Franju was there – I remember that he was slightly tipsy and insisted on dancing a polka with Nigel, who remained as imperturbable as ever. I also saw my first glimpse of Martha Graham on film one evening, and knew that I had to see more.

Nigel was widely read, and his interest in the new went hand in hand with his admiration for the great works of the past. But he never flaunted his knowledge at any time or in any place. And though he was intellectually my superior, he created an atmosphere in which I could talk to him freely and on equal terms. He always managed to do this – to find a language compatible with those around him. To me he seemed like a Francis of Assisi, who could even talk to the birds and the beasts. He never tried to influence or to hand out advice, but encouraged one to develop and express one's own ideas – to let one's imagination run free and to take risks. He rarely talked about himself but, if asked, would give his own views clearly and then dismiss them as quite irrelevant. Above all, he was fun to be with, with his incredible quirky sense of humour, his unfailing youthfulness of spirit. He always said that he would love to live to be a hundred, life was so fascinating.

The relationship between us as critic and performer was never difficult. There was a tacit understanding between us. The friendship was far more important. I try not to read dance criticism by anybody. But for those who are not as involved as I am, his writing on ballet will be as illuminating as his writing on art was for me. His ability to put the essential concept of a work into words was amazing. He made everything fall into place for me. He always had his finger on the pulse.

Nigel was far more than just a friend. He and Maude were like my family, a foundation stone in my life, a base which I could pull towards or push away from. He was a man to love.

*Rudolf Nureyev*

# The Fifties and Sixties

# The Dancer's Art (Extracts from *The Dancer's World*)

Ballet is above all others an art which conceals itself, which keeps its heart up its sleeve. In spite of its dazzle and showmanship it is a reticent medium. At his first visit the viewer may hardly disentangle even its basic principles.

The fundament on which all ballet is built – and which even a moderately shrewd eye will have discerned behind the panoply of physical beauty, surprise, drama, spectacle and personality – is simply movement. Painting cannot move, literature does not, drama need not (though the cinema must, proving itself ballet's near relation) and music moves only in that temporal way which makes it a dancer's perfect partner. But dancing *is* movement. A motionless ballet is a contradiction in terms.

The basic element of movement itself contains, in dancing, a mysterious and fascinating duality. This ordered energy incarnates the secret marriage of mind and matter, of reason and emotion – of geometry and the human heart if you prefer.

Ballet is a three-dimensional art and, though the laws of gravity compel it to be, in general, no more than high relief, individual dancers can and do scoop out of the air as they move forms and volumes as amply satisfying as those of sculpture. The voids held between classically rounded arms or between the two partners in a *pas de deux* speak as eloquently as the hollows in a figure by Moore; and the way in which they merge and melt into one another is something which no sculptor can achieve.

In dancing there enters the almost unanalysable attribute which we call 'quality of movement'. This quality, which suffuses every gesture of a dancer from the simplest walk to the most intricate evolution, is without much doubt rooted in the area where physical and spiritual meet. Proportion, fitness and training play a big part; but intelligence, emotion and moral – even social – background contribute as much.

A great role demands that its interpreter should at least be enough aware of greatness to be able to portray it.

It is certainly true that tension – the result of two opposing forces – is the key to classical ballet. It is the 'pulling up' of the muscles of the back and legs, the tightening of the spring running through shoulders, spine and pelvis, which creates that firmness underlying a soft outline which we admire here as we do when we find it in a musical phrase or in a line of poetry. It is this duality, which Marxist philosophy might call the dialectic of dancing, on which the choreographer plays, mingling sharp accents and slow gliding and curves, rough energy and melting liquid grace in the proportions he desires. And it is above all the precious instant when, at a moment of climax, a great dancer (balancing subconsciously each muscle in the body at the right degree of tension) executes a motion of extreme difficulty with tender precision which affords the ballet-lover his supreme pleasure. He partakes in perfection.

In ballet (as in all arts) there are no rules, only risks.


## The Critical Tightrope

'Critic' is about the spikiest word in the language, and criticism the most unlovable of occupations. It is often held to be also the most useless. Couldn't the whole practice be abolished, letting the creator speak directly to his audience?

Whether or not this might be a good thing, it is obviously a dream situation – a dream evoked more often by the artists than by the audience. But certainly the system, which has jellified into a fixed convention, needs looking at. To begin with we might disentangle the two fundamentally different branches of criticism. Confusion between them often leads to ill-aimed discussion.

The true, or academic, critic – usually a hard-cover performer – starts from a special premise. He chooses his own subject. Naturally this is usually somebody he finds especially admirable or interesting. He will take the sculpture of Donatello or Rossini's operas or the novels of Fielding and subject them to new analysis and appraisal. He can assume that his readers are already interested in the topic (otherwise they wouldn't be reading the book), and roughly familiar with it. He does not have to inform – he explains and persuades. He is both deeply sunk in his subject and detached from it. He is not taking part in the mysterious flux of producer-consumer relationship which, from day to day and week to week, imperceptibly marks the course of any art's progression.

How different is the task of the journalistic-critic! He is first and foremost a reporter. He is sent out to survey a specified territory and to come back with an account of what he has found. In this capacity he performs an essential distributive role: whether we ignore his assessments or not, most of us make our actual first acquaintance with a work of art via a critical review. Only when he has reported it can he go on to analyse and evaluate it. And in so doing he has to bear in mind that he is not only holding it up to the judgement of history; he is also acting as instant adviser to some reader who may be wondering whether to spend money on it or not.

This immediate, practical reaction involves a persistent breaking of that pseudo-rule of journalism, that news and comment should not be confused. In this the journalist-critic resembles his colleagues on the sports, fashion or business pages. In fact his role might be clearer if, like them, he were labelled Drama-Correspondent, Music-Correspondent, Art-Correspondent and so on, distinguishing him from the academic critic.

The journalist-critic is involved with several other complications from which his academic colleague is free. In the first place the intermittent reporting and discussion of an artist as he develops may actually affect this development – not by his influence on the artist, which is absolutely minimal, but indirectly, through his influence over his readers (including other critics). And secondly, he operates in a competitive framework. He has to compete for readers. He must draw them from rival attractions in other parts of the periodical in which he is writing, and even on the same page. He has the marvellous chance to make converts; but he is subject to the quick switch-off. And in the same way the artists about whom he writes are mostly struggling for survival – Rossini and Fielding are safe, but new talent can be extinguished.

Dealing as he does mainly with living people, the journalist-critic faces another problem – his personal relations. It can be maintained that he cannot judge a man's work unless he knows the man and his problems; it is also true that knowledge of these problems (the artist's wife may be dying of cancer) may cloud his judgement or affect his

5

recording of it. There is no completely good answer; each critic must tread this tightrope in his own way.

And of course there is the basic rough and ready form in which he has to work, involving a snap judgement on a complex work which may have taken years to create – a judgement of whose limitations he is constantly aware, and which is further open to editorial cuts which, however carefully made, may alter the whole tone of the piece. If the journalist-critic is sometimes guilty of insensitivity, it must be remembered that he himself has to make regular public appearances in postures over which he has no final control. He must accept this as part of his job; it presupposes a basic and very wholesome humility which is one of the best aspects of his profession.

The two different varieties of criticism demand of course totally different qualities in the critic. The academic critic needs the virtues of a good retriever – perseverance, concentration, patience, reliability. The journalist-critic is more of a hunting-dog. He must be alert, active, wide-ranging, with a good nose and a strong voice; he may follow some false scents, but he should keep our interest riveted on the chase and be relied on to flush every bird in the covert. He is not a volunteer like his colleague. He is a mercenary – but he chooses which side he is fighting on.

Few people object to reporting, though there is a natural resistance to that kind of shorthand description which amounts, in the eyes of the uninitiated, to jargon. This is naturally commoner in the journalist than in the academic – he has to express himself in frequent short bursts rather than in a long single exposition, and cannot pause each time to explain himself – and is common to all subjects. Readers tend to get a bit huffy about the subjects they know least about, as can be expected. They sometimes object too, to the tone of the report. Good criticism is based on good writing, and writing is a craft. Like all crafts it is highly traditional. For instance it is a practice in almost all journals that the theatre and film critics should be witty fellows, hard hitting and given to extremes. At least one joke is expected in every piece – often in every paragraph. Such an approach applied to music, or art or ballet, would seem painfully brash – even Shaw's scintillating somersaults sometimes have an exhibitionist air.

An essential part of the journalist-critic's craft is brevity – which inevitably means over-generalisations which would be unforgivable in an extended study. Even a 'long' article by newspaper standards (1,000 words), amounts to only three pages of a normal book, and regular pieces seldom exceed 500 words. Few editors, moreover, will

6

put up for long with measured, cautious judgements. They (or their readers) demand that the critic's neck should be stuck well out – and left there.

But the real hostilities arise when the critic moves on from information and interpretation into consumer-guidance, in other words evaluation. Here an irrational movement often takes place in the reader's mind. Though the opinion is obviously solicited and palpably personal and fallible, something of the collective authority of the organ it appears in rubs off on it. Views which, if expressed in conversation, would be received with calm interest, even gratitude, tend to take on the air of volunteered ex cathedra judgement. The answer to the simple question which must lie behind any critical review – What's on? What's it like? Should I spend my time and money on it? – turn into some kind of bogus schoolmasterly mark-awarding.

The ways in which a journalist-critic circumvents these snags, which are inherent in his middleman's position, together with his ability to fan the coals of his art without betraying long-term values, are what make him more, or less, effective. If he is faithful to high, idealistic standards he may be denounced as disliking his subject; if he consistently enthuses he runs the risk of being dubbed superficial and modish. In the long run his most important role is probably just to keep his readers paying attention to the works he is discussing – whether his own view on them proves correct is a very minor importance. To be wrong is the critic's occupational risk – none has ever escaped it completely. But who cares now about Baudelaire's misfires? The important thing is that he encouraged Delacroix.

Two simple steps could be taken to reduce the animosity which seems to extend, in a very understandable way, to all critics. The first is that more facilities should be provided for the artists and their supporters to answer back. The second would be the setting up of a really objective critic-critic. Most artists think critics are too severe, while audiences, in my experience, invariably think them too kind. I hope one day to see a powerful figure – quick to spot errors of fact or taste or integrity – lambasting us all on the TV screen. He would surely become a much-loved Television Personality overnight. And he would be performing a useful service.

*It is every ballet company's dream – indeed necessity – to build up a steady audience. But once there, this audience may grow into a furry monster whose*

7

*affectionate, inevitably conservative, hug will strangle the life out of its loved one. Once ballet was in the nose itself of the cultural missile. How many of the intelligent young go to it now? It has become trapped in a band of balletomanes.*


## Anniversary of the reopening of Covent Garden

The tenth anniversary of the reopening of Covent Garden, which was celebrated last Monday, was a modest occasion for joy, but a real one. During the war it had looked as though this beautiful, draughty, uneconomical old theatre was lost to the jitterbugs.

A medium-priced box of fireworks would have been appropriate. Instead of which the evening was illuminated by a performance by Margot Fonteyn of dazzling candlepower. *The Sleeping Beauty* had been the ballet chosen for the reopening in 1946 and here it was again, hardly changed.

Hardly – but how much that little is. Margot Fonteyn was already in those days an admirable Princess Aurora. This role – generally considered the supreme test of the classical dancer – is one on which she kept her eye firmly fixed in the intervening years. It was obvious that she was studying patiently and doggedly to perfect it. The details became more delicate, the style in the three contrasting acts more consistent, the mime more natural, the technical feats more and more invisible. At last the whole performance was all of a piece. And then at this point she paused. The tiny gap between the perfect dancing of the part and the perfect theatrical performance of it remained unbridged.

What was lacking was suddenly revealed on Monday night. No dancer to-day can match Margot Fonteyn in the simple gift of natural line and movement; to this she now triumphantly added theatrical *excitement*, a glow of dancing for the love of it, an inner *bravura* which stung the audience into enthusiasm. To see this unique combination of restraint and exuberance was a memorable experience. The rest of the company stood up heroically to this high standard. Somes was a noble and reliable Prince. Ashton injected new life into old Carabosse. Beryl Grey waved a graceful wand as the Lilac Fairy. Rosemary Lindsay and Annette Page were charming in their Fairy variations; but these

8

were all exceptionally good. Ten years have certainly improved *this* ballet.

26.2.56

## Twenty-fifth anniversary performance, Sadler's Wells

Looking back on this twenty-fifth anniversary of its opening perform-ance (the pedant will note that this took place at the Old Vic: the first performance at Sadler's Wells being ten days later) it is hard to see just where the company crossed the canyon between 'arriving' and 'arrived'. Perhaps during the war. Before this, ballet had its enthusiasts and connoisseurs, its experiments and small gallant ventures: after-wards, the picture had changed. Every girl in Britain seemed hell-bent for ballet. The company moved from Islington to the splendours of the Royal Opera House, the Arts Council weighed in, and the audiences rolled up in their thousands.

It's a remarkable achievement. From the little group of dancers pio-neering in Rosebery Avenue through the early years with Markova and Dolin in the lead, to the massive modern organisation with its junior company, school, enormous staff and international reputation – all this in one short lifetime. There is no question whose lifetime that is. It was Ninette de Valois who started the venture under the wing of Lilian Baylis, and it is she who still sits very firmly in the directorial chair. She had a notable collaborator in Constant Lambert, and she still has one in Frederick Ashton. But the hallmark of the company is her own.

The chief among many reasons for her success has been her steadiness of aim. In her short association with the Diaghilev ballet she became aware of the value of the classical tradition which lay behind all his experiments, and it has been her constant determination to plant this tradition on British soil so that all future generations might benefit from it. From this heroic task she has not been diverted by the tempting rewards of novelty or foreign stars. Indeed one has the impression that, like a gardener, she sometimes tends to nip off to-day's buds in order that later blossoms should be more magnificent.

That she should thus devote herself to the classical tradition is in some ways strange, as her experience of ballet started with the wild experiments of Diaghilev's last years, and her own bent as a choreo-grapher is distinctly unclassical. She has been rewarded with the god-send of a prodigious star in the person of Margot Fonteyn, and with the

9

firm establishment of a State-recognised company and school, with a staunch public to support it.

Dame Ninette would be the first to admit the dangers inherent in this institutionalised system. Rigidity, bureaucracy, ossification – these are the attendant evil spirits which hover perpetually over a State theatre, and which Diaghilev fled to escape from. Let us rejoice in the fact that they have got something so substantial to hover over, and pray that they may long be fended off.

6.5.56

## Symphonic Variations, The Royal Ballet, Covent Garden

The programme at Covent Garden on Thursday was like a Blake sandwich – one Song of Innocence spread rather thin between two fat Songs of Experience. It goes without saying that, this being an English company, innocence won hands down. Ashton's *Symphonic Variations*, presented now with a new team, remains one of his most satisfying works. The English are not adept at abstract art. Yet here is the most abstract of ballets, empty of story, character, even atmosphere: and it brilliantly succeeds.

The truth is, of course, that it *has* an atmosphere, though a very elusive one. It is the daisy-pied English lyrical simplicity which shines through Chaucer, English madrigals, or Blake. 'When the voices of children are heard on the green' – well, they sound something like this looks (how right Sophie Fedorovitch was to choose turf colour for her famous setting). The spare choreography lies lightly on the music, firm enough to support the occasional sags yet supple to follow its delicate line.

16.9.56

## The Bolshoi

Though the Bolshoi ballet season is not yet over, we have seen all its four ballets. It may seem premature to rush into generalisations. But the impact of the visit has been severe enough to make it worth while to try, as we get up and dust ourselves down, to make a snap analysis of what it was that hit us.

The first quality, which stood out a mile, was sincerity and moral earnestness. There was no trace anywhere of the happy accident, of trickiness or high jinks. Every detail of theme and performance had been, one felt, seriously – not to say solemnly – discussed. All those taking part seemed confident that they were doing something important. Never for a moment was there any sign of doubt that ballet is a Great Art, and that these were great ballets. This sublime confidence lent punch to the production and strength to the dancers.

There is a reverse side to this picture. Confidence leads, as we know, to sluggishness. The civic pride which lends such weight to the ballets imposes on them also something of the music-bound unwieldiness of a Lord Mayor's Show.

The basis of Soviet ballet – as apparently of all art in Russia at present – is literary. Much attention is paid to the story, to find 'themes that not only provide a spectacle, but carry a deep philosophical message,' to quote the Soviet ballet critic Slonimsky. Great respect is paid to 'The Classics'. A ballet based on a story from Shakespeare or Pushkin has an added glamour.

In the new Russian ballets such as we saw, the tendency is to eliminate all dancing which does not carry the story forward or create character. To our eyes the extreme application of this doctrine (first preached by Noverre and revived by Fokine) leads to a limited and monotonous dance mime.

'Realism' is, of course, the war-cry of Soviet art (with 'formalism' on the enemy's flag). In the ballets we have seen it paid high dividends. One was convinced again and again by little details of production or movement, by the ease with which costumes were worn, by the way a man led his partner into a dance. But in the new productions one saw how hampering a style it is. The classical dance is based on a deeply worked-out stage convention which creates a world where everything is possible. It is paradoxical to find that Russians, whose folk art is steeped in Byzantine art, should be turning away from formalism.

A certain earthbound quality seems inherent in the Soviet approach to ballet. The great achievement of Diaghilev was to splinter it off from opera and drama, to let it loose to develop its own idiom. In doing so it has shot off to some odd extremes; it is often artificial, whimsy, chi-chi, hysterical or brash.

But its virtue is an immediate sharp impact whose nearest

11

equivalent lies in poetry. Accustomed to the stabbing daggerstrokes of short one-act ballets, we find these Russian productions diffuse, long-winded and rather pedestrian. It is only fair to say that in Moscow our ballets may seem meagre, heartless and exaggerated. It is the confrontation of something short, sharp, imaginatively bold and if necessary expendable, and something laboriously and solidly-carpentered, heavy but built to last.

The forward-looking face-to-the-sun attitude of official Russian artistic policy is carried, in theory, into the ballet – sometimes to extreme lengths. 'To the heroes of Tchaikovsky's ballets life is worth fighting and dying for, and this is typical of the hero of Soviet ballet.' It seems almost impossible to make this formula fit the melancholy hero of *Swan Lake* (or indeed the whole outlook of the composer, a neurotic pessimist who committed suicide). None of the works we have seen fit, as it happens, the official heroic mould.

Though we may have doubts about current ballet aesthetics in Russia, there can be no two opinions about the standard of dancing and mime. The vast size of the Bolshoi theatre has surely been an important factor. It has made the stage action more self-contained than it is in our theatres, where performers project themselves all too actively over the footlights. It has also allowed the dancers a much freer way of moving than we are accustomed to. They sometimes lack the precision which we rightly value; but in exchange they have a natural, loose style and an exuberant bound which make our dancers look as though they were in corsets. The girls can be more feminine, the men more manly. The corps-de-ballet moves not like one, but like many with a single thought. Warmth and humanity are breathed into every step.

Immense stress is evidently placed on that flowing quality known in singing as 'cantilena'. The different steps melt into each other, the jump into the arabesque, the arabesque into the turn. Supple backs, soft feet, generous arms, high arabesques, mobile (to our eyes, sometimes too mobile) hands, above all a magnificent soft, strong *plié* – all play their part towards giving that superlubricated quality which is the hallmark of this company. This is not the only way of dancing. Sometimes, indeed, in the newer ballets, the eye tires of the serpentine curves. But it gives a wonderful velvety finish to a classical step.

One thing which we had expected to find was missing – the so-called 'Grand Manner'. This queenly dominance, so perfectly displayed, we are told, by Diaghilev's stars, was no doubt a product of the Imperial Theatre in St Petersburg. Such of it as remains is probably in the West. At its best this style has the austerity and authority of a thoroughbred performing *haute école*. But it is certainly undemocratic, and also opposed to the looser, more natural style which was always typical of Moscow dancers.

The girls are long-limbed and elegant, but at the same time gentle and simple. (Not all, of course, are paragons. It was nice to notice now and then a more homely style in the back row, or occasionally even nearer.) The men are more thickset than we are accustomed to; but this enables them to be unostentatiously strong, and soft without being sissy. Their larger limbs fill out the movements in a three-dimensional way to which we have become unaccustomed. Western male dancers have become, perhaps, too concentrated on line. There is no male posturing or hauteur. The same effect is achieved by proper carriage. Concentrating on big, simple steps, they jump prodigiously, finish honestly (what Western dancer habitually finishes a double turn with a deep *plié* in fifth?) and the best have a relaxed control even in the air, which gives the true classical touch.

When it comes to 'character' dancing, the superlative skill of these Russians is equally marked. Nowhere in the world (except maybe in Africa) will you find men with such savage, virile rhythm. And nowhere – but perhaps this isn't surprising – will you find girls to dance a mazurka with such a suggestion of fire blazing behind an elegant etiquette.

Taken all in all, the visit of the Bolshoi company has given British ballet the biggest shaking-up for many a long year. And not only ballet. After many stops and starts it so happens that this monumental sample of social-realism has arrived at a moment when Millet is being brought out of the cellar and George Eliot put back on the shelves. We can now all think clear and argue louder while we await the second visit, which must be the hope of every lover of ballet.

21.10.56

*Doubtful, however, as we may be about* Romeo *and* Juliet *as a work of art, it is fascinating as a sincere utterance in a strange, half-forgotten tongue: and as the vehicle for a star-performance of the first order by Galina Ulanova.*

13

## *The Prince of the Pagodas*, The Royal Ballet, Covent Garden

It is often asserted that a fairy-story makes the best ballet. This seems to fix the art at a fairly low level, and I would accept the theory only in so far as it can be stretched to include the unnaturalistic or even surrealistic. Straightforward fairy-tales come to life only when they have some contemporary application; this usually means in practice that they can be interpreted in Freudian terms.

For *The Prince of the Pagodas* – the first British three-act ballet with specially commissioned music (score by Benjamin Britten) and therefore something of a landmark – John Cranko has bravely devised a new fairy-tale, compounded of several old ingredients. A modest and father-loving young Chinese Princess, Belle Rose, is bullied by her sister, Belle Epine, until she is snatched away by a magic Salamander. She repels his reptilian advances until he has mortified the wicked sister, and released her father from the cage where she had imprisoned him. Belle Rose thereupon embraces the Salamander, he is revealed as a Prince and wedding bells (presumably) ring out.

The tale stands up to the psychological test bravely, is clearly enough told to save us from a programme scenario, and offers scope for plenty of variations. In fact Cranko has hung so many on it that it sags at times like an over-extended clothes-line. The first act, after a bottom-slapping start, goes well. There are a sprightly courtiers' dance, strongly contrasted solos for four visiting kings, a romantic *pas de deux* in front of a truly magical cloud and a fine conclusion as Belle Rose flies aloft on a frog-propelled carpet.

The second act, where we see her gliding through air, water and fire, is less happy. Men do not make an effective *corps de ballet*, even with the aid of chiffon, and acrobatics are no substitute for poetic feeling. In vain one looks for the solemnity and wonder of a night sky or the tender rippling of the sea: one wishes indeed that Belle Rose would descend from her carpet and relieve some of the jumping and twirling. As it is, she touches down in Pagodaland, an arid country where automation seems well advanced. As the Salamander goes through his rather leisurely courtship, spikes revolve and grow, windows open, fans spread out – but it is slow work and invention is thinly spread.

14

The last act is in the classic *divertissement* tradition including an extended *pas de six* and no less than three *pas de deux*. It contains some lively numbers, but lacks the variety needed to refresh our spirits at the end of this overlong evening. One's final impression is of a somewhat disjointed, overgimmicked, uneasily balanced affair in which the story is lost and spectacle not quite gained.

Much of the choreography is in the sharp modern manner, but the part of the heroine, Belle Rose, has been smoothly and beautifully written by Cranko for Svetlana Beriosova, and she amply rewards his pains. Her pure open line, velvety arm and head movements and gentle feet make her appear composed of a softer, richer material than everyone else on the stage. She has the quality, all too rare in this company, of seeming to dance from the heart. Her partner, David Blair, makes an amiable batrachian, but does not quite fill out the princely part of his role. Of the rest of the company, honours go to Julia Farron, a fierce but rather common little Belle Epine; to Pirmin Trecu as a faithful Fool and also one of a nimble pair of Fishes, to Maryon Lane, outstanding in the *pas de six*; and to that rarity, a promising new male dancer, Gary Burne, who might, with a scrap more *plié* and less smile, go all the way.

The décor (by John Piper) and costumes (by Desmond Heeley) make only scant allusion to *chinoiserie*. The Bakst-ish dark blue and apricot colour scheme of the palace is rather cramping and crowded and the pagodas are decidedly drab. But the final scene is bright and beautiful in an imaginative way, and one would like to see more of many of the costumes.

6.1.57

## *Petrushka*, The Royal Ballet, Covent Garden

No ballet evokes the originality, magic and finesse of Diaghilev and his Russian Ballet so strongly as *Petrushka*, which on Tuesday was at last added to our national company's repertoire. Its dizzy growth, from a short piano piece (now the music of Act II Scene 1), struck off by Stravinsky while working on *Les Noces*, to the final mankind-enfolding drama: its multiple parentage, with Stravinsky, Benois, Fokine and Diaghilev each making his unanalysable contribution: its international organisation, with scores, designs, telegrams and

15

contracts flying between Rome, St Petersburg and Paris: this is the epitome of the Diaghilev spell.

*Petrushka*'s richness springs from three separate sources. From Stravinsky's score, with its miraculous blend of sweetly-solid folk-music, pathetic dissonance and dazzling shower of bumps, grunts, buzzings, cries, pringles and hums such as had never (anyway in the year of George V's coronation) been heard before. From Benois's inspired vision of the tragedy of the favourite Russian 'Punch and Judy' drama contrasted with the jolly Butter Market crowd. And from the extraordinary insight of the movements devised by Fokine for the puppets. Petrushka, the weak-kneed introvert, shambling around with turned-in toes and fumbling hands, or leaping, trapped like a cat, in a cell whose walls turn out to be only paper (yet when he breaks through there is nothing outside: he is still imprisoned). The strutting extrovert Blackamoor, splaying out his hands and knees in bovine stupidity, clutching gluttonously at his wealth – his coconut – which he half hates and worships. The Ballerina, too dumb to understand her power. The Showman-Magician, whose spells are only a trick (but are they?). And, milling all round, the figures in the crowd, in whose lives this seems to be just a moment we have the luck to watch.

These are the ingredients of an undeniable masterpiece. How did they fare on Tuesday? Although the company seemed not quite at home with Sir Malcolm Sargent's *tempi*, the complicated production, with its eddying whirlpools of dance and emphasis, was marvellously smooth – and small wonder, as it had been in the hands of Serge Grigoriev (with the help of his wife, Tchernicheva), who had been Diaghilev's *régisseur* for the original. Though we might criticise details (not enough red noses and apple cheeks for a Russian winter and many characters – especially the coachmen – several stone underweight) the general effect was impressive and will certainly get better.

The principals had also not yet settled down. Margot Fonteyn was still tentative as the Ballerina, Ashton's Showman was unalarming, and Peter Clegg, as the Blackamoor, was too neat for the rolling muscleman he represents. Alexander Grant is a promising Petrushka, but he has not yet learned to conceal his natural strength: those pinched little feet and wavering limbs, from which the stuffing has leaked out, seemed from the very start too sturdy and co-ordinated.

Benois's new sets and costumes stick closely to the original and are as cunning and charming as ever. The weakest (or rather the

16

strongest) element in the production was the lighting, which opened in a golden blaze of Neapolitan sunshine and closed with a dusk so bright that Petrushka's ghost was hardly visible. Either for this, or for some more deep-seated reason, this first production failed in the final test. Magnificent as a spectacle and convincing as a reconstruction, it did not touch the heart. It had magical moments, such as the entry of the carnival giants. But recent, less authentic, productions have been more moving. The final cry from Petrushka's ghost, which should send a shiver of anguished triumph up the spine, was unconvincing. This *Petrushka* is a splendid puppet, but it has not yet grown a soul.

31.3.57

## Beryl Grey

On Thursday Beryl Grey, appearing at Covent Garden for the first time for many weeks to an enthusiastic audience, took her leave as a regular member of the Royal Ballet. Henceforth we shall see her only as a guest-artist. It is twenty years since she joined the Sadler's Wells School. From the start she was groomed as a pure classical dancer; in fact she danced her first full-length *Swan Lake* (which she performed with her usual fluidity on Thursday) at fifteen. In a company which in general tends towards lightness and neatness, Grey stood out by the smooth Bolshoi-like way in which she would carve a movement out of the air in a huge gesture like the swing of a ship's sails. Unusually tall for a dancer, she has a magnificent technique, with a long, eloquent line. Her weakness is in interpretation, which is perhaps the reason why only one ballet has ever been created for her in the principal part – Death in Massine's *Donald of the Burthens*. Otherwise one remembers her best in *Swan Lake*, *The Sleeping Princess*, *Les Sylphides*, and most of all as the second ballerina in *Ballet Imperial*, a role which she danced with breathtaking ease and grandeur. She is a serious loss.

21.4.57

## John Gilpin with Festival Ballet

In these desperate days, when ballet companies are mostly kept afloat on the heaving waters of inflation only by regular pumping in

17

of public money, the Festival Ballet (which started a nine-week season at the Festival Hall last Tuesday) has always been rather a heartening sight – a gaudy, dashingly-cut craft skidding along through the shallows with an alarming spread of canvas and no help from anybody. Admiral Dolin may not open up any uncharted oceans, but he certainly knows how to impress the ladies on the pier.

The company has just returned from a successful European tour and now has a distinct feather in its cap in the well-merited Nijinsky Award to John Gilpin – undoubtedly the most naturally gifted mover among our male dancers. Three-quarters of our artists of both sexes give signs of having had dancing thrust upon them: rare is the individual who – whatever use he or she may make of the gift – is born with the priceless temperament that makes leaping, running, bending, beating, spinning as natural and easy as breathing. Gilpin is one of the lucky ones.

14.7.57

## *Ondine*, Royal Ballet, Covent Garden

Ballet is a short-winded art. Its heartbeat is fast, like that of a bird; its natural reactions are intense and sharp. A *pas de deux* will say in a minute what may spin out in an operatic duet to ten. No other theatrical art can match it for concentration. Can it compete equally on a broader front, stretched out over the whole evening? In spite of those inspired scrap-books *Swan Lake* and *The Sleeping Beauty* (sole survivors among a host of similar productions), I am not convinced that it can, except on the level of mild entertainment. Ashton's new work, *Ondine*, given at Covent Garden last Monday, is a new challenge – charming, distinguished, skilful, intelligent. But, as evidence, still inconclusive.

The ballet is very much a star vehicle, a Fonteyn-concerto. From the moment the water-nymph steps timidly out from the waterfall, feeling with wonder the texture of dry rock and foliage, her character is established. The solo which follows, as she darts around, a delicious sex-minnow, shaking drops delightedly off her fingers and flirting with that mysterious acquisition a shadow (this is Ashton's version of Cerrito's famous *pas de l'ombre*), is enchanting. From then on Fonteyn hardly leaves the stage. Whether she is luring the hero

18

into the magic wood, trying to soothe the storm which threatens their ship, or – finally – reappearing from the depths into which she had been snatched, to give her faithless lover the kiss of death, she never loses for a moment the shy grace and little-girl tenderness which are her special qualities. Her part, largely written in variations of *arabesque* and *attitude* which flow liquidly across the music, requires acting and an effortless smoothness. It gets both. This is a fine performance.

All the same there is a flaw in the role. It exists in a vacuum. The hero, Palemon (Michael Somes) is a handsome dummy: Berta, the land-based Other Girl (Julia Farron) is a conventionalised hard nut, whose relationship with Palemon is not explored (she doesn't even have a *pas de deux* with him, while Ondine has no fewer than five – one of them of inordinate length). Tyrrenio the Sea-God (Alexander Grant) and the Hermit (Leslie Edwards) are understandably impersonal. Not surprisingly, drama languishes. The story proceeds, but the urgency which arises from the clash or attraction between real characters is totally lacking. We are beguiled, but never moved.

In his last three-acter, *Sylvia*, Ashton produced a direct period pastiche, following both the form as well as the character of nineteenth-century ballet. His new work is different. It is an attempt at a new interpretation. For the most part the choreography is restrained and classical: sometimes, indeed, he seems to have disregarded hints in Henze's score of a more adventurous style. Compared with some of his works it is rather lacking in invention: the *corps de ballet* dances for the sprites are surprisingly ordinary, and the temperature drops whenever they appear. The second act, with its pantomime tempest set in a cut-out cameo (surely the Trust could have raised a puff of real wind?) relies somewhat heavily on the scenery. The last act is filled with the usual divertissements, some with the slightly incongruous cuteness of the Cranko-MacMillan style. The variations are not outstanding, except for a *pas de six* (excellently danced by Misses Lane, Grahame and Wells and Messrs. Shaw, Clegg and Trecu) and a remarkable solo full of original twists and changes, brilliantly performed by Shaw.

It lacks, then, dramatic or choreographic highlights; but the general effect is wonderfully sensitive and tasteful, with a consistent low-velocity beauty. This is carried through in Lila di Nobili's sets. Apart from a masterly gauzy forest, they are unremarkable – operatic-romantic in brown-gold, silver and black (always

19

beautifully lit). Evocative, certainly, but a bit devitalised. Think of the salt spray which blew through Orson Welles's 'Moby Dick' sets!

Already at a second performance the ballet, inclined to be over-melting, was beginning to take on sharper outlines: but its muted impact rises largely from a basic fallacy – the belief that you can take the myths of another age and present them as living, emotion-rousing symbols to a new generation. This is aesthetic taxidermy. The nymphs of the nineteenth century are as dead as the shep-herdesses of the eighteenth. Only the violent twist of a Picasso or Cocteau can revive them. In spite of the superimposition of contem-porary music, Ondine, with her grottoes and amulets, is rooted in the dead past. To have her displayed before our eyes so exquisitely is an extraordinary achievement for sputnik-year. But one day ballet will sink altogether if it does not shed its cargo of Victorian clichés.

2.11.58

## Frederick Ashton

When a theatrical company is being built up, the works it performs have a decisive effect on its character; this is obvious in enterprises like the Moscow Art Theatre, the Old Vic, or the Comédie Française. In the case of the Sadler's Wells, company and repertoire grew to-gether, interacting on each other. To begin with, most of the ballets were provided by de Valois, but for the last twenty years by far the chief contribution to the repertoire has been from Ashton.

A choreographer not only arranges the steps in a ballet but super-vises the whole production – in stage terms, he is both author and producer in one. This means that Ashton has coached successive 'generations' of dancers in executing the kind of movements and emotions he specialises in. The style of the company to-day, hall-marked as it is with the personality of its famous director, reflects even more strongly the tastes of its official choreographer, Ashton.

This style is often alluded to as particularly English. Frederick Ashton is certainly as British as a Briggs umbrella. But, as so often happens with successful English artists, a foreign strain has been added. Ashton was born in 1906, in Guayaquil, Ecuador. When he was three his family moved to Lima. Here, in the old capital of the Spanish Viceroys, he was put to school with Dominican monks and served as an acolyte in their huge Baroque church. He admired the

20

altars ablaze with saints, the vestments and the ceremonial. At week-ends he was taken bathing in the Pacific by his Inca nurse.

It can hardly be doubted that the Sitwellian splendours of this background struck deep into his imagination. But soon another influence appeared. When he was ten he was taken to see Pavlova at the Teatro Municipal. 'Is it her? Is it her?' he asked eagerly as each dancer appeared on the stage. When she finally appeared he was momentarily disappointed: but from the moment she started to dance his future was settled . . . [An] emotional reserve, which may in some respects be called English, is deeply ingrained in Ashton's character. He has embraced the classical ideals of good taste, good craftsmanship, elegance and stylish finish to counterbalance a cast of mind which is by nature spontaneous, romantic, comfort-loving and malleable.

He likes to live quietly, but impeccably, whether it is in his tiny London home with its red 'Covent Garden' wallpaper or in his beloved country cottage. Worldly, intelligent and well up in contemporary culture, he combines a childlike enjoyment of simple pleasures with a languid sophistication. His friends are chosen with care, and he enjoys the comforts of moving in society. The administrative side of a big company means little or nothing to him, though he is a percipient critic and a helpful supporter of talent he admires.

A sad, witty talker and a devastating mimic (he still enjoys playing the grotesque parts of the Witch in *The Sleeping Beauty* or a Comic Sister in *Cinderella*), he has a love for the French values of elegance and clarity. Easily the most fertile of living choreographers (*Ondine* is his sixtieth ballet) he is exceptionally versatile. He has worked in films and opera, and his balletic moods range from the frenzy of the wartime *Dante Sonata* to delicate satire, period romance or sophisticated abstraction. Horror, realism, psychological problems or jazzy experiments are utterly alien to him. He does not accept 'pretty' as a term of abuse.

He is one of the few men living who can be relied on to manoeuvre a large company through a whole evening's entertainment without faltering. Yet he is still shy and secretive about his work while he is creating. Quiet spoken, modest and totally undogmatic in his approach to his work, he will jump down from the high chair from which he directs rehearsals to seize on a chance movement made by a dancer and adapt it to his own purpose.

It is this direct approach, working without preconceived ideas straight on the dancer before him, which makes him write so well for

21

individual performers. His sensitive ear makes his work acceptable even to those fiercest of ballet-critics, musicians.

It is certainly without intention that he has impressed his personality, for good or for ill, on the company he works for. (He seldom writes for other companies.) If the Royal Ballet is criticised for being under-emphatic, out of touch with reality or tastefully brittle, that is the unfavourable way of expressing his dislike of melodrama and his love of style and detail. When it is praised for its discipline, brilliant footwork and classical poise, that is due to his tastes, too....

... His matchless gift for lyrical *pas de deux* and his deft inventions for light-footed girls has made the company's team of ballerinas a unique precision instrument. He is that very rare English bird, a completely professional artist.

14.12.58

*Ballet is all dreams. They can be sharp or misty; reflections of yesterday's headlines, ecstatic flights, terror-dramas, or those uneasy lingering ones from which the sleeper wakes crying, without knowing exactly why. But the essential dream logic, dream-space, dream-rhythm, dream-reality must be there if a ballet, a work of artifice and convention, is to come alive: all else is mere entertainment or theatre manqué. The task of choreographers is to summon up new dreams.*

## The Firebird, The Royal Ballet, Covent Garden

Is there a difference between romance and romanticism? You might say that the second is a conscious effort to achieve the first. Examples for those who wish to brood over the distinction were provided at Covent Garden last week in Ashton's *Ondine*, a super-skilful exercise in the romantic manner, and Fokine's *Firebird*, a magic tale in which every step and gesture is as sincere and convincing as an old soldier's yarn.

This ballet emerges more and more as a masterpiece, and perhaps the best thing in the present Royal Ballet repertoire. The heady Russian atmosphere which has proved so obstinately elusive in the case of *Petrushka* rises off the production like steam from a samovar. The story and the music unwind with inexorable excitement, a

22

fireside tale told for the hundredth time. Goncharova's exquisite sets and costumes fill the darkened stage with mystery (but could we not have a glimpse of those apple orchards stretching into the night?). Nothing is omitted, nothing excessive.

What price your three-acters now? Is it unambitious, flighty or 'immature,' as one writer has suggested, to admire so short a work as this? If maturity means preferring some of our three-acters, then I suggest we should return to the nursery to join Diaghilev, Stravinsky and the other tots.

The success of this ballet is not entirely a production-trick, of course. It provides a full ballerina role; and – a little unexpectedly perhaps – it proves to be the role of Nerina's career. Her strong technique enables her to dominate the scene as a magic figure should, with no visible effort. Ronald Hynd, as the Prince, was acceptable and will improve. Is it ungrateful to long for the day when we can, with pride, introduce this work to the company where it belongs by blood – the Bolshoi?

9.11.58

*What a master-choreographer Fokine was.* Les Sylphides *for classical perfection – infinity glimpsed through geometry –* Petrushka *for gutsy realism, with a thread of bitter magic, and* Firebird *for romance and legend. What a range!*

## Danses Concertantes, The Royal Ballet, Covent Garden

One of the pleasurable consequences of the amalgamation of the two Sadler's Wells troupes is the steady flow of works from the repertoire of the smaller theatre to that of the big one. Old friends reappear, larger and smarter. *Danses Concertantes*, which we met again on Friday, came up looking like a champion.

This was the first ballet Kenneth MacMillan wrote for Sadler's Wells (in 1955) and it remains his best. We find ourselves confronted by an entirely new dance language. It is an idiom based on the old classical style, but on only one element in it – the sharp accented movement. Ashton has, of course, experimented widely in this direction, but he has usually set it against soft, melting passages. In this ballet sharpness is all.

The work consists of an intricate suite of dances. There is no plot, no characterisation in the ordinary sense. Yet the soloists quickly establish personality, of that indefinable kind one ascribes to a tune or a bird. In fact there is something birdlike about the whole work, with its darts and quirks, its cocked heads, flashing hands and sudden scatterings (in his next ballet MacMillan was to make this bird quality explicit).

In all this he seems to follow a trait in the music. It may be that Balanchine has found more lyrical elements in the lively score which Stravinsky wrote for him in 1942; but there is no doubt that it contains a sharp-eyed mischief as well. And this MacMillan has exploited in a chain of wonderfully witty and inventive variations.

15.3.59

## *Cyrano de Bergerac*, Ballets de Paris, Paris

Perhaps international cross-fertilisation in the arts really does work. At the very moment when the Bolshoi company in Moscow was putting on (at the demand of its younger members) a programme of short ballets, Paris plunged last night into the first full-length work by its best-known choreographer, Roland Petit.

He has chosen as subject a popular French theatrical favourite, *Cyrano de Bergerac*. Petit has kept closely to the play. The rowdy opening scene in a theatre auditorium is splendidly done, ending with a lavish criss-cross of plastic swordplay. Then comes the eating-house act, used to introduce some variations for *croissants* and *brioches*. Petit here uses tumblers, in the Chinese fashion, and Tessa Beaumont, besides an interesing *pas de trois*, executes a skit on the rose adagio with four tiny boy-pralines. The famous balcony scene, where Cyrano makes poetic love to Roxane in the darkness and Christian claims the reward, is presented as a *pas de trois*, with ingenuity if not much passion. But the second half of the evening (there is only one interval in this long programme) is in many ways the better.

When the curtain rose on the battlefield where Christian is to die, the imaginative set and grouping won a round of applause, and so did the final battle when the acrobats came into their own. But the climax was the last scene of all, in effect a protracted *pas de deux* between

24

Roxane – now, years later, retired to a convent – and Cyrano, who comes to visit her. The stage is dominated by a huge plane tree, set dead centre. Beneath it the story suddenly takes on dignity and humanity, as Cyrano's secret is finally bared. In this scene Petit is superb. He moves around clumsily – not aping an old man's gait, but having lost all spring and grace. His gestures are real – stiff and anguished. When he goes into his final paroxysm of dancing, you felt the emotion bursting at last through the ice pack in which it has been frozen all those years. Cyrano is, all through, a plum part for Petit, and he carries it off with great conviction. He does not quite get the full range of swagger and aggressiveness, but you feel all the time a real heart beating behind the 'fatal cartilage'.

The trouble is that (as in the play) there's not much for anyone else. Roxane is a feeble, pretentious creature and work as Renée Jeanmaire may, she cannot make her come alive. She danced beautifully, but romantic daydreaming is simply not her line. George Reich makes a handsome Christian, but he too has a dullish part.

It is the large, excellently drilled company which is really Cyrano's partner. There is not much detail in the acting, but Petit has an eye for mass effect, and in this he is much helped by Basarte's beautiful, sparely designed Clavé-esque sets and Yves St Laurent's costumes (though Jeanmaire's are too like dresses). The weakest link was an important one – the score. On a first hearing Marius Constant's music, though theatrical, seemed to lack character. But London audiences will surely have the chance of judging this spectacle for themselves.

19.4.59

## *Hazaña*, Ballet Rambert, Sadler's Wells

Under a spell cast by that old Carabosse of St James's Square, the Arts Council, the Rambert company is condemned to hover continually outside the magic circle of Greater London. The reason behind this injunction is presumably to keep it out of the magnetic field of the Royal Ballet. Should the two bodies approach they would, one supposes, rush inexorably together, meet near Streatham, and in the fearful blaze of the collision we should all be burnt to cinders. Providentially some good fairy stepped in according to tradition, and once a year the company is permitted for two weeks to alight among us.

We know by now more or less what gifts Madame Rambert will bring – a gold mine of a repertoire; that almost amateurish integrity which one would say, were it not for the Bolshoi, is for ever denied to mammoth companies; and an exceptionally sure touch with the classics. All these qualities have been shown during her first week at Sadler's Wells. *Giselle* and *Coppélia* were the two classics, and within the limits of her dancers, and more especially of her orchestra, they were quietly satisfying.

But it is as the conjurer-up of new talent that Madame Rambert is justly most famous. This season's first new work, *Hazaña*, by Norman Morrice, will add another notch to her score. Set against an effective scaffolding background (by Ralph Koltai) the action concerns the building of a church in some unspecified South American country. A vast stone cross which is to crown the edifice is too heavy for the lazy, sulky workmen to move. One man, however (well danced by John Chesworth), by a near-miraculous effort of strength and will, succeeds in dragging it inch by inch to the top by himself.

The heat-sodden atmosphere and the shifting moods of the workmen and their womenfolk are conveyed with beautiful fluency. Morrice has a rare sense of the theatre and a feeling for gesture and the small suggestive movement. His style – the spasms of energy and sudden stops, and above all the way he sets his choreography against Surinach's telling music, as though only half aware of it – is very reminiscent of Antony Tudor. More and more one recognises Tudor's as the missing voice in our national repertoire.

The climax of the ballet is an anticlimax: it needs some re-thinking. But to see this work as a whole is a genuine experience. Also it does a rare thing. By the success with which it tackles a curious subject it expands the expressive range of ballet as a whole.

31.5.59

## Martha Graham, 'The Dancer's World', BBC TV

A short (not *very* short, about half an hour) film at the Academy should be visited by everyone – and particularly by every dancer – who may feel the weather overpowering his faith in ballet as a serious art form, a common condition these days. It is called 'The Dancer's World'. It depicts that celebrated American, Martha

Graham, explaining what a dancer is trying to achieve, and how he sets about it. It is a work of art in itself.

The script, emerging from the amazing oracle herself as she transforms herself, in her dressing-room, into a strange oriental priestess, is spare and high-minded – no apologies, jokes or embarrassments. The class-room illustrations and examples she has choreographed herself, and these are a revelation. The arrangements are both beautiful and appropriate, and they reveal a whole range of movement unexplored elsewhere. Rich though it is, the classical vocabulary to which we are accustomed is very far from exhaustive.

It is not only the supple, controlled style which strikes an unfamiliar note, but the use to which it is put. We are familiar with the romantic, sad, dreamy ballet, the sexy ballet, the witty ballet, the harsh or jolly ballet. But Martha Graham goes back to a tradition which has become overshadowed – the dance as ritual.

In all ritual, movement plays a dominating part, and religious manoeuvre is the root from which ballet springs. Yet how rarely is this great and solemn power exploited! The marching and countermarching of military formations, the rolling tide of a funeral, marriage or coronation procession – these move us in a profound and simple way which has been replaced by shallow theatrical effects. De Valois reflects the mood in parts of *Job*: Tudor explores it wonderfully in *Dark Elegies*; Ashton turns it to a subtle lyrical effect in *Symphonic Variations*. But in some odd way it is implicit in all of Martha Graham's work. She insists (like oriental performers) that dancing can be as profound and serious an art as poetry or music. In a world where cuteness, cheapjack drama and soppy romanticism run riot this is a salutary lesson.

28.6.59

*The vocabulary [Martha Graham] has invented to exploit the expressive powers of the whole body have become a modern text-book of movement, a store which will enrich the future language of dance.*

# The De Cuevas Ballet, Coliseum

Confronted by the sudden banquet of ballet spread before him last week in London, the kindly critic is in the happy position of being able to pass over his sadder hours and count only his blessings.

Several of these came from the Coliseum where the de Cuevas Ballet returns after four years' absence from London. As a company it shows signs of its gipsy character, with nowhere it can call home. But even its first programme gave us two outstanding performances.

The first was by Nina Vyroubova as the sleepwalker in Balanchine's *Night Shadow*. This exquisite part has been well danced before, but never better. Apparently simple, it is actually extremely taxing. The long, serpentine movement must be unwound as smoothly and delicately as a thread; one false move and it snaps, with no hope of repair. There is nothing to help the dancer: no change of expression, hardly a gesture. The mood must be sustained entirely from within.

Vyroubova has just the right gentleness and pale moonshine glow. From the moment she glides out into the night until she disappears with the dead poet in her arms, she completely embodies Balanchine's poetic vision of Love and Death as identical – a sleepwalker, blind to this world but intensely living in another, in whose arms we are quietly folded at last. Unfortunately, the rest of the production is by no means up to this standard. Muddled and haphazard, with a fussy, trivial décor, it has neither elegance nor tension.

As the Poet, Serge Golovine was acceptable in a part for which he is not really suited. It is a measure of his versatility considering the really astonishing display of pure classical virtuosity he gave later on. Already accomplished on his last visit, he has made immense progress, and now takes his place among the greatest names of male dancing. Small and neatly built, he has a phenomenal jump, speed, softness and control. But what makes him exceptional is that he puts his technique at the service of the choreographer. Beautifully musical, he can turn a double *tour en l'air* into a deep *plié en arabesque* as trimly as if it were a phrase in a Mozart sonata.

As an extra treat, the de Cuevas company presented us with Massine as the amorous Peruvian in his own *Gaîté Parisienne*. Spry and nimble, he dominated this light-hearted romp as easily as a cockerel among a bunch of chickens. Hightower was light and lively as the Gloveseller.

Among other pleasures of the week was Yvette Chauviré's *Sleeping Beauty* with the Royal Ballet: it was hard to believe that this was the first time this eminent ballerina had danced the part: it suits her so well that the Paris Opera will surely mount it for her. The assurance and poise with which she tackled the Rose Adagio, her confident characterisation and her attack in the last act were exemplary. Rassine was a stylish and unassuming partner, but it seems odd to have called in a guest artist to dance opposite such a distinguished visitor. Moreover the noises emerging from the orchestra pit were below any acceptable standard. The company (particularly Anya Linden) deserves medals for steady, and often excellent, dancing in the face of such opposition.

14.9.59

*Nobody who saw [Massine] on stage can ever forget the electric charge of his personality or the dynamic vitality and agility of his dancing. He was a master of perfectly timed grotesque movement and of a tension which gave the impression that every nerve and muscle in his body was pulled up like a spring.*

# Jerome Robbins, Ballets: U.S.A.

Firing the second shot (the first was *West Side Story*) from what appears to be a twenty-five-barrelled gun, Jerome Robbins dealt London audiences a knock-out last week with his Ballets: U.S.A., the company which had stunned Edinburgh the week before.

The encounter was both decisive and short. The company (nineteen dancers selected for a special mission to the United States-Italian festival at Spoleto last year) operates under remote control by the State Department, which understandably wants this intercontinental balletic missile to strike as many targets as possible in the shortest possible time. Already it has taken off again, this time for Copenhagen and Warsaw.

The commercial world hasn't hardened Robbins in the least.

29

Though a professional to his eyebrows, he is saturated with sincerity, and demands the same from his dancers – all of whom, incidentally, have the same background as himself, half-ballet, half-Broadway. He is no slave to the audience (he has clung to *Moves* in spite of pressure to abandon it for something more popular) but he has learned the hard way to win and hold it – not by extra dollops of charm and daintiness, but by expert knowledge of timing and style.

Nor is he a rebel in a sense of wishing to overthrow other traditions. A devoted admirer of Balanchine, whose work is often held to be cold and geometrical, he will wax enthusiastic over a performance of *Swan Lake* or *Giselle*. He looks back with detachment to psychological ballets like *The Cage*, the last work of his seen here, which showed him in a bitter mood. He feels that he has developed since then. He knows what he wants, and how to get it. In spite of successes in the omnium-gatherum world of the musical, he still clings to pure dancing – pure in the sense that everything must be expressed through movement. He has no great interest in glamour, spectacle or star temperament. The instrument he has forged is designed to put over his own individual formula – no showing off, no hysterics, no otherworldly mystery of portentous star-rapture. Real cool, in the words of *West Side Story*, it seems to hit a note we have been waiting for. The only pity is that more people could not have heard it.

20.9.59

*In this country ballet has become more and more centred around one great fetish – the opera house. Essential though this institution is for the production of the epic masterpieces of nineteenth-century ballet, it is very far from ideal for modern works. Vast in size, portentous in atmosphere, its velvety decorum is out of tune with an age which finds genuine poetry in a fag-end or a kitchen sink. Robbins's little company – tight-knit and bearing the stamp of a single personality – is a far better instrument and underlines the sobbing need for a London-based company not reliant on churning out the classics and geared to contemporary tastes.*

*To [Robbins] the two worlds are one. In New York there is no such barrier between the opera house and the music hall. Top dancers, designers or composers work for both.*

## La Fille Mal Gardée, The Royal Ballet, Covent Garden

The ups and downs of the rustic in the theatre would almost make a subject for a ballet. Shakespeare's rude mechanicals still trailed in their matted hair hayseeds left over from the Middle Ages. But times changed, and country complexions with them. It was a gentler, paler swain who toyed in the eighteenth century with his shepherdess. The Romantic revolution came, and once again the countryside became the haunt of rugged simplicity. What a gulf lies between the elegant young farmer hero of *La Fille Mal Gardée*, originally presented in Bordeaux just two weeks before the French Revolution broke, and the boorish woodcutter in *Giselle*, born some fifty years later!

The fascination of this work, now revivified at Covent Garden with new choreography by Ashton, lies in the fact that it is poised on the very brink between two ages. It preserved the conception of the country as the home of charming lusty sexual innocence (the episode where the heroine is locked up in a bedroom where her forbidden lover is already hiding is unimaginable in a romantic work); but it shed both the idea that common folk are fit only for sub-plots and also formal court-bred dance-suite conventions. In so doing it let in the full flood of dance-drama which has not yet subsided.

In the history of ballet it is, then, an important work, well worthy of a place in a national repertory founded on the classics. It is entirely to Ashton's credit that he has concealed this solemn aspect. The ballet emerges in its true natural shape – gay, charming, lively and trivial. Its form – the lyrical-comedy – is a natural for ballet, and has been so much exploited that it needs great invention to make it seem fresh. This quality Ashton (aided by Karsavina, a former star of the old Maryinsky version) has supplied in good measure. From the moment the rumpled poultry hop off their perch in the farmyard, the succession of small happy thoughts which make up a live production never flag. There are some moments of real excitement (how well Ashton knows how to exploit a dancer's special qualities!), especially at the end of Act I, and the character roles give splendid opportunities to the performers – particularly to Alexander Grant, unique master of the grotesque, as the goofy

31

suitor and to Stanley Holden as a *travesti* mother who can raise a laugh with the smallest flash of her button-boot.

Blair is an honest, straightforward lover and dances excellently: as the heroine Nerina looks enchanting and performs her difficult solos with breathtaking virtuosity. Yet she lacks at present (particularly in the *pas de deux*) the tender, sensitive delicacy of feeling needed to give the true pastoral quality. *Mal gardée* is not the same as *mal élevée*.

It may be chiefly this failing which opens the whole production to the criticism that though the comedy is strong the lyricism is decidedly weak. The hotch-potch score devised by Hérold for a 1828 revival, well freshened up by John Lanchbery though it is, stands miles away from Adam's expressive *Giselle* music, composed only thirteen years later, and adds little. But in general Ashton has chosen to stand back from the subject, and present it, as it were, between inverted commas. In this he is more than abetted by Osbert Lancaster, whose costumes are excellent but whose knowing décors are, consciously or not, mocking at the whole conception.

31.1.60

## *Le Sacre du Printemps*, Maurice Béjart, Coliseum

In 1913 Diaghilev, though already far ahead of the world of fashion, was still lagging behind the Parisian circle of creative artists. He was still tied to his Russian folk-background. His newest creation (what would one not give to see it now!) was to be a reflection of the *fauve* or 'wild-beast' movement which had been current in Paris ten years earlier, an exercise in primitivism located – naturally – in Asia.

'I saw in imagination a solemn pagan rite: sage elders seated in a circle watched a young girl dance herself to death,' writes the composer, Stravinsky. 'My object was to represent a number of pictures of earthly joy and celestial triumph as understood by the Slavs,' adds Roerich, the designer. The choreography was entrusted to Nijinsky. There were 120 rehearsals. Marie Rambert was brought in to help disentangle the complicated rhythms. The ballet was finally launched in Paris to howls and catcalls. It revolutionised ballet permanently and it ran for six performances.

It was entitled *Le Sacre du Printemps*, and it has been revived since by Massine and by Mary Wigman. Astoundingly, nobody else has tackled it, nor had it been performed here for thirty years until last week, when it was the chief attraction of the painfully brief visit of the company from the Théâtre Royal de la Monnaie in Brussels.

Maurice Béjart, the new choreographer, is an impassioned radical and we should not be surprised to find that he has thrown overboard the entire original conception. In his version there is no vestige of Asia, no sage elder, no young girl dancing herself to death and no solemn rite, pagan or otherwise. Instead, he has taken the 'wild-beast' element in the music and used it as the basis for a mass spectacle of striking impact with sex as the overt driving force and, for the climax, copulation as a substitute for death.

Though the shedding of the ritual element is an irrecoverable loss, lowering the target to the belly (or even lower) rather than the heart, Béjart's approach makes a sort of sense. He has merely put back the clock ten thousand years to a time when man was still nine-tenths animal. In the first (all-masculine) part this works well. Crouching, pouncing, and panting movements vividly suggest a herd of rutting males in the throes of spring fever, and the final scene where they bound off, rigid with excitement, through the legs of Pierre Caille's great stone female idol is a fine theatrical stroke.

But inevitably the quiet female opening of the second part loses drastically in interest. The famous Dance of the Chosen Girl will hardly make history, either, as its predecessors have done, but the *dénouement* with the Chosen Boy is well worked out and the finale makes, perhaps not surprisingly, a strong impact. The general effect is like swallowing a tremendous slug of gin.

The megaton score carries the great bulk of the striking power. Indeed much of the ballet could be criticised as a rather crude, simplified exercise in eurhythmics, a mere parallel of the music. Béjart has no gift for grouping or choreographic phrasing – he is content with small clumps of steps in varying styles bolted strongly on to the music. But each step is conceived (and danced) with conviction and undeniable force. The sculptural décor is suitably brooding and heavy but the costumes are a serious mistake. The plain skimpy fleshings worn by both sexes deprive the dancers of even normal bulk and weight. Moreover they reduce everyone to the appearance of a teen-ager: how infinitely more exciting are the genuine tribal rites of Africa or Polynesia, with adults and old people welding the present to immemorial custom! Finally, they are the most sexless of all costumes; in the circumstances this is hardly appropriate.

24.4.60

33

*[Béjart] is less of a choreographer than a man of the theatre, groping towards new forms. His ballets have the touching clumsiness of primitive machinery: it is easy to laugh at them, but future inventors, as they soar into the sky, may well look back at them with respect and amazement.*

## The dancer as hero

In a recent number devoted to ballet, that go-ahead German magazine *Magnum* quoted a remark by Otto Reger. 'Der unbesiegte Mensch,' he says, 'ist der tanzende Mensch.' This untranslatable phrase conveys a belief that man in his heroic aspect – an aspect, he adds, neglected nowadays by painters and sculptors (and, he might have added further, writers) – survives to-day only in ballet.

What a noble thought! It makes our chests swell to think that red blood still flows, thank God, through our dancers' veins, whatever may be happening elsewhere. The only snag is that it is not true; in fact, the very opposite is the case. It is man the sufferer, man the sensitive, man the agonised bewildered victim of life's brutality and love's sweet torture who swoons nightly on the Covent Garden boards or is carried out prostrate, bludgeoned by a cruel fate.

The reason is obvious. Ballet was to all intents born at the heyday of the romantic movement, when pale complexions and lovelorn sighs were at a premium. It is a sign of the rather feebly creative pulse which beats through the art that the ghost of this etiolated period figure still haunts all but a fraction of our dance dramas.

As a matter of fact the hero of the earliest ballet in the repertoire, *La Fille Mal Gardée*, has one of the few really integrated personalities in the business. Colas is a simple and reasonably determined young man who cheerfully contrives to get himself locked in a bedroom with the heroine.

But this (in 1828) was a hangover from the eighteenth century. Thereafter it's all waltzing and *Weltschmerz*. The heroes of *La Sylphide* and *Giselle*, archetypes for hundreds of later models, are weak-willed cads who end up, as they deserve, aimless wrecks. Suicide (*Swan Lake*) seems a comparatively positive conclusion.

Only one hero of this period strikes a reasonably extrovert note – Franz, in *Coppélia*, who is a direct descendant of Colas. Not the man for a statue in the town square, perhaps, but he does at least go after his girl, and get her, which is more than can be said for most of the prancing princes who succeeded him. They rely confidently on rank, elegant legs and help from the fairies.

We know, of course, that the nineteenth century was the age of the heroine – the male dancer was a mere attribute of the ballerina. With the new century you might expect a change. But, though the girls shed their wings and came down to earth from their supernatural element, the young men stayed as limp a lot as ever. One effort, it is true, was made to introduce a more virile figure. In his three 'Russian' ballets – the *Polovtsian Dances*, *Firebird*, and *Thamar* – Fokine presented warrior heroes who might, one feels, have tackled Wyatt Earp himself if occasion demanded. But Diaghilev's attempt to reinstate the male dancer was pulled sideways by the peculiar genius of Nijinsky – an artist who evidently combined in an astonishing way the fey and the voluptuous, but hardly the bold and manly. The result was a succession of melting, whimsical or half-human roles (*Les Sylphides*, *Carnaval*, *Schéhérazade*, *Spectre de la Rose*, *Petrushka*, *L'Après-Midi d'un Faune*.)

Since then things have hardly improved. In fact in this country our devotion to neo-classicism has made the Prince or the Poet, in one guise or another, the normal (if that is the word) male lead. One waits with confidence for him to keel over, like a heavyweight boxer, at the first sign of trouble.

There are minor exceptions. De Valois, for instance, has thought up some men's roles which have the right ingredients. In *Checkmate* the Red Knight is a proper champion, and Satan in her *Job* is a noble and spirited creature, even if he is on the wrong side. Lifar perhaps, in an egocentric way, in *Alexandre le Grand*; Loring's *Billy the Kid* or the Bolshoi *Mazeppa*. But the outstanding choreographer in this respect is Massine. Delving, no doubt, into his own hard masculine character, he has given us the only ballet heroes who, one feels, could talk to Achilles or Henry V or Robin Hood in their own language. Even he has failed to create a true heroic role. But Lichine in *Les Présages* or *Choreartium*, and he himself in *Tricorne* or *Beau Danube* are made of the true steel. In other circumstances, one feels, they might have been given the sheriff's badge.

This may reveal a childlike set of values, but it is not a negligible or disgraceful one. A sophisticated devotion to the dreamer and mixed-up neurotic has done a serious disservice to ballet. But a new wind can be felt blowing through the art. It is time it swept away some of our weak-kneed lovers and replaced them with a new,

35

active, two-fisted breed. There *is* real blood in our dancers, if it were allowed to show.

3.4.60

## *The Invitation*, The Royal Ballet, Covent Garden

Writing in the current issue of *World Theatre*, a German critic gives one of those brutal laconic side-swipes which make one gasp and open one's eyes. 'The public does not know,' he murmurs, 'what it can and should expect from ballet: a substitute for operetta or a dramatic digest.' Is this all it's about, then? Is it for these meagre prizes that dancers sweat and bleed, and the faithful public queues in the sleet?

The definition is obviously unfair. But it is too near the normal run of things for comfort. We have ourselves basketfuls of operetta-substitutes (it is a genre in which Ashton is unsurpassed), and it is natural that the up and coming generation of choreographers should lean towards digested drama. After Cranko's *Antigone*, with its crushing load of myth, Kenneth MacMillan now, in *The Invitation* (what invitation?), plunges into the steamy swamps of Tennessee Williams country, where corruption rules and innocence is shown only as a decoy pigeon to bring the falcons in.

The theme is of a young girl just awakening to love (the process is illustrated by her unwilling initiation into the revelations of classical sculpture). She is attracted by the mature charms of a married man. He responds all too warmly and flirtation flares into rape. Meanwhile his wife comforts herself by seducing the girl's young boy companion. When the two children, shattered, come together again everything has changed. As the boy bends over to kiss her she is suddenly repelled. The whole thing is nasty, and that's the way, we know, it will stay for her all her life.

The scene is Edwardian, the prim background forming an ideal foil for the scenes of passion. Inevitably one is reminded of Tudor's *Lilac Garden*. This is the kind of territory he was exploring twenty-five years ago. (One is reminded, too, of the astonishing absence of any work by this most distinguished English choreographer from the national repertory – an omission which history, notoriously dis-interested in reasons, will not forgive.)

MacMillan tackles the theme in a looser style than Tudor would

36

have done. The five scenes vary from the first shifting, delicate, uncertain passion of children playing in a garden to the concentrated fury of the rape: and he has inserted, rather abruptly, a *divertissement* sequence in a totally different style. This last seems, at first viewing, a mistake; it does not contrast the mood so much as dissipate it. There are, too, dashes of bathetic realism. And there are moments which come near to Victorian melodramatic farce. One cries out repeatedly for a pull on the snaffle. But in general the fluency and delicacy of the writing and the succession of exquisite solos and *pas de deux* – there is plenty of dancing as well as drama – make this MacMillan's best ballet to date.

He has dropped the jerky articulated movements, interspersed with jazz references, which he has often employed in the past, keeping this style for the Entertainment (which includes a striking Melanesian-type cockfight). Instead we have something smooth and inventive, yet never strained.

Above all he has written superbly for Lynn Seymour. She is the lucky possessor of a tender, expressive, liquid movement astonishingly similar to that of Fonteyn: she can act: and she is very young. From the moment when she runs on and gently plays (flirts would be too grown-up a word) with the boy – sensitively danced by Christopher Gable – to the beautifully arranged twisting rape-scene and her last empty gesture, a modern Giselle, fractured by lust instead of by love, he never puts a foot wrong for her. And she responds with a performance which puts her straight into the ballerina class. This is an interpretation which connoisseurs will treasure. Desmond Doyle could do with more restraint as the Husband, and Ann Heaton, in an unfortunate costume, has to struggle with the part of a *grande dame* totally lacking in sophistication or elegance.

For once the other elements concord happily with the choreography. Georgiadis's series of tachist sets are his best yet – evocative, practical, positive and yet unobtrusive: and Matyas Seiber's skilful score is full of happy invention, neither turgid nor wan, nor sentimental. This is drama well digested.

1.1.61

# The arrival of Nureyev in the West

Russian newspapers did not carry any mention yesterday of the defection of Rudolf Nureyev, the brilliant young dancer of the Leningrad Kirov ballet who sought political asylum in France as his company was about to leave Paris by air for London.

He left Paris yesterday morning for an undisclosed destination, after the French authorities had granted him permission to remain in France. Meanwhile, thirty members of the Kirov ballet visited the Golders Green Hippodrome last night to see the Royal Ballet perform *Les Deux Pigeons*. The company opens tomorrow at Covent Garden, but Nureyev would not have been required until *The Sleeping Beauty* began on Friday night.

The defection of Nureyev will rob London – at least for the present – of the chance to see one of the three or four best male dancers in the world. Even Russian authorities describe him as 'a great dancer with a brilliant future.' He was the sensation of the company's Paris season and was to have danced a number of leading roles in London.

Twenty-three years old, slim and fair, Nureyev has high cheekbones and slanting eyes which reveal his Tartar ancestry. But in his street clothes – tight trousers and sweater – and 'forward-cut' hair he could be mistaken for an English art student. In fact, he speaks good English (but not a word of French) and was much looking forward to his visit to London. Like others in the company, he is something of an Anglophile.

He is not a product of the Leningrad school. He began his career with a provincial amateur troupe and joined the Leningrad company only three years ago. Evidently he did not fit into the ensemble too easily: he has been criticised for having failed so far to learn 'that the leading role is after all only part of the artistic whole to which even the most gifted *premier danseur* must subordinate his individuality.'

Curiously enough, his style is very much of the kind which has been associated with Leningrad (as opposed to Moscow), possessing a striking elegance and authority. To this he adds superb technique and a compelling dramatic power.

He is one of those lucky performers who have only to walk on to the stage to command it. His startling new interpretation of the fairy-tale prince in *The Sleeping Beauty*, with its foppish wit and royal disdain, would be keenly appreciated by Covent Garden audiences.

In Paris yesterday Serge Lifar declared that Nureyev's decision to remain in France was a 'disaster for the Leningrad ballet, of which he was the unquestionable star. Nureyev recently received the Nijinsky Prize – the No. 1 award for dancing in the Soviet Union. Serge Golovine and he are, in my opinion, the two best male dancers in the world.'

18.6.61

## The Kirov, Covent Garden

Five years ago that great juggernaut from Moscow, the Bolshoi Ballet, rolled into Covent Garden and out of it. The state of dancing in Russia had been revealed to us by the mightiest of all ballet companies. Yet audiences in London have been awaiting the arrival of the much smaller Kirov Ballet company from Leningrad with almost as much excitement as they felt in 1956, and with even a special nervousness. Why?

The short answer is: family curiosity. While the Bolshoi was the magnified version of what had always been an idiosyncratic company with a special Muscovite style of its own, this troupe is the true descendant of the imperial company from which (via Diaghilev) our own Royal Ballet springs. How far apart would the two companies prove to have diverged?

The test lies in a single work – *The Sleeping Beauty*. To understand the key place which this ballet holds one has to glance at history. Born in Italy, ballet was brought to France in the sixteenth century. With the westernisation of Russia, dancing spread eastwards and soon a French ballet master was installed at the head of a Russian company in St Petersburg. It had a succession of foreign directors and reached its peak at the end of the nineteenth century.

The culmination came on January 15, 1890. On that day a Russian-ised Frenchman, Marius Petipa, combined with a Francophile Russian, Tchaikovsky, to produce a masterpiece which seized on the pomp and panoply of the court and raised it to be an image of something noble and rare – *The Sleeping Beauty*.

The event took place in the very theatre where the visiting Leningrad company works from day to day – the Maryinsky, now

39

renamed the Kirov; and the ballet has stayed in the repertoire ever since. But in 1917 St Petersburg became Leningrad; the princes and princesses disappeared; foreigners were discouraged; the capital shifted to Moscow. Finally, in 1952, the ballet was largely re-choreographed. The spirit of the original had, it was claimed, been respected; but the straight stream of descent had been slightly polluted.

If *The Sleeping Beauty* is a peak, it is also a watershed, and it was Diaghilev who divided the streams. He lured away the principal dancers and choreographers – Pavlova, Karsavina, Nijinksy, Fokine and the rest – and toured them round the world, leaving, like a profligate prince, heirs wherever he stayed.

Our own Royal Ballet is a specially pure-blooded descendant for here (unlike France for instance) there was no already existing company before his arrival. And our *Sleeping Beauty* has special claims. In that original production one of the 'rats' was a child named Nicholas Sergeyev. He grew up to become *régisseur*, and supervised the ballet many times. He followed Diaghilev out of Russia and produced it for Diaghilev in 1921. He settled in London and it was he who, in 1939, directed our production. This is our stream, our claim to be an authentic heir of the Russian Ballet.

This phrase has a precise meaning. The Russian artistic character left to itself is (as can be seen in the modern Bolshoi company) free and strong as a herd of wild horses. Magnificent though a galloping mustang can be, there is something even more satisfying. That is when the same horse is tightly controlled by the sensitive rein of an expert rider. In St Petersburg the Russian horse had a Latin rider. The result was the tense, vital art which we call Russian Ballet. It has been aptly described as 'three parts French, one part Italian, seen through the Russian temperament and shown through the Russian physique.'

The magnificent Russian temperament and physique are still there. One has only to watch this company's *Stone Flower* to enjoy it. The zest of the Gipsy scene makes Western orgies look like a parade of pansies and debutantes (with Irina Gensler and her partner almost stealing the show). The lubricated athleticism of the men sets a standard beyond the West's present reach, whether it is expressed in the heroics of Soloviev or in the villainous antics of Anatoli Gridin, while the touching, sensitive, fragile-footed Sizova adds to a lively spring that simple *naiveté* which is the special Soviet gift to art. (Evil, perhaps because it is more complicated, they seem less good at: as the seductress Alla Osipenko was over-exhibitionist and lacking in musicality.)

The ballet itself is not distinguished. The Gipsy sequence is brilliantly arranged, but otherwise the choreography is unimaginative, and somewhat cloying. Moreover the whole conception is tired and second-hand – a story expressed in other people's images in the same way that Prokofiev's score veers (again the Gipsy scene is an exception) from weakly derivative waltzes to Hollywood heroics.

25.6.61

*Almost all good art is held in a balanced tension between opposing principles – Appollonian and Dionysian, classical and romantic, or whatever you like to call them. The fact that Russian culture sprang from its medievalism bang into the nineteenth century, the high noon of the Romantic age, has suggested a special and rather inaccurate imbalance in what we think of as typically Russian art. The unlucky fact that Pushkin (so far) has proved untranslatable while Dostoevsky's flavour runs steadily into English has thrown most of the limelight onto the wilder shores of the Russian literary landscape. The deeply romantic idiom of the age in which he worked makes us overlook that Tchaikovsky's great love was Mozart.*

*This is what Stravinsky has written: 'If I appreciate highly the value of classical ballet, it is not simply a matter of taste on my part, but because I see exactly in it the perfect expression of the Apollonian principle.' It is this principle – the classical canon of order, harmony and proportion – which lies at the back of ballet, the intensely arduous discipline concealed under the deceptive ease. This quality is exactly what seems to emerge from Pushkin's poetry, and it is a quality which has run through all Russian art just as strongly as its more demonic energy. Maybe it is because we too have always valued undemonstrative excellence that the English are now the nation which comes next to Russia in its love for, and understanding of, classical ballet.*

## Nureyev in London

From the top of a Tower-bound bus last week peered a dramatically un-English face with strong Tartar features, alert dark eyes and a

41

mop of fair hair. It belonged to Rudolf Nureyev, the twenty-three-year-old Russian dancer who made his dash for freedom at the airport at Paris a few months ago just as his company, the Leningrad Kirov Ballet, were taking off for London.

Nureyev was in London to make arrangements for his official visit next month, when he makes his first appearance here at a Gala at Drury Lane on 2 November. Quiet, elegant, soft-spoken, he walks with the fastidious intentness of a cat – one of the larger, wild cats. His manner is gentle, with a hint of something formidable behind; his style is 'cool'; his physique, slight-seeming from a distance, looks tough as you get close.

It is not surprising that he broke with his old masters. He is exceptionally exceptional; and in Russia, even in the theatre, orthodoxy is in strong demand ('I do not like to be pressed'). But he is understandably reticent about the details of his defection. 'I forget quickly,' is his comment on his Russian past.

His parents are peasants in a small village in Tartary, three days' journey from Leningrad. When he was six he was taken to a dance recital and later he joined an amateur folk-dance troupe. But he was seventeen – almost middle-aged for a dance student – when he was spotted and whisked away to Leningrad. Within half a dozen years he had crashed through the barriers of long service and seniority which guard promotion in the Soviet theatre.

Hours after reaching London he was finding his own way round. Hyde Park ('very nice – especially for dogs'); Covent Garden (several times, once accompanied by Margot Fonteyn) and the National Gallery, where he was impressed by the free admission.

His natural expression is one of faint amusement, puckering into a grin. The lowering of the safety curtain at the Opera House made him laugh. A road sign – Dead Slow – sent him into fits.

His English, though he taught himself only last year, is good. But he is greedy for new words. 'Scatty? What is scatty? Ah, yes – that is what I am!' And he beams like a child with a new penny.

1.10.61


## Fonteyn and Nureyev, R.A.D. Gala

The annual matinées organised by Dame Margot Fonteyn in aid of the Royal Academy of Dancing have established themselves as

42

something rare – galas to which even blasé *aficionados* can look forward.

This year a real balletic missile was sandwiched in amongst the fireworks, in the shape of Rudolf Nureyev making his first London appearance: but it would be unfair to let the fall-out from his detonating performance totally obscure the other performers.

First among these is Margot Fonteyn herself. In *Le Spectre de la Rose*, in which she played the tender young girl opposite Gilpin's agile rose-apparition, she has refound a role which suits her marvellously – girlish innocence conveyed with perfect proportion and timing. Gerard Ohn and Claire Sombert offered a nice, quiet *pas de deux;* and a company of Danes, dazzlingly led by Solveig Oestergaard and Niels Kehlet, displayed the speed, lightness and clean *batterie* of the Bournonville style.

But, of course, Nureyev was the star of the occasion and one, clearly, of a magnitude to pale the sky. This was not the kind of programme to prove, as he did in the Kirov *Sleeping Beauty*, how he can create a psychologically true role and sustain it through a whole evening. But what we did glimpse was enough to show that he is not just one more skilled dancer but something utterly different – a strange, haunted artist whose medium happens to be dancing.

The savage intensity with which he flung himself into his first solo – an odd affair in which one could feel the romantic Soviet style run on a loose rein by Ashton – produced the shock of seeing a wild animal let loose in a drawing-room: while the blend of gracefulness and strength (more of each than we are used to) in the Black Swan *pas de deux*, in which he was expertly accompanied by Rosella Hightower, displayed what I believe to be the true Maryinsky touch, in which Slav temperament is drawn tight by Italian formality.

He has the unmistakable Kirov style and dignified stage manners, a dazzling technique and, rarest of all, a potent stage presence – a Babilée with a Soloviev technique. Now we all eagerly await the chance of seeing him in a full-scale setting.

5.11.61

# Nureyev's debut at Covent Garden, in *Giselle*

Everybody knows that it is men who are, in life, the dreamy crea-tures, relying on the solider sex for practical aid. How wrongly this is reflected in ballet! For every hundred feminine fly-away romantics there is hardly one male able to project even the faintest gleam of the true consuming fire. One who excels in dancing as well is, of course, even rarer – not more than one or two in a generation.

The last great romantic male dancer, anyway in the West, was perhaps the young Lifar. Now we have Rudolf Nureyev. His début at Covent Garden last Wednesday should be recorded as clearly as the appearance of a new comet.

*Giselle* is essentially a long *pas de deux*. Unlike later classical works – *Swan Lake* or *The Sleeping Beauty* – in which the hero is just a packet of instant nobility, this ballet offers two parts of equal dramatic depth: the wronged Giselle and the deceiving Albrecht. Its full con-tent cannot emerge unless both roles are satisfyingly worked out. The vital importance of each to the other was spelt out for all to see on Wednesday by the sudden gain in Margot Fonteyn's interpretation. We have had many good Giselles, including hers, but at Covent Garden the ballet has never quite struck fire. That it does now is simply due to the appearance of an Albrecht of equal stature.

We have had all sorts of Albechts – noble ones, ardent ones, weak ones, manly ones. Here is one who combines all these elements and adds a vital ingredient of his own. This is a streak of post-adolescent instability which arouses mixed feelings of anxiety and protec-tiveness. It is the James Dean charm of a boy who will always be in trouble and always forgiven.

This excessively youthful interpretation makes the story wholly believable. Here is one of those all too real tragedies arising from the selfish, unreflecting infatuation of a first affair. The emotion is abso-lutely genuine (how tenderly Nureyev dances to Giselle in the first act, an earnest adoring puppy-soft lover) and so is the agony of self-reproach when he is faced with the consequences.

Fonteyn has always excelled in portraying youthful innocence, but it was uncertain how the visitor's more exotic style would marry with our production. It worked out miraculously well. The changes are almost all for the better and the company gave sturdy support.

Anya Linden is an ideal Myrtha and Shaw and Lane did a spirited Peasant *pas de deux*.

To say that the two stars were well matched is to compliment each. Both are musical to their finger-tips, and it is long since such delicacy of phrasing – not just here and there but sustained through long sweeps of movement – has been seen at Covent Garden. Fonteyn also added to her customary waif-like lightness and charm an extra cleanness of technique to give an outstanding performance.

To innate romanticism Nureyev adds a variety of gifts. Technically he is endowed with a neat figure, natural turn-out, exceptional elevation, impeccable turns and beats, strong but sensitive feet (rare in a man) and a suppleness laced with a fiery dash of Slav temperament which permits him more grace than most men could get away with. When he makes one of his great loping runs round the stage like a cheetah caught behind bars, he seems to be made of more elastic material than normal humanity.

Almost all his variations differ from the ones we know – neither better nor worse. He makes them seem right, which is what matters. An example is when he is commanded by Myrtha to dance till he drops. He immediately does thirty-two *entrechats* in a row – a simple but startlingly effective response.

Dramatically he is both powerful and subtle. He can afford to underact. The reason why, when he stands clutching his throat, he expresses such anguish is a matter of fine interplay of angle and line and twist, something which any sculptor can understand. He is lucky enough to be born with the instinct to compose it unconsciously. From the moment of his first entrance – sliding in unobtrusively as though he really *was* anxious not to be caught – the acting element was secure. It was clinched by a marvellously sustained performance. He appears unaware of the audience. Caught up in the greater reality of the drama, he does not actively project emotion; he enables us to look in on it (this is Ulanova's style).

As for the dancing, this was better than those who had glimpsed his gala turns could have foreseen. A strong and attentive partner, his own solos were done with perfect smoothness and control, meticulously measured to each dramatic situation, with a modest but aristocratic elegance. What is most impressive, though, is the way in which acting and dancing are held so tightly within the same style that they flow imperceptibly into each other. This is the true sign of a great artist greatly taught.

23.2.62

45

# Erik Bruhn, *Giselle* at Covent Garden

'There is nothing particularly interesting in a jilted girl having her heart broken.' Few people will be ready to push misogyny as far as this extremity, recently reached by a colleague discussing *Giselle*. All the same it is true that if, as is often claimed, *Giselle* is the *Hamlet* of ballet, there must be a good male dramatic part in it somewhere. Too often this is glossed over politely to make the ballerina shine more clearly. Nureyev showed the other day how a strong individual rendering plus a supercharged stage personality can make Albrecht jump into the foreground of the picture: on Tuesday Erik Bruhn gave a second remarkable interpretation of a totally different kind.

Apart from the exhilarating rectitude of his dancing (how can he move his trunk and arms so freely and yet so correctly?) this was a splendidly well-thought-out characterisation. The Barrymore profile which sometimes lends a sort of stiffness to his acting here becomes an asset. He suggests just the kind of over-handsome charmer who would let a girl down; nothing vicious about him – probably a bit spoilt.

Bruhn is an intelligent rather than a natural actor and there were rare breaks in the 'line' of his performance (the naturalistic walk-on at the start of Act II was one) but there was not a moment when he fell below the level which puts him in the very front rank in this exacting part.

Nerina, in response, gave one of her best performances. A charming and touching little simpleton caught in a situation too big for her, she went mad movingly and bounded and floated through the second act like a real guardian angel, comforting yet unearthly. Sibley and Usher made a dashing peasant couple and the production went well. As he lets a flower from Giselle's grave fall from his grasp his gesture expresses a double finality – good-bye both to his love and to the ballet.

8.4.62

*Erik Bruhn dominated the ballet world of his period like a rock: granite-hard, smooth, dizzily high, inscrutable, unscaleable.*

*Bruhn embodies all the qualities the English hold most dear. Decent and correct as a Georgian crescent, with a fresh-laundered purity of technique and the unobtrusive distinction of a Savile Row suit, he could be called the first gentleman of ballet. Like a Danish Scarlet Pimpernel, he conceals his fiery deeds beneath an almost glacial elegance. His dancing has an almost moral quality. He is an artist of virtue rather than a virtuoso.*


# New York City Ballet, Hamburg

Igor Stravinsky, justly fêted during the last few weeks as a musician, has another claim to our homage. He is the most important living figure in the world of ballet bar none. First, of course, because of his contribution as a composer, but also just because he *has* contributed.

Every ballet-lover has to endure from time to time the slings and arrows of outraged musicians. He can endure the buffeting with fortitude, strong in the knowledge that he has a giant-sized fifth-columnist on his side. Stravinsky neither despises ballet as an art nor thinks it demeaning for music to accompany dance. That he has held to this view through his 80 years is in itself a major blessing.

His offerings on the creative side are astonishing, far exceeding in importance those of his only rival, Tchaikovsky. Almost by chance Tchaikovsky stepped in and in one work (*The Sleeping Beauty*) set up a summit in an existing style, and in another (*Swan Lake*) founded a future one. But then death intervened. Stravinsky, on the other hand, started young and his 12 ballets – not counting works arranged to random pieces – have carried ballet through at least three revolutions; he has taken it from *Firebird* (written when he was 27) via *Petrushka* and *Sacre* to the neo-classical *Apollon* and on to the latest, *Agon*.

The last two were both choreographed by Balanchine, and there can be no doubt that it is the mutual respect and sympathy between these two men which has kept the balletic spark alight in Stravinsky. It was a graceful thought on the part of the Hamburg municipality (any red faces at the L.C.C.?) to stage three of their joint creations last week as a birthday tribute to the composer.

A somewhat superfluous unity was lent to the programme by selecting ballets with Greek associations, though one of them, *Agon* has (in spite of a programme boldly announcing 'The Greek Myth Ballets') nothing remotely Greek about it beyond its title. Balanchine brought over 12 of his New York City company to ensure authentic performance. The result was a rare and fascinating evening, a glimpse of three ages of two great artists.

The earliest work – lucidly conducted on the opening night by the composer – was *Apollon Musagète* (1928). With two supremely Apollonion temperaments at the helm, this was a sure-fire hit. It is at the same time a pure reflection of the twenties and (like so much in that period) a foretaste of the sixties. In fact, some hindsight seems to have crept into the production. Jacques d'Amboise and his three Muses are a fine set, but classical polish has been replaced by something sharper, more edgy. The sidelong approach to classicism gives the dancing now an ambiguity I do not feel in the score.

But this is a ballet to last. The fate of the next one is more doubtful. The tale of *Orpheus* (1948) and his Eurydice might be expected to have evoked some marvellous manoeuvres. But the score is muted and the dancing almost non-existent. The ballet is dominated by the designer, Noguchi. His wonderful inventions (who can ever forget those planets floating behind the great, white, silken cloud?) still resound like a gong.

It was the third ballet, *Agon* (1957), which clinched the evening. It is a remarkable work, quite different from the Royal Ballet version. No quirks or fancies here; instead, a straight suite of dances as prescribed (performed, as Balanchine always prefers, in simple practice dress) with no connecting link other than that of style. This matches that of the music miraculously.

It is not a matter of slavish eurhythmics. Invention runs free, but the dancing seems to move always in the same dimension as the score – epigrammatic, stripped, short-breathing, held-in emotionally yet curiously relaxed and airy. An elusive note of self-mockery hangs in the air. All the numbers (that is how they are presented) end with a sharp and witty pay-off, like a sudden drop in the voice.

The dancing in this ballet – by Balanchine's own team, of course – mirrors the choreography and catches the contemporary mood to perfection. The girls are given classical, high-kicking athletics. The men are wary and limber, a bit exaggeratedly wholesome now and then – not camp but campus, in a style strongly reminiscent of Jerome Robbins.

Balanchine's control of his performers is acute. It is stylistic rather than mechanical. There is little individuality and no great unanimity either, but each dancer seems to understand perfectly the tensed knife-edge poise between dignity and insouciance which is his imprint.

Seekers after what corresponds to *bel canto* or *belle peinture*, a rich flow of movement, will be disappointed. The dancing is dry and calculated, sometimes so detached that one feels the movements are being described rather than executed. As Stravinsky has foresworn sumptuous texture, so too this dancing is, compared say with the Russian style, like a dry-point beside an oil painting.

It is hard-edged puritan art in which the flesh is refined away. These dancers speak with their bones, and they have marvellous things to say.

1.7.62

*Agon, that balletic Everest whose peaks seem to reach into a clear stratosphere where mortal struggles fade away: Stravinsky's thin, passionate sounds from the orchestra, tense as wire, manifest themselves in diagrams of movement as open, but as complex (and difficult), as a constructivist mobile.*

## Fonteyn and Nureyev, *Le Corsaire* at Covent Garden

The curtain came down at Covent Garden last night to cheers, shouts and flying carnations. The Fonteyn-Nureyev combination (a pairing which will surely go down in ballet history) had brought off another knock-out performance.

The *pas de deux* from *Le Corsaire* lasts for only eight minutes, but it is worth going a thousand miles to see.

In a way it is more astonishing than their famous *Giselle*. That is an extraordinarily subtle piece of character interpretation, an extreme example of a genre our own dancers often make quite a fair stab at. But this is something quite new to Covent Garden, something, in fact, still far outside the range of our home team – the sheer percussive impact of a bravura-cum-style which makes the heart alternately freeze with awe and race with exhilaration.

*Le Corsaire* is an old Petipa dance, a fragment from a romantic tale of a maiden carried away by a pirate. The maiden was Fonteyn in an enchanting little sequin cap, and she seemed to be mightily enjoying her misfortune. Far from languishing, she sparkled and spun and dipped like a filly loosed out to grass. The bubbling dash with which she tackled her *fouettés* made one feel good.

49

Nureyev, lithe and hungry-looking in silver Turkish trousers, stunned the audience with what was probably the finest piece of male dancing seen on the Covent Garden stage in this generation.

Leaping and turning like a salmon, soft as a panther, proud and cruel, never for a second relaxing his classical control – this was a spectacle which made one believe (the comparison is inevitable) those legends of Nijinsky.

It was hard to believe that this was the same dancer who had wandered, rapt, beside Giselle's grave. On Thursday we had seen him in yet another guise, taming his fires to fit the wholesome, modestly extrovert style of Bournonville's *Flower Festival at Genzano* with Anya Linden (who proved badly miscast).

It is not long since we saw the role superbly danced by Erik Bruhn. He himself had built individually on the Bournonville tradition, giving it extra breadth and expressiveness. Nureyev does the same but – not surprisingly – departs further from the original idiom. This idiom is essentially a sharply articulated affair – a chain not a rope. Nureyev danced it with such smoothness, ease and perfect timing that the separate links became almost invisible. The definition of the choreography was harder to grasp. But he introduced a new singing element which was a rich compensation. This was not quite Danish but it was something just as good.

4.11.62

# Revival of *Ondine*, The Royal Ballet, Covent Garden

In the same way that a little learning is dangerous, a medium acquaintanceship with a ballet is misleading. The first impact will tell a great deal. Not until much later do valuable new revelations emerge.

It was obvious at first sight that *Ondine* was a magnificent vehicle for Fonteyn. Subsequent visits gave the impression that this was almost all – that much of the rest of it was confused or only half-realised. Its revival last week raised different reflections. The first impression remains. There can be few modern works more marvellously and lovingly devised to draw out and show off a dancer.

In her new flowering Fonteyn could hardly fail to excel, and in fact this was one of her best performances to date. Emerging as sleek as a silvery minnow from the stream, she played with her new-found shadow like a squirrel chasing its tail: lost and bewildered in the shipwreck scene, she reached a new height of Racinian tragedy in the last act when she returns, thaws into humanity and accepts her role as her lover's executioner. She danced like an angel throughout.

But she did not eclipse the rest of the show. The variations in the last act were given with a fine billiance, especially by Shaw and Park. Linden was a human if an anachronistically Edwardian Berta, and Somes and Grant shone in their old roles. All these have reached a point where they reveal the true potentials of their parts. Now one can see that there is even more here that has not yet been brought out.

18.11.62

*[Fonteyn has] that marvellous control which dovetails movements when others would show the joins. She has* in excelsis *the typically English quality of poise, in which all display – even that of reticence – is consciously concealed. The nearest analogy I can think of is Wren's architecture.*

## Alicia Markova, on her retirement

It is obviously premature to use the past tense about Alicia Markova, but as a performer we must now say 'did' instead of 'does' or 'will do' about our first international ballerina – a sad change.

She has had a fantastic career. It started so far back that by rights she should now be a silvery old lady; but she had the luck to be a young prodigy just when young prodigies were in demand. When she made her début with Diaghilev in 1925 she was only 15, young enough to start a new career after his death as ballerina of the Ballet Rambert and then as the key luminary round which the newborn Sadler's Wells Company revolved.

From the start, lightness and a fragile poetry were her speciality. Exceptionally slight in build, with the oval face and delicately sloping shoulders of a Victorian heroine, she naturally found her favourite territory in the nineteenth century. Bravura display was the opposite of her approach, but her technique was, at its prime, con-siderable – how easily and elegantly she executed the nowadays often omitted double-turns in the *Façade* polka solo. Her musicality and

51

feeling in romantic roles like *Swan Lake* and *Les Sylphides* were inimitable. She also had a delicious streak of mischievous comedy – a quality never fully exploited – and in Massine's *Rouge et Noir* showed she could sustain a lyrical role at symphonic level.

But it is with *Giselle* that she will always be most associated. In this ballet she developed her fey, ethereal stage personality to reach an interpretation which has been compared to Taglioni's but which is probably unique. She was not so much a human who became a spirit as the reverse. The tender, trusting peasant girl seemed no more than the temporary condensation of the vapour into which she later melted.

6.1.63

## *Cinderella*, The Bolshoi at Covent Garden

Seeing the Bolshoi's *Cinderella*, like seeing most of their productions at Covent Garden, gives you the sensation of an air journey on a rough day. There is a sense of weightlessness and loss of aesthetic bearings. Euphoria induced by repeated glimpses of intoxicating splendour is punctuated by drops into banality so sudden and precipitous that they take the breath away. You stagger out at the end feeling exhausted, elevated and a trifle air-sick. It is a memorable experience.

Like *The Humpbacked Horse*, this ballet had the bad luck to be introduced to British audiences in an inept film version. On the stage it is far more impressive; in fact, it is the most satisfactory production all round which the company has presented this season. It differs from Ashton's ballet to the same Prokofiev score by playing down the comedy. The heroine's step-sisters are silly, not ugly, and the grotesquerie is confined to an extra character, her stepmother (wittily played by Elena Vanke). Some of the fairy-tale ingredients we love most, the pumpkin, for instance, have disappeared, but the story otherwise proceeds with the charming earnestness of a child's narrative. The finale shows Cinderella in her fireside rags held aloft in triumph, the very apotheosis of the working-girl.

Raissa Struchkova raises the heroine to a figure who verges on the heroic. In the kitchen scenes she is no bashful, half-starved waif but a sturdy unsophisticated girl who would wield a useful broom. Transformed for the ball, she is a real dazzler. Serenely confident that she can out-dance them all, she promptly does so. She is one of those lucky performers with ideal all-round proportions, and she has an amazing all-round technique – jumping and spinning, darting and poising with breath-taking ease. When she is let loose from the corner she flies like a whippet (the Covent Garden stage is visibly too small for her): she is all spring and feather-weight control, with marvellous steel ankles, supple arms and a calm smile.

On the opening night her Prince was the dashing Mikhail Lavrovsky, who brought a hot-blooded attack to both his dancing and acting which completely convinced. In a later performance Vladimir Vasiliev, making his début in the part, introduced even more superb breadth and style and a handsome presence. His consistently left-handed turns are disconcerting at first, but he is an amazing dancer, combining strength and elegance in a way we in the West have not got round to.

The choreography by Zakharov (who arranged *The Fountain of Bakhchisarai*, which was shown here on their last visit) is very uneven but by no means to be despised. The solo numbers may not be original but they are never dull. The four 'seasons' dances are charming (and irresistible when performed by such delicate artists as Bessmertnova, Maximova, Sorokina, and Samokhvalova): the Jester, especially as interpreted by Georgi Soloviev, is a quicksilver conception and the Prince's entry, with its final backward leap on to the throne, is a fine imaginative stroke. Though the whole ballroom scene runs with excitement, where the choreography falters is in the arrangements for the *corps de ballet*: what the poor 'grasshoppers' and Spanish dancers have to do is funny and sad.

The costumes in *Cinderella* are unobtrusive but it is impossible to ignore the sets. A huge area of the already cramped stage is reserved for the display of cloth after cloth of indistinguishable feebleness: rigging and trellis work, light-machines and false mirrors are heaved up and down to absolutely no effect. I have never seen in Covent Garden uglier sets than those for the Oriental and the Andalusian scene, in which bullfighters in gold straw-hats prance about holding parasols. I would gladly have scrapped the lot for black curtains, a big stage and the whole company gloriously let loose upon it.

14.7.63

*There were half a dozen superb dancers here and at least one potentially great one. She was in the corps-de-ballet, moving like a crescent moon among the stars. Her name is Natalia Bessmertnova.*

53

# Martha Graham in Edinburgh and London

Martha Graham is revolutionary, ruthless and prodigal. To encounter her work for the first time is one of the most stunning experiences the theatre has to offer. Her person and her productions are so much of a piece that in a way all her work seems one. She employs different composers, yet her scores are like siblings. No matter who designs her sets and costumes, they look excellently alike. The nine ballets she brought to Edinburgh (and brings this week to London) could, without a nonsense, be performed as a single colossal programme. The series on Greek legend makes up, indeed, a unit as solid as *The Ring*.

This is not accidental: in more ways than one she could be described as a modern Wagner of the dance. There is a ponderous element in her thinking, and an obsession with dark forces symbolised by the conspiracies of ancient gods. Like Wagner, she tackles solemn themes in an outrageously serious way, and is uninterested in coquetry, prettiness or wit. And the comparison relates her to contemporary choreographers who may be thought of as successors to Bach or Mozart, carrying forward subtleties of form, stylish delicacy, individual observation and mathematical precision which are simply not within the Graham range.

When the curtain rises on a Graham ballet you will probably find the stage empty except for a few strange bits of modern sculpture (usually by Noguchi) bathed in a mysterious light. As your eyes become accustomed to the gloom you will see that entangled in one is a half-naked human body. Another may turn into a figure unrecognisably bundled in a cloak. Graham herself may be stretched in a corner like a dark stain. There is a feeling of awe as though the stage were deep underground, a cave in which some slightly unpleasant rite was about to begin.

When the shapes move (and to Graham a 'prop' must be as beautiful and as able to act-through-movement as a human) they do so in a tense, angular way which reminds you of Japanese theatre. Faces are mostly dead. Limbs seem propelled by violent mental or physical stresses, the incisive gestures of a drowning man or a woman in labour or the act of love.

The figures stand and sit, manoeuvre around, stamping or twisting or jumping, falling to the ground or swinging from the sculpture. When they, rarely, come together it is usually for lust or a killing. The rhythms are individual and convulsive, never jazzy. Graham has (unlike Wagner) rejected altogether the traditional language of her art and heroically fashioned one of her own. The dancers are barefoot and their movements natural. In the wide sense of stage picture and space awareness she is unmatched and her ingenuity endless. Yet the dance vocabulary is narrow, in spite of borrowings from various national styles.

Basic it may be, but the new language has opened up new and vital ideas of stagecraft, both dramatic and formal. Graham does not set out to grip you with a mounting narrative climax, to charm you or to carry you romantically away. She evokes the vaguer, more timeless emotions inspired by a great building or monumental sculpture.

Her dancers are superbly trained to follow her demands; they moved as though they understood why each muscle works as well as how. When stripped (as they mostly are) her nine men look like Olympic athletes and their grace is of the same order. Her ten girls skip like deer, and writhe and posture with passionate control. In the centre is Graham herself, a tormented spider at the heart of the net she has woven.

The ballets in the programme London will see divide roughly into the Dramas (*Legend of Judith, Phaedra, Clytemnestra, Night Journey*) which are ominous, ritualistic and as richly complicated as a dead queen's shroud; and the Diversions (*Secular Games, Diversion of Angels, Acrobats of God*) revealing a choreographic invention which makes you wish she gave herself more dancing latitude in her dramas. Somewhere between are *Embattled Garden*, a variation on the theme of innocence and experience, and *Seraphic Dialogue*, a vision of Joan of Arc.

There is not a work which would not grip any student of dancing, drama or art (music students might be less impressed). For sheer originality and power, the cumulative majesty of the three-act *Clytemnestra* might come first. For celestial perfection *Seraphic Dialogue*, which turns the whole stage into an altar. For pure pleasure, *Secular Games*, as fresh and strong as a morning breeze.

1.9.63

# Interview with Dame Ninette de Valois

*When you founded the company in 1931 did you want to create a specifically English style of dancing?*

No. I felt that a British school would come naturally out of a tradition. Even at that early time our dancers had a style which the Russians – Diaghilev, for instance – regarded as English. It comes from the classical schools of Western Europe and from our own temperament, which is quite different from the temperament of the Russian dancer.

Just by looking at a person, you can tell the way he's going to dance. And there's no question that physical make-up in Western Europe is not quite the same as physical make-up in Eastern Europe. Eastern Europeans are a more plastic type, they're nearer the Oriental feeling of relaxation. The farther east you go, the more you notice this thing. You can see it in their folk-dances.

*Does this mean that we never could dance in quite the same way as a Russian?*

Yes. And I don't see why we should. It would be boring if you weren't able to recognise different schools. You can't possibly rid yourself of your own style. You can expand it and enrich it by outside influences, but to lose it would be an entirely false thing to do. Anyway, it'll never happen.

*Do you think there's any danger of our style being upset by Nureyev coming in as guest artist?*

No, I don't. I think that's just the way to develop it. And I don't understand the attitude that he should 'fit into' the company. When you take an individual from another environment and place him in the middle of a large company with a different tradition you're very aware of the differences. That's the whole idea of having a guest artist. Every school can give another something. It happened in reverse with the Russians in the last century. They were tremendously influenced by the Italian teacher Cecchetti and by the Italian dancer Legnani, who went there in the nineties.

*It must have been disturbing for the local artists.*

Oh, very painful. They discuss it to this day in Russia. Some of Cecchetti's principles have gone on, but they've all been absorbed into the strength of their own school. And it should happen with us in reverse now. It's like flavouring food. You put something special in to bring out the basic flavour of what you're actually cooking – I regard it rather like that.

I don't expect everyone to understand at the time and I do expect quite of lot of people to be upset. I know that people call me unpredictable. If anyone is first of all given a reputation for having rather a strong mind they daren't ever change it without being called unpredictable. Well, I shall continue to be 'unpredictable' when these occasions arise because I am convinced that they are of real importance.

Of course I would have been stricter in the beginning. When I was with Diaghilev I learned the importance of tradition, of a background. That's what gives you the confidence to experiment.

*You said when you started the company that it must be based on the nineteenth-century classics. Will this go on for ever?*

I believe in going back, if you can, at the very start. But whether *Swan Lake* and *The Sleeping Beauty* will be as important in the repertoire in 50 years' time as they are now, I don't honestly know. The classics are at the height of their popularity here at the moment, but I think a time may come when they will drop down. Remember, nobody in Paris or London wanted them 50 years ago. In Russia, of course, they have carried them on continuously. They have several versions running in different places. That applies to everything they do, even new works. If they produce a new ballet in Moscow, and it's reproduced in Leningrad only six months later, it will more than likely be by another choreographer. This, to us, is quite extraordinary.

*Are there no definitive versions of the nineteenth-century classics?*

Probably the nearest were the ones Sergeyev originally gave us. He was very well known for fighting anything being changed and, as notation master in Leningrad, he had a certain amount of control. But people don't realise the big changes we've introduced into ballets like *Giselle* and *The Sleeping Beauty* and *Swan Lake* during the last 15

57

years. Nureyev's alterations have really meant very little to me, because I know the enormous changes we've made over the years without people noticing.

*How many of the changes which Nureyev has introduced are his own?*

I would say very few. There are so many versions and, of course, we don't know how accurate his version is in comparison with what he either learned or saw in Leningrad. All I know is that in style and approach and musicality they are like everything I've ever seen over there. Without talking of details of left leg or right leg or both arms up or one arm up – leaving all that sort of nonsense out, and thinking of the phrasing and the general style, he's carrying on the tradition of the Russians, that's quite obvious.

*What about contemporary work?*

We've had Nureyev in only two contemporary works and there was nothing changed in either of these. I think he recognised, as a very professional person, that this was our tradition and something that he had to accept if he went into it. He's a most disciplined artist and thinks everything out with the greatest care.

Frankly, I'm just as interested in his mind as in his feet. He's an extremely intelligent young man and has strong convictions. Occasionally he's arrogant, but it's the arrogance of a young man who has broken away from some of the artistic principles of his own country and feels he needs further development. But it's a genuine search on his part and there's a genuine intellect behind it. I find it an exciting mind, responsive and very stimulating.

*You don't seem as shocked as some people are at Nureyev's un-English approach.*

That comes in for more attention than it deserves. I just accept it. Unless it becomes uncomfortable and then I try to explain why. Early on I taught him the saying 'When in Rome, etc.' It appealed to his sense of humour – though without, I should add, any apparent results.

Of course, you'll never get him anywhere on time. You can't get the Chinese to time, you can't get the Spanish to time, you can't get the Russians to time. It's no good worrying. That's the way they're made. I got to know the Russian temperament with Diaghilev.

*Do you think, as some people do, that having stars is a disadvantage?*

That's quite absurd and the most appalling admission to make. A ballet company develops in certain directions at certain times. There will be a period when the stress is on the choreographic side, on theatre production in general. Then there may be a lull when you have the uprising of dancers of genius. These are very rare – perhaps a dozen in 100 years – and of course when they do appear the theatre may have to submit to them, just as it has to submit to that even more rare event – the great choreographer. Then you have another period when strides are being made behind the scenes in teaching. These things hardly ever progress together, there's always one pre-dominating. You have to consider a long period to get things in perspective.

*Can our teaching be improved?*

Of course. The British school of teaching is very sound in its theory, if not yet so sound in practice. It has reached a stage now when it can well afford to develop a few highlights. Foreigners may notice, per-haps, that our dancers don't have, in general, a very high jump. My answer is that this is quite true. But when I go to Russia I don't see general neat footwork.

We want to meet halfway on this. On our side we want to forget how well we can dance Scottish reels and spread ourselves a bit, and the Russians could give up some of their everlasting hurdle-leaping for a little neater and stronger ankle-work. In Russia there appears to be a tendency to make the women as strong as the men. I find this, after a time, a little bit exhausting, and monotonous.

*Do you think the company will continue to develop on the same lines as you have laid down?*

It's not for me to predict the future. That's the business of the people who are taking charge of it. I am being followed, luckily, by England's leading choreographer, Sir Frederick Ashton, who must have theories of his own, and these theories must develop the com-pany and bring it one step further forward. He has no reason to look back on me and bother about what I've said or thought. That won't help the company. Things change and that's good.

There's always a danger of a National Ballet becoming too institutionalised. What is so interesting about innovation is that in the end, after you've absorbed anything new, you return refreshed to your own school. Instinctively you have all this time been strengthening your work basically.

It shows a great weakness if you daren't take in something new. You must be able to say: 'For a moment we'll upset this applecart and see what happens.'

15.9.63

*The English have always been good at lyric poetry and it is perhaps not surprising that they have excelled in an art which is fundamentally lyrical – ballet. Good fortune produced at a critical moment a personality who could concentrate and establish this national gift – Ninette de Valois – and a star performer to interpret it – Margot Fonteyn.*

## Nureyev's production of *La Bayadère*, Act III, Covent Garden

'Jan. 23. La Bayadère: music by Minkus. Benefit of Mlle Vazem. Great success.' So runs Marius Petipa's diary for 1877. He would have been gratified if he had been at Covent Garden last Wednesday when the 'vision act' – always a steady favourite in Russia – was mounted by Rudolf Nureyev for the Royal Ballet.

With two small qualifications it is a totally enjoyable production. The famous repeated-arabesque entry goes on a good deal longer than the music will support; and the work, torn from its context, imposes a strain on a new audience without any scenic clue to place or period. Apart from this, it is a fascinating addition to our historical repertoire.

It also gives rise to wry reflections. First, at this vivid demonstration of art history's eternal spiral twisting back on its own tail; for this is exactly the formal archaic stiffness against which Fokine and all his heirs, from Nijinsky to Robbins, reacted so fruitfully. Yet here we are eagerly reverting to its qualities, the pure structure, disciplined invention and concealed virtuosity which best guarantees survival. In a way *La Bayadère* is the most up-to-date ballet in London.

Another odd reflection. For years we have talked of the great moment when the West would impart to the Russians the fruits of Diaghilev's revolution. Now it turns out that the first exchange is in the other direction; it is we who are holding out welcoming arms to a work from the old Russian Establishment. Odder still, this proves to be that Soviet anathema – a purely abstract creation.

The final wonder is the source of the production. What Nureyev originally brought to our home company was a flourish of romantic fire bordering on the exotic. Yet his first contribution as producer is of a stern severity unmatched by anything in our own repertoire. The golden boy of ballet has added a new, unexpected dimension to his achievements.

Basically this *ballet blanc* consists of geometric cat's-cradling by a large female *corps de ballet* which forms a frame for fluid dances for three girl soloists and for an extended and very beautiful *pas de deux*. It is all as clear and cold as crystal, a distillation of dancing. There is no set. Minkus's music is a mere feeble trellis. No breath of character or drama or atmosphere clouds this Kingdom of the Shades in which an Indian prince pursues the spirit of his beloved.

The long white lines of girls acquitted themselves valiantly and the soloists – Park, Mason and Seymour – span through their exquisite variations with a newly blossoming verve. At the radiant centre Fonteyn – neat, quick, poised and fluent – shone like a diamond, while Nureyev himself (though he had the bad luck to miss out on a series of leaps *en attitude*) formed a proud princely pivot.

How much of the choreography was Petipa and how much was Nureyev only he could say, and there could be no greater compliment. He has given us a glimpse of the spare simplicity which forms one often unnoticed side of the Russian temperament. 'I love thy severe harmony' wrote Pushkin of his adored home city and he might well have been talking of *La Bayadère*. It is a little chip of Leningrad.

1.12.63

## *The Sleeping Beauty*, The Royal Ballet, Covent Garden

The hypnotic fascination which classical dancing holds for its followers lies in its combination of precision and evasiveness. Each new ballerina contributes, by her idiosyncrasies, towards that final definition of the 'true classical style' which always eludes us.

Two of them did so at Covent Garden last weekend in *The Sleeping Beauty*. On Saturday afternoon we had Antoinette Sibley, young and fresh and dowered by the good fairies with a basketful of natural gifts, relatively narrow in experience but dancing in a ballet and a part in which she had grown up. In the evening we had Violette Verdy, trained in France and America, with a broad background but appearing for the first time ever with a strange company and in a ballet unfamiliar in both style and production.

The result was perhaps foreseeable, but also revealing. Sibley darted through the part like a swallow, never putting a foot wrong. Sparkling at the start, she added a touch of dignity at the finish, and at every second she made you feel relaxed and confident. With Verdy the whole effect was reversed. Her own nervous tension when she first ran on generated an electric atmosphere, but produced a technical awkwardness and uncertainty. She never blended with the production, but every minute her tenseness melted until in the last act she suddenly opened up like a rose. In every superficial way her performance was less successful than Sibley's – yet its effect was mysteriously greater.

The fact is that Aurora is a part demanding an adult approach. This precious quality often comes simply through growing older. In five years' time that capacity to make a small movement important, to render a piece of phrasing a matter to take seriously, will almost certainly be added to Sibley's other gifts. In the meantime it is good to have with us an artist who possesses it so strongly, for it is the keystone of real classical style. Perhaps Baudelaire inadvertently came nearest to defining it, with his 'luxe, calme et volupté'. Nobody could have been, on that Saturday evening, less calm than Verdy; but richness and sensuality were equally missing from Sibley. So we go bracketing on round that elusive perfection.

On Tuesday came what looked like being the crucial test of the new production of *Swan Lake*, when the pair for whom it was originally tailored, Fonteyn and Nureyev, finally appeared in it. On this occasion it remained obstinately what it had always been: more entertainment than drama. It goes without saying that the standard of the dancing was high but, apart from minutes of glorious anguish in the last act, the evening never took fire. It turned out, however, that this was not much more than a dress rehearsal. The real performance came on Friday, and it developed into a purple-letter experience. Nureyev's slightly uncertain first-night prince turned into an ultra-subtle and crystal-clear study – a still innocent youth, friendly but *distrait*, pining secretly for he is not sure what. His vision of love once glimpsed, he is only partly misled by its false, glamour-coated image and it is with almost joyful impetus that he hurls himself into eternity in pursuit of the true ideal.

His rendering fitted perfectly into the delicacy of Fonteyn's swan-princess, the fleet embodiment of every lover's romantic phantom. The first encounter between the two beside the lake was touchingly fresh and tender, and the Black Swan act went like a bomb. Fonteyn, dark and dangerous as a mountain tarn, exulted like a girl with a diamond necklace in her back pocket. Nureyev, who continually dares everything to go right, struck an evening when it did. Loping and leaping, twisting, spinning and soft-braking with elegant ease, he made this one short concentration of dancing expand into a whole evening's enjoyment.

The last act became a riot of passionate despair. For the first time the duel between Rothbart and the lovers took on the quality of tragedy. *Luxe* and *volupté* were flying off in handfuls, and the apotheosis which follows the double suicide ended with a consummate calm. The new *Swan Lake* had emerged looking like the season's winner. But with performances like these, even *Charley's Aunt* might masquerade as a masterpiece.

8.3.64

*If* Swan Lake *is a greater ballet than* The Sleeping Beauty *(same composer, same choreographer for the most part) the basic reason is simply that one is haunted by failure, death and despair while the other is not. One is a living myth, the other a mere fairy tale. Swan Lake's marvellous musical unity and choreographic expressiveness flow directly from the haunting presence of the forces of negation, the menacing yawn of the gulf into which Tchaikovsky felt himself (and his hero) inexorably drawn.*

# Nureyev's production of *Raymonda*, Spoleto Festival

Gian Carlo Menotti's annual festival at Spoleto is devoted to celebrating the ties which bind together the 'two worlds' which lie on each side of the Atlantic. The theme was illustrated all too vividly this week, when the echoes of a revolver shot in Panama suddenly rang round the steep and narrow streets of this little town. Margot Fonteyn's enforced withdrawal at the last minute from *Raymonda* meant the disappearance of the star from an avowed star-vehicle. Would it all fall to pieces at this cruel thrust?

That it did not is a huge tribute to the participants, but is fundamentally due to the merits of the ballet itself. For lovers of Petipa's choreography (or of Petipa-style choreography, because Nureyev has cunningly inserted a good many invisible patches of his own) this is a regular blow-out. For the whole long evening the dancing never stopped.

*Raymonda* is frankly a display-piece in the *Sleeping Beauty* manner, in which more or less abstract dance numbers are stitched together by a romantic story – in this case a medieval tale of a young girl who is menaced by a sinister Saracen in the absence of her knightly fiancé, who returns in the nick of time. The original must have contained long patches of mime, but Nureyev has obliterated these in his version, which avoids all pastiche nineteenth-century echoes. No attempt at realism is made, and dramatic strokes are shunned as firmly as are effects of stunning splendour. Like Balanchine, he has reversed the Fokine clock and we are back in a formal world where the only language is that of pure classical ballet.

Here at last is an alternative to the splendid but overworked *Sleeping Beauty*. It contains less spectacle than that ballet but correspondingly more dancing. Number succeeds ravishing number to exploit a surprisingly wide range of new movements – many of them of a difficulty which stretched the young Royal Ballet Company up to, and sometimes beyond, its capabilities. But this is going to be a testing work at all times – and as such it is doubly welcome in the repertoire.

The role of Raymonda is a plum ballerina part – one which incidentally suits Fonteyn in her Bayadère style to perfection, as could be seen at an open rehearsal. It is long and immensely taxing. Doreen

64

Wells, stepping into Fonteyn's shoes at a moment's notice, won a deserved ovation in it, her sure technique standing her in good stead. Nureyev has not much built up his own role, which allows him two virtuoso solos, both done with his customary dash, style and an elevation which belied the strain he must have been under. The company, though foreseeably a bit rough at this performance, showed a pleasing new plasticity.

Glazunov's lush and hummable score lacks the brilliance of Tchaikovsky, but is always adequate and occasionally beautiful.

12.7.64

## The Merce Cunningham Company, Sadler's Wells

Merce Cunningham and his company have burst on the British scene like a bomb, for a simple reason. At a blow, ballet has been brought right up in line with the front-rank experimenters in the other arts – something which has hardly happened since the days of Diaghilev. Here is heart-warming proof that it is an art with a future, opening up ranges of possibilities which stretch out of sight; it ought to be celebrated with champagne in every dancing academy in the land.

Diaghilev would have loved Cunningham. Besides admiring him as an artist he would have respected the seriousness and discipline of his company, the spare wit and style of Rauschenberg's costumes and lighting, the consistent invention of the choreography and the provocative strangeness of John Cage's musical accompaniments. Above all, his acute artistic antennae would have tingled at the sense that Cunningham was talking in the language of today.

It is a voice which comes to us borne on that mysterious stream of thought which seems (whatever Sir Charles Snow says) so often to penetrate artists and scientists simultaneously – in this case an interest in the fact that within the apparent orderliness of the material world lurks a fifth column of indeterminacy, of which random chance is ruler.

This opens up again one of the oldest of man's problems, round which all his social and artistic manifestations revolve – the struggle between freedom and order. It has stimulated new approaches in every art. The doodling pencil, dribbling paint-can, and wobbly, hand-held camera, William Burroughs's chance-assembled books, improvised stage dialogue, far-out jazz cadenzas, sculptural collections of

65

random-chosen objects – all these follow the same trend towards some mystically unobtainable target and away from strait-laced mechanisation. There is an affinity with Oriental thinking, and a worship of the act of creation – fresh and unrepeatable – as opposed to the thing created. The movement's motto might be the two words of Rauschenberg's answer to a question whether he always improvised the lighting. 'Never always,' he replied.

Now, with tremendous effect, ballet joins the field. Through its link with music, ballet has developed since the Renaissance a classical framework capable of a wide range of subtle variety. Cunningham has jettisoned this structure altogether. He has substituted a much looser system based on the rhythms of human movement itself – the rhythm which makes us swing our arms as we walk. Instead of a steady beat he uses a sense of time. Like experienced runners completing a track-circuit his dancers (who rehearse with a stopwatch) can perform a sequence to split-second accuracy.

He extends this limited freedom to the individual dancers, who cue each other as they move, and to whole episodes in a ballet, which he may present in a different sequence on different nights. The whole thing adds up less to a blueprint than to a programme in the scientific or industrial sense. It is like getting up in the morning; the order in which you put on your clothes may vary, but the result and the time remain constant.

The relationship of the dancing and the accompanying music (much the most formidable element in the whole affair, consisting frequently of spasmodic squeaks, drones, thumps or wails which somehow intrigue without obtruding) is of the same order. While each individual player has considerable latitude as to what he does, the conductor ensures that the sound and the visual events coexist, though with no attempt at synchronisation. Dance and music, too, must be allowed to keep their own identity. We have very nearly reached that goal so ardently preached by Marie Rambert – the total emancipation of dancing as an independent art.

Counteracting these liberties are extraordinary restraints. We are in a taut and cagey world very similar to that of much modern painting and writing and music. The dancing is agitated but unemotional, interacting but uninvolved; like the widely spaced notes of the music or the scattered shapes on one of those huge American pictures, the boys and girls retain intact their impassive individuality. There is a take-it-or-leave-it attitude. There is no passion, far less a story. In an extraordinary flow of original movement (derived from Martha

Graham, but less positively 'ugly') the figures run or walk, curl up, jump, pass, interlock or briefly skip in unison like parts of a giant mobile moved by the wind.

We are not so far here from the world of Petipa and Balanchine, and the total effect has the aloof conviction of the best classical dance. The element of ritual, so vital to a theatrical performance, is strong and the dancers themselves exude a powerful stage presence. Cunningham himself is one of the most gifted dancers to come out of America, a natural mover with a subtle sense of timing and flashes of wit as quick as they're surprising in such a serious type. Carolyn Brown is gorgeously lean and supple, with a line both eloquent and elegant; Steve Paxton has a quick, virile precision: and the whole company is trained to perform technical prodigies of balance, slow control and logical muscular progressions.

The cloud of theory in which the company moves may look alarming, and the programme notes are not aimed at tempting the timid (though they make some shrewd points – Debussy's inability to detect any shape in one of the two amiable pieces of normal music employed, Satie's 'Three Pieces in the Form of a Pear', and a quote from Ivan Karamazov, 'Let me tell you that the absurd is only too necessary on earth').

The apologia are often, in fact, strangely remote from what we actually see. Art is no respecter of ends and means. What counts is the soup not the recipe, and the dishes served up by these dancers are as nourishing and lovingly concocted as a finely rendered *consommé*. They vary from the faintly solemn to a high-altitude comedy-belt unattainable by more conventional methods.

They are austere to the point of monotony – bagfuls of babies have gone down the plughole with the bathwater of classical ballet – but they are so full of invention that they will be a mine for imitators for years. And they are beautiful in the disturbing way which makes you feel your angle of vision has been permanently shifted, which is a kind of beauty you don't get often.

2.8.64


*'Rest and motion! O ye strange locks of intricate simplicity, who shall find the key? He shall throw wide the portals of the palace of sensuous and symbolical truth ...' Yes, that is exactly the palace where the secret lies. Coleridge would have made a good ballet critic.*

# Nureyev's production of *Swan Lake*, Vienna

The Vienna Opera House is not normally renowned as a ballet centre, but its first full-length production of *Swan Lake* – mounted last week – turned out to be a fascinating and important event. It was choreographed and produced by Rudolf Nureyev, designed by Nicholas Georgiadis and the company was led by the choreographer and Margot Fonteyn.

This is no piece of minor refurbishing, no ingenious mish-mash of East and West, but a totally new creation. Drastically original, personal, single-minded and intense, it is hell-bent for controversy and history. Opinions will certainly differ about the acceptability of its approach; but of its artistic stature there can be no question.

Nureyev has seized *Swan Lake* by the throat and bent it to his own shape, taking Tchaikovsky's score as his basis and bearing Petipa's style in mind. As might be expected from the dancer who also fills the hero's role, his angle is that of the Prince.

*Swan Lake* is no longer a general myth or fairy tale. It has become the passionate, subjective expression of a young man's despairing idealism. The Swan Princess is here the creation of the Prince's own imagination. It is he who clothes her with gentleness and beauty, he who twists her into a projection of his own black thoughts. Rothbart is also himself and, poetically speaking, it is he who finally rejects her and in so doing rejects himself. It is a conception which has the sustained intensity of poetry and the realism of deep pessimism, and it marvellously echoes Tchaikovsky's music.

This vision has been miraculously embodied in Georgiadis's designs. Grand and brooding, the darkly burnished sets are charged with atmosphere – probably the best designs for a full-length ballet since the days of Bakst.

To heighten the poetic temperature Nureyev has pared down the narrative to a minimum. It is told in four acts, ending with a spectacular flood which drowns the hero and bears Odette away. Apart from the White Swan act which remains almost intact (Kirov style) he has rewritten the whole ballet.

The idiom is that of Petipa and Nureyev has used it with a splendid unity of breadth and flow. There are some beautiful details, which included a fine solo for the Prince in act one and a completely new

'Black Swan' *pas de deux*. But it is the pervasive unity of style which is most striking – a style which reaches its climax in a magnificent *pas de deux* before the final parting. Here intensity of feeling has broken through the Petipa mould and produced a plastic, supercharged duet which embodies the whole production and which feels like unalloyed Nureyev.

The crux of this version is the new emphasis on the Prince, who now dominates both in dance and drama almost every moment of the ballet. This is perfectly valid theatrically, but it has its disadvantages. The Swan Princess, who is now only a kind of mental image, loses both character and dimension: the incidental story shrinks and the minor characters fade into shadows. Like Hamlet, the Prince has withdrawn into a private world in which nobody exists but himself and his fancies.

There is little explicit drama. This has been replaced by a mounting psychological development which was beautifully carried forward in Vienna by the two principals. Fonteyn contrived to shed the emotional warmth she usually brings to the part in favour of a disembodied purity, and Nureyev himself was in stunning form. The Vienna company acquitted itself remarkably well. It is a smallish troupe but it has good style and several artists of real promise. Unexpectedly the orchestra proved a weak component: its thin tone and prissy phrasing never came near to the generous heart of Tchaikovsky's score.

This large and bare-breasted emotionalism is the quality which permeates the production and gives it a kind of nobility. Beside it our own new adaptation shrinks into a suburban entertainment.

18.10.64

# Revival of *A Wedding Bouquet*, The Royal Ballet, Covent Garden

Ashton's *A Wedding Bouquet* is a comedy. It is also nearly thirty years old, dotage for a joke. To revive it, as was done last week at Covent Garden, might seem an act of madness, yet it came up as crisp and fresh as in its salad days. What is the preservative? Craftsmanship, of course – there is never a sag in this daisy chain of airy ridicule. Style, of course – the dotty off-beat note is held with precision. But this ballet has a third and secret ingredient. It is a poem.

This is easier to say than to explain. Perhaps the best way of putting it is that Ashton makes us aware of the many levels which lie beneath the surface. Gertrude Stein – begetter, if not the only one, of the proceedings – was a real poet, of course, and anybody with an ear for words will feel the shadow-meanings which haunt her astringent prose.

Ashton must have had a peculiar sympathy for this oblique and witty approach. The novel form, pastiche of a pastiche: the deceptive innocence of the setting, a provincial wedding about as rustic as the marriage ceremony of Figaro: the brittle chatter and farcical embarrassments beneath which hearts crack like saucers – these add up to a fantastic confection which could have been whipped up by no other choreographer and at no other time.

After a shaky, over-emphatic start the new cast managed the elusive idiom splendidly, with the intoxicatedly beautiful Josephine of Deanne Bergsma as a special benefit. Lord Berners's décor is delicious. His score – rightly kept in the background as Robert Helpmann superbly dishes out the verse from a side-table – is, as Miss Stein might have said, not too bad but it's not too good but it's not too bad.

29.11.64

[Helpmann's] line was always elegant and harmonious, his style lofty. But his real strength lay in sinister and comic roles: his range stretched from romantics to buffoonery, from pathos to sophisticated clowning, and he revelled in grotesque elderly roles like Don Quixote. As a classicist he conveyed a kind of vulnerable poetry, as a dramatic character dancer he has seldom been equalled and probably never surpassed.

## *Les Biches*, The Royal Ballet, Covent Garden

The versatility of the Royal Ballet is remarkable. It must by now have far the widest range of ballets of any existing company, and last week yet another choreographer with another style was added – Bronislava Nijinska and her *Les Biches*.

Cocteau accurately described it as a kind of *fête galante* of the twenties. It is a deadpan satire perched on a stylistic point as sharp as a

70

needle's. Round this minute focus Diaghilev concentrated three wildly incongruous talents. The result is a triumphant fusion.

The ballet consists of an almost plotless suite of dances. The atmosphere is elegantly decadent 'smart society' with a hint of self-aware nostalgia. The characters include females – a bevy of ostrich-topped flappers, their impressionable hostess and a pair of mutually amorous girls; three ultra-masculine males, all muscles and self-admiration; and a figure neatly poised between the two, a page-boy not yet qualified to join either lot. They cluster round a sofa, flirt together like butterflies, exchange bitchy jokes behind smiles of angelic innocence, make their exits and their entrances.

The choreography, like Poulenc's ravishing score and the pink and blue Laurençin decor, has an aristocratic spareness which permits passages which might easily have been saccharine or over-simple. The widely spaced groups are calculated with nicety and the ensembles demand consummate unanimity. The female parts are seductively feminine and the men's movements are slow and manly, while the page is turned into a strange, pure creature with an impersonal radiance which easily dominates the ballet.

Basic to the whole piece, of course, is the twenty-ish style which Mme Nijinska has handled with unerring and reticent skill. It involves a special use of head and neck and shoulders while the lower part of the body nonchalantly performs the most complicated classical manoeuvres.

It is choreography which demands every ounce of technique the company has got. Stylistically speaking the level was uneven at the first performance, with few girls coming up to Fenella Fielding standard; but the groundwork is secure and the rest will surely come. Svetlana Beriosova as the hostess managed her pearls and her cigarette holder with *sangfroid*; Merle Park and Maryon Lane were a touching pair of best-friends; and David Blair, with his gift for comedy, was a fine upstanding athlete virilely backed up by Keith Rosson and Robert Mead.

But the evening's honours went to Georgina Parkinson as the page. Cool and withdrawn in her blue tunic and white gloves, she traced the sharp angled choreography of her part with exactly the right firm, light touch. Quick in her turns, dead accurate in her *posés*, she caught the half-tones of adolescence with poised detachment – calm and remote as a night flower.

5.12.64

# MacMillan's *Romeo and Juliet*, The Royal Ballet, Covent Garden

Nine months late for the anniversary celebrations, the Royal Ballet's biggest chunk of Shakespeareana so far rolled on to the Covent Garden stage last Tuesday – Kenneth MacMillan's *Romeo and Juliet*. It is his first three-acter, his first excursion outside this century and a venture in that breakneck exercise, the recreation of a work already tackled by other choreographers. Altogether a major milestone.

Prokofiev's exquisitely dovetailed score, with its intricate pattern of leitmotifs indicating moment-to-moment stage action, makes an exceedingly tight framework, and the new ballet closely follows the general line of the Bolshoi version. The street affrays, the Capulets' ball, the balcony scene, the bedroom *pas de deux*, the chapel, the tomb – they are all there. But the result is very different.

Few works of art fall more neatly than *Romeo and Juliet* into the dialectical mould. The two opposing forces clash, and out of the white-hot explosion rises the phoenix of peace. The Soviet version has grasped the simple formula with masterly firmness; MacMillan follows a different path. He paints on a wide screen a disorderly, rather insensitive, society and then slowly zooms in till we are watching the intimate beating of two young and tender hearts. Their 'death-marked love' is not so much snuffed between social pressures as bruised to death by life itself.

The tone is set from the start, where Verona is portrayed (slightly in the Zeffirelli style) as a raffish metropolis in which almost good-natured gang mix-ups are part of the local amenities. There is little sense of pent-up hatred. Romeo is one of the lads, currently making a pass at Rosaline. When he meets love for the first time he is confused; he can still be persuaded to join in a hoe-down with some tarts. But the world and its recreations fade away. Private passion takes over and runs its short downhill course to death. The general glow has been narrowed to a small, bright flame. It flickers, and goes out.

In the last act this approach brings big returns. The bedroom scenes are imagined with a clear, sharp eye which allows music, action and dance to claim their own worlds. But in general the lifting of the cloud of public hate from over the heads of the innocents robs the love scenes of poignancy. We are in the area of pathos, not tragedy.

It may be that the production will acquire a bigger dramatic punch when the general scenes have tightened up. Where it already scores is in choreographic subtlety, especially in the smaller parts such as Rosaline, Benvolio or Tybalt. No British ballet offers richer chances for the supporting artists to build up their roles.

For this mammoth undertaking MacMillan has reverted to pure traditional classicism. For the first two acts it would need an experienced eye to detect his own personal idiom beneath the *arabesques* and *pirouettes*. Juliet has a delicious solo in the ballroom and the two big *pas de deux* – in the balcony scene and bedroom – are beautifully flowing and free. Margot Fonteyn brings to the part her inimitable mixture of elegance and naiveté: even in the nursery she has an aristocratic delicacy. Though she graduates rather abruptly from dolls to guys her divided loyalty to her parents and her lover is childlike and clear.

MacMillan's Romeo is very different from Lavrovsky's. In the Soviet version he is something of a sixth-form hero, a Steerforth endowed with all the doggy virtues. Here the part has been sharpened and enlarged into a more casual and credible character, with much more dancing. Unfortunately the score does not provide for this and the borrowed excerpts are mainly in light, quick tempi which inspire dexterity *à l'anglaise* rather than broad movements expressive of a big manly heart. Nureyev, succeeding astonishingly well in shedding his natural romantic aura, did not seem comfortable in the first allegretto numbers but took fire in the genuine balcony solo with some tremendous swinging leaps, and the final passion and death were of course a natural for him.

His wayward plastic style competed with Blair's nicely exhibitionist Mercutio and Dowell's nimble Benvolio, but made a fine foil to the upright single-mindedness of Doyle's Tybalt. The much-improved Keith Rosson brought a Russian breadth to the Mandoline dance. Julia Farron and Gerd Larsen mimed middle-age convincingly, and the company whacked their swords with vim.

All this takes place in a setting of breath-taking richness. Avoiding the temptation of polychromatic prettiness, Nicholas Georgiadis has proved – as he did in his Vienna *Swan Lake* – that period can be conveyed without detail, variety with subtlety. High and deep and handsome, the stage looks enormous, and the company glamorous. When the lights finally turn up on the Knights' Dance the scene gives off the genuine glow of the Renaissance, a moment when solid money bore fruit of gold.

The score's flavour of pomp and sentiment smacks of Cecil B. de Mille. MacMillan has bent it to a more honest human scale. The result is not a revelation, but it is the next best thing; professional, consistently absorbing, a feast for the eye, rich in good detail – a spectacular asset to the repertoire.

14.2.65

## *Romeo and Juliet*, The Royal Ballet, Covent Garden

Kenneth MacMillan's *Romeo and Juliet* is to be shared by a syndicate of dancers. The first new pair took over last Wednesday – Lynn Seymour and Christoper Gable. It was in a way as memorable an occasion as the first night, for it confirmed what had been suspected, that Seymour as a dramatic dancer has few rivals if any.

It is a rare and rather special kind of gift. In this ballet she has, like her partner, the advantage of much previous experience with the choreographer. The result here runs so smoothly that it is hard not to take this as the definitive reading – though other interpreters will obviously find new angles to explore.

In the Fonteyn-Nureyev version Juliet was a shy, fey little creature carried away unwillingly by the force of a lively young cynic suddenly struck down by genuine passion. Seymour's Juliet is innocent in a different way. She surrenders to her feelings with complete and guileless abandon. Her whole life is freely offered, and when she is baulked she plunges into desperate measures with equal violence. You feel that she would sacrifice her nurse, her parents – anything or anybody – in her determination, and in the end she reaches death as naturally as a sexual climax.

Placed at the receiving end of such drive Romeo inevitably fades into a slightly negative role. Gable's simple, wholesome stage personality fits this honest Romeo like a glove. He had only to be true to himself which he admirably was. The only doubt which lingered was whether such a nice well-balanced youngster would have gone as far as suicide – he was somewhat more loved against than loving.

His low-key acting was consistent, well timed, easy and sympathetic, matching his dancing. Seymour, moving with marvellous eloquence and sensitivity, contrived to extend the intensity of her acting into every passionate *arabesque*. In this performance the

74

public feuding seemed weaker than ever; but private suffering was conveyed with riveting conviction.

21.2.65

## Ballet Festival in Stuttgart

Ballet has its own geography, with only a handful of cities shown on the map. Now a German town has begun to make itself noticed – Stuttgart, which has just finished its fourth Ballet Festival.

British chests can swell in the reflection that this is largely the work of John Cranko who has built up in five years a company and a repertoire which any city would be proud of.

It has three full length Cranko ballets. The brand-new *Eugene Onegin* has a specially piquant interest for Londoners since (if rumour is to be believed) it was originally on offer to the Royal Ballet. To tackle a theme already successfully explored in another medium would seem rash if *Romeo and Juliet* had not shown the way . There will certainly be some yelps of pain from opera-lovers, but Cranko has cunningly forestalled them. Although the ballet relates the same Pushkin story, he has not used a note from the Tchaikovsky opera. Instead, his colleague Kurt-Heinz Stolze has constructed a completely new score by the same composer, mainly from piano pieces.

It may not be a great new Tchaikovsky ballet-score, but it works well to support what turns out to be an excellent ballet scenario. Cranko unfolds its dark, romantic line with exactly the right period atmosphere. There is plenty of dancing for the principals, but it is always in character.

The saturnine, magnetic, anti-hero Onegin is played by Ray Barra with an uncanny resemblance to Pushkin himself. His friend, Lensky, is danced with vitality and understanding by Egon Madsen, the bubbling Olga is just right for Ana Cardus, and Marcia Haydée makes a bewitching Tatiana, an amalgam of modesty and naïve passion who develops into a woman with an adult will, able to turn the tables on her former idol in the dramatic finale. These are four plum parts, juicily filled, and the action swells out naturally in the two well-contrasted ballroom scenes. Jürgen Rose's costumes and designs are beautiful and true. Choreographically Cranko has broken no new ground here, but this is a production with the makings of a balletic best-seller.

The other long ballets showed up fresh facets of Cranko's invention and the company's talent. His Prokofiev *Romeo and Juliet* is very close to MacMillan's (which it preceded), with a stronger start. It has many shrewd small touches but perhaps a less personal style, and tends to fade away, just where this occasionally over-dramatic choreographer might be expected to have excelled, in the melodrama of the final scene. Juliet was danced with melting charm by Carla Fracci from Milan; Ray Barra's solid Romeo was too much in the *West Side Story* key, accentuated (as with all the male characters) by anachronistic modern haircuts, but Egon Madsen made a splendid Mercutio, witty and virile.

The Cranko *Swan Lake* is more dramatic than Helpmann's, less romantic than Nureyev's. The first act is rechoreographed to allow the Prince to take a cheerful part in a last fling before he comes of age, interrupted by a real row with his mother which casts him into the despondency necessary for the next act. The ballroom scene is a bit of a muddle, but the last act – pessimistic ending with the Prince drowned and defeated – makes a punchy climax.

Odette-Odile was a local girl, Birgit Keil, who, dancing it for only the second time, showed technical assurance and a style which only needs interpretative experience. Her Prince, the young American-born Richard Cragun, has immense promise. He already has a clean technique and a broad, soft, strong style which might come out of Russia. Not much of an actor yet, but a manly young dancer of an all too rare kind.

He showed up well in a mixed programme. This gave a splendid chance to Haydée in Balanchine's *La Valse*, revealed Madsen as a born comedian in Cranko's *Jeu de Cartes* and gave the rest of the company an opportunity to show its paces, which, though sometimes over-energetic, are well up to international standards. Cranko is clearly not only a talented choreographer but that equally rare phenomenon, an inspired director.

6.6.65

# The Bolshoi season, Festival Hall

Each time the Bolshoi comes to Britain it leaves a trail of punctuation behind it – half exclamation marks, half queries. It would be a blind, biased or incompetent critic who did not salute the dancing; but anybody concerned with the future of the company and of ballet in general must feel germs of anxiety wriggling in his benevolent breast.

This year's visit brought its own worries. The Festival Hall stage was lamentably small for a team which excels in big movement and the scenery had to be left behind because of fire regulations (an old booby-trap). More serious for the future was the fact that these conditions maimed items like *Swan Lake* and *Giselle*, so that – coming on top of the Albert Hall concert programmes last year – they tended to fix the image of the Bolshoi as a purveyor of sensational acrobatics, as opposed to the more serious and solid offerings of Western companies.

A side effect of this diet of scraps (which, we are assured, will not be repeated next time) was a whole evening of second-rate music. To hear the Royal Philharmonic Orchestra under conductors like Rozhdestvensky pounding out ice-rink pot-pourris was distressing.

The Russians' devotion to the kind of ballet-music which belongs in the classroom is a major cause of their cliché-ridden choreography. To them the score is the real 'text' of a ballet, of which the steps are only the visible (and variable) expression. Until, therefore, they use music which expresses the spirit of today they are inexorably condemned to carbon-copies of grandma's emotions and grandpa's heroes – even if they are dressed up as spacemen or geologists.

The mildly modern scores of Prokofiev have inspired many of their most interesting ballets. It will be fascinating to see the new production of Stravinsky's *Rite of Spring* (apparently the two young choreographers, Vasiliov and Kasatkina, have followed the original 'primitive' idiom) and to learn which modern composer Sergeyev has chosen for his new three-act *Hamlet* for the Kirov company. And when shall we see a Shostakovich ballet at the Bolshoi?

It is obvious that choreographers are just as rare in Russia as in the West (it was interesting to see the veteran Goleizovsky – clearly an original and important choreographer in his day – reinstated for the recent season). They seem particularly rare in Moscow: *Romeo and Juliet*, *The Stone Flower* and *The Fountain of Bakhchisarai* were all born in Leningrad. It is becoming equally obvious that the attempt to subsist entirely on home-grown works – a policy as unjustifiable artistically as maintaining an orchestra devoted to local composers – is leading to choreographic anaemia.

The custom also leads, in the long run, to some limitation of the artists. Since all Soviet choreography is basically similar, the dancers learn to excel in a single style, but a certain mechanicalness, detectable in this year's *corps de ballet*, inevitably creeps in. How much the dancers

77

would enjoy, benefit from and shine in a Bournonville ballet, or something by Massine – to say nothing of Ashton, Balanchine, Mac-Millan, *et al!*

This is not to want this great company to 'internationalise' itself under its new director Grigorovitch. As the interchange of companies becomes easier, it is more and more important that each should preserve its own character, even its own imperfections. It would be disastrous if the Bolshoi were ever to drop, in the face of superficial sniping from the West, such typical numbers as *Spring Waters* or *Walpurgis Night*.

Of course these are not masterpieces; but they are unique and inseparable facets of a genius which produces masterpieces. Shortsighted pleas that the Bolshoi should Westernise itself are like the exasperated, loving, but finally idiotic complaint of Professor Higgins in *My Fair Lady* when he asks why a woman can't be more like a man. The Russians are just different from us, and long may they remain so.

29.8.65

*Ballet is a mixed dish. The proportions of the ingredients can be varied with impunity; but each ingredient must be of top quality. It is quite legitimate to give over-riding preference to the dancing, but there is a point where weakness of choreography, music and production become intolerable.*

## New York City Ballet at Covent Garden

After the chuckle-headed reluctance of the paying public (and of some critics) to enjoy Balanchine some twelve years ago, it was good to hear the cheers ring out at Covent Garden last week for the New York City Ballet. After a long period of coy flirtation between the two managements what must, for most of the audience, have been legend at last became reality.

As usual in such cases, some reassessments have had to be made. Blinking away the stardust after a dizzy succession of new programmes, we can perceive one major truth – the perhaps rather obvious one that Balanchine is made like other choreographers. He is not a

78

Mozartian miracle-man incapable of mistakes. Indeed when his inspiration fails, as, of course, it sometimes must, his craftsmanship seems to flag too. When he is good he is sublime. But he can also be mediocre.

To be able to present even a handful in the first category puts him high on the roll of honour. In the first week two ballets stand out supremely – almost his first and almost his last. *Apollo*, written in 1928, is an unqualified masterpiece. Its relaxed originality and streamlined flow of invention build up a strange mood which marvellously reflects Stravinsky's marvellous score. It was not exceptionally well danced, and the Bauhaus-style decor is a far from perfect setting (Diaghilev was surely right to give it a Mediterranean flavour). But it emerges each time as a miniature giant amongst ballets.

Whether *Agon* will look as good in 30 years' time is hard to say; it certainly looks good now. Each short piece seems to get inside the music and open it up for our enjoyment. Serious but not solemn, terse but not brusque, remote but not unearthly, it explores in a new idiom one of the more impressive veins in contemporary sensibility. It was beautifully danced by Suzanne Farrell, Gloria Govrin and Arthur Mitchell.

Just below these two peaks lies a range of lesser but seductive works. *Bugaku*, for example, is a Madam Butterfly of the dance which turns Japanese ritual into a perfumed garden of movement. Mimi Paul and Edward Villella (outstandingly the stars of the company) were exquisite in the long sexy duet – she all tendril, he a rugged male oak. The music and the decor were just right.

In the same slightly exotic vein is *Liebeslieder Walzer*, a dreamy evocation of old Vienna worked out as a series of linked ballroom variations by four couples. The decor is pure *kitsch* and fifty-five minutes of Brahms in three-four time is enough, but the ingenious dancing patterns run like water and come to a close with a stroke of quiet magic.

There is pleasure to be had from *The Prodigal Son*, a very early narrative piece which offers Villella a fine role and has the added attractions of a score by Prokofiev (interesting) and a decor by Rouault (rather ugly): from *Symphony in C*, a slightly dated 'abstract' piece to Bizet which stands up only when it is immaculately danced: and from *Episodes*, an austere and intriguing setting of some Webern pieces. At first sight it yields a splendid *pas de deux*, well done by Patricia Neary and Conrad Ludlow, among some rather dense tanglings.

Against these must be set the brash *Tarantella* danced by Patricia McBride and Villella with exaggerated salesmanship; *Western Symphony*, a ballet copy of Agnes de Mille and not suited to the company; and *Stars and Stripes*, the kind of send-up which Massine has done so well but which here emerges as long and unfunny. Jerome Robbins's *Fanfare* is inconsiderable.

The dancing has been as uneven as the choreography. At one end of the scale is the lovely Miss Paul, supported by Gloria Govrin and Suzanne Farrell, with Edward Villella and Jacques D'Amboise as the outstanding men. At the other is a very mixed *corps de ballet* which shows signs of wear after a long and exhausting tour. Ironically, this victorious company has so far not shown up as strong as the one which failed to galvanise London in the bad old days.

Such inequality adds to the interest of the future rather than detracts from it. Which dancer will this week suddenly emerge triumphantly from the ranks, and in what masterpiece? We can be sure that the great Russo-American maestro has a few aces up his elegant sleeve.

5.9.65

*George Balanchine – a great choreographer with a flavour all his own and a searching, sensitive talent which is leading ballet – a tradition-clogged art by nature – into our own time.*

## *Raymonda*, Australian Ballet, New Victoria Theatre

If Marius Petipa had been a painter his smallest sketch would be fought over at Sotheby's or Christie's. A major work would bring the museum directors flocking in. The ballet world is still novelty-fixated partly owing to lack of authentic records – the new Institute of Choreology may begin a revolution in taste – or queues round the New Victoria Theatre would be longer. For there a full-length ballet by the great Franco-Russian master, written at the height of his powers only a few years after *The Sleeping Beauty* and *Swan Lake*, can be observed – if not yet fully savoured – *Raymonda*.

It is odd if understandable that this ballet has remained almost unknown in the West (a Lithuanian company gave it during a brief season in 1935) until Nureyev mounted it on the Royal Ballet touring company at Spoleto last year. Understandable because it represents everything against which Diaghilev so fruitfully rebelled. Odd because it is packed with genuine Petipa jewels of dancing, set to a rich, tuneful and very Russian score by Glazunov and because it contains that rarest of assets, a supremely testing and therefore supremely rewarding virtuoso ballerina role.

The revival of the old 1898 spectacular presents great problems. It was criticised even on its first appearance for its foolish story, which included a young girl, a mysterious lady, an evil Oriental and a knight who timed his return from the Crusades to a fortunate split second. In many ways it is both complicated and dated.

Nureyev's version – it is a tribute to this whiz-kid turned wizard that his own contribution and additions are mostly undetectable – deals with this problem by dismissing it. What we have now is a glorious necklace of varied choreography linked by the thinnest of narrative threads. The result is a ballet with plum dancing parts for a dozen artists – difficult and dividend-paying roles which any classical dancer must envy.

The romantic *pas de deux* in Act I, the *pas de sept* in Act II (surely a bit of Nureyev, whose plastic asymmetrical style dovetails into Petipa's rather as Ivanov's does) and the *pas de six* in the finale are all show-stoppers. Fonteyn here seizes on a part which shows every facet of her genius, from the softly romantic to the aristocratic fire of the Hungarian solo with its cymbalum-sounding accompaniment, while Nureyev has expanded the hero's part to include some breath-catching solos, breathtakingly danced.

Yet there is a feeling that this is not the total picture. Nureyev's production has not yet struck the perfect balance (after all this was Petipa's fifty-seventh ballet while it was only Nureyev's second), and this results in muted entries and climaxes, while Ralph Koltai's handsome metallic sets are monotonously weighty. The ballet's successive moods are clear: Act I majestic leading to romantic, Act II dramatic, Act III festive. These changes are not taken advantage of, the dream-effect of the first act especially being lost in cumbersome scene-shifting. The last scene, with its Hungarian setting, is the most perfectly successful as it stands.

19.12.65

81

# *Romeo and Juliet*, The Royal Ballet, Covent Garden

It is the contrasts which stab home in *Romeo and Juliet*, the dark passions in the sun-drenched streets, the tender adolescents caught in the mesh of power politics. And of course the metamorphosis inside the lovers themselves under the stunning stroke of passion – little Juliet with her indoor dreams turned into a rebel, a schemer, a heroine deliberately skirting the edge of death and the flip young Romeo eagerly tangling himself in the marriage halter which is to lead him inexorably into the crypt.

Each production, each player brings out one element or another in this mixture. Kenneth MacMillan's version, with its strikingly intimate bedroom scenes written in a kind of film close-up, emphasises the personal drama. This makes it a rich vehicle for the two lovers – richer than the Lavrovsky production, unmatched though that may be as a piece of total theatre – and we have seen an impressive succession of them.

It was fascinating to watch, at last week's Covent Garden gala performance, the original pair who launched MacMillan's work a year ago. First performances are rarely best performances, and both Fonteyn and Nureyev are artists with resources which are not tapped fully after a few rehearsals. Rumour had it that they had developed much since that first evening in 1965, and rumour was right.

Fonteyn's natural stage personality is divinely feminine – quick to spark, to melt, to glitter or maybe scratch, but ultimately (and this is her deadly female weapon) helpless. In any tragedy she will be the sacrifice. This fits her perfectly for half the Juliet role. She brings a marvellous combination of pathos and elegance to the scenes with her parents, and her surrender to her endocrine glands is sweetly done. She simply does not carry a big enough charge of masculine resolve to explode the full emotion of the final scenes, but she has beautifully simplified her playing of them. She moves through them like a bird circling round the fatal lighthouse beam.

Nureyev is pretty far from the simple Zeffirelli-type honest-Joe Romeo, graduating straight from the campus to the counterpane, whom we sometimes meet – a sympathetic modern conception probably remote from Elizabethan, not to mention Veronese, ideals. His Romeo, which has greatly increased in definition, is altogether more

82

mercurial – a fusion of fiery particles off whom passion might well strike poetry; wayward, worldly, a discothèque charmer before his time. The change into the single-track romantic is even more striking.

In a way it is easy for Nureyev to excel in the big balcony scene. The solo with its huge swinging leaps and melting turns *en attitude* is in the Russian style, and passion is his playground. What is now extraordinary is his second act in the market place, through which, dizzy with requited love, he flashes – tender heart showing only in soft-edged movement – with a stylish mischief which is entirely personal. Sliding effortlessly from power to delicacy, from mockery to sentiment, he now brings to the part a uniquely generous range.

The rest of the cast (as originally, with the exception of a sadly missed Blair) played with their usual style and assurance.

27.2.66

## Antonio's Flamenco company at the Cambridge Theatre

Antonio is back in town (at the Cambridge Theatre) as good as ever. To say this is to say something special. He is an extraordinary performer – as personal and inimitable as any ballet star, with an electrically mercurial personality and a technique which enables him to dance the tightrope of parody with impeccable mastery. His speed is undiminished, and not to have seen him do one of his whispering *zapadeados* or one of his flamenco-gone-crazy antics is to miss much.

20.3.66

## Revival of *Les Noces*, The Royal Ballet, Covent Garden

It is getting late. As Nastasia Timofeyeva and Fetis Pamfilovitch, the bridal couple in Nijinska's *Les Noces*, rise from their bench and slowly pass through the bedroom door the shrill singing stops at last. The final cracked-bell chords of Stravinsky's miraculous score strike into the air and the company congeals into ritual groups. Those at the back look up to the sky; those in the middle twine themselves into a human knot; those in front kneel and slowly, humbly bow their foreheads to the earth. Something is finished, something is beginning. The wedding is over.

*Les Noces* (revived at Covent Garden last Wednesday) is a rite, a celebration, a rustic sacrament – and being ritual and rustic, movingly estranged from its solemn origins. Stravinsky, a religious man brought up in the Orthodox Church, perfectly understands the 'coolness' of a holy gesture, and so does Nijinska. Together, with Goncharova's help, they have translated a peasant feast into the summary of a national soul. It is a folk image. Yet there is hardly a recognisable folk-motif in it. The steps are stylised; the tunes (except for the final 'My dear little bed!' which Stravinsky characteristically borrowed from a factory song) are invented; the flower-bright palette of the Russian people is reduced to monotones.

The history of *Les Noces* is almost as fascinating as its performance – how it was conceived by Stravinsky in 1914 and Diaghilev burst into tears when he heard it ('it was very surprising to see this huge man weep,' notes Stravinsky); how it was first scored for a mechanical piano, electric harmonium, percussion and two cymbaloms; how Nijinska obstinately changed the original idea (a throwaway piece like *L'Histoire du Soldat*) and worked with Goncharova to replace the colourful folksy element by browns and blacks and bleakness; how it was launched in 1923, rejected by London in 1926 as 'drear ceremonies' and defended in *The Times* by H. G. Wells.

All this set the scene for the first piercing half-Oriental notes as Stravinsky's weird accompaniment – chorus, percussion and four pianos (played, as at the first performance, by four eminent composers) – whirred into lively action under John Lanchbery.

The curtain rises on the Bride flanked by her companions holding her long ritual pigtails. 'Oh fair tress of my hair!' sings the soprano – and this could be the motif of the whole ballet. The score weaves a crisp embroidery of words and music, poetry and slang. On the stage, in place of delicate classical curlicues and filigrees, Nijinska plaits her dancers together, kneads them into knotted mounds, tugs them backwards and forwards like lengths of thick hemp.

The patterns are stiff as new linen. The steps are complicated but rough, repeating like a sampler pattern. The groups are blunt and tight and rounded. Without a hint of rural charm, she evokes a peasant world where a wedding means – not the champagne and nylon veils of its witty Western equivalent, Ashton's *Wedding Bouquet* – but a vow, a bed, having children, dying and leaving them money and a cow.

*Les Noces* is a superb sample of the Diaghilev ideal – contributions of individual, almost independent merit bound together into a single

84

perfect skein. Stravinsky's astonishingly original conception for a 'Cantata depicting peasant nuptials', with its dry, virile poetry and rhythms, catches exactly the right mood. Goncharova's designs – anonymous stylised dresses, two backcloths (a plain wall with one window, another plain wall with two windows) and a tiny corner-set – are unobtrusive but stunningly firm.

In her groups and dances Nijinska goes on her own harmonious way. She follows the scenes but not the words of the score, and some of the characters, for instance the delightful couple of official bed-warmers, have disappeared altogether. The idiom is turned-in, crouching, crab-like, rhythmic, twisted as a Scythian brooch – some-times recalling her brother's *L'après-midi d'un Faune* and fiendishly difficult to dance, with point-work, jumps and runs in fantastic distorted poses – all excellently done by the company, to a nice crisp accompaniment.

How could the same mind create this solid sacrament – surely a gentle cousin of her brother's legendary *Rite of Spring* – and also *Les Biches*, in which innocence and vice, prettiness and perversion are distilled into a sophisticated Parisian nectar? To see them together in this same programme – the foundation-stone of neo-classicism and a fountainhead of Modern Dance – was to set Nijinska securely in a top choreographic niche. They are enough on their own to mark Ashton's directorship of the company as memorable.

27.3.66

.

## *Song of the Earth*, The Royal Ballet, Covent Garden

With the triumphant notes of *Les Noces* still ringing in our ears, it seemed too much to hope that the very next Covent Garden produc-tion would hit the jackpot. But it has. MacMillan's *Song of the Earth* is undoubtedly the best work of one of the best living choreographers.

*Song of the Earth* is a long, gentle elegy dedicated to the sweetness of life and inevitability of death, a balletic intimation of mortality. Mahler's song cycle, to which it is arranged, is a pessimistic, swir-ling, richly loaded score applied to a set of Chinese poems whose dry resignation gives an edge to the emotion. Oriental overtones are deftly retained in the music, like a cherry-blossom motif in an art nouveau design, and MacMillan has followed the same pattern.

The six songs are sung by alternating male and female voices

85

(Vilem Pribyl and Yvonne Minton) and MacMillan has similarly divided the action equally between men and girls. Two in particular, Donald MacLeary and Marcia Haydée – ballerina of the Stuttgart Company, which created the work six months ago – embody the joy and hopes of humanity. And one figure obstinately haunts the scene accompanying every movement, the Messenger of Death (Anthony Dowell).

The episodes are presented as self-contained choreographic pictures, cued by the music but subtly referring to the text. Plainly but effectively presented in practice dress against an almost but not quite anonymous background, the dances have a solid but constantly changing shape, mostly slow but not sagging, with sudden bursts of violent energy, in a mixture of Modern Dance and classicism neatly blended through the Oriental references.

There is no miming or agonising; a proper Chinese formality is preserved. There are explicit moments – when Jennifer Penney jumps into Death's arms as lightly as a bird, when a group of men get lost in the mists of drunkenness, or when Death finally steals away with MacLeary and restores him to his love only when he has put on the ritual white funeral mask – but what holds the attention is the extraordinarily sustained, apt invention of the choreography.

Its scope, which ranges from intense introverted posture to the softest plasticity or dizzy aerial spins, makes enormous demands on the dancers. The company responds remarkably well, but is overshadowed by a stunning performance by Marcia Haydée. Slim and sure, she has an electric energy which wraps up emotional tension in movements of total accuracy. With lightning twists and leaps, long line, virtuoso technique and a darkly dramatic personality, she gives her part an edge of steel. She faces death as she faces love, not as a victim but as an equal.

Anthony Dowell, nowadays a rapidly developing artist, makes a beautifully clean, darting figure of Death, and MacLeary is a virile foil to him, all warmth and vigour. Jennifer Penney is enchanting as an innocent adolescent, and Georgina Parkinson aptly represents imperishable beauty.

*Song of the Earth* is a major work and marks a new peak in MacMillan's career. That it was turned down by Covent Garden, which has now imported it ready-made from Stuttgart, and that MacMillan himself is being lost to the Royal Ballet at this moment is more than tragic – it is alarming.

22.5.66

86

# Nureyev's production of *Tancredi*, Vienna

In the nineteenth century Vienna may have been the home of wine, women and waltzes; in the twentieth it is known as a hotbed of art and thought. From the rotten stump of the Austrian Empire sprang not only Klimt and his art nouveau, the *angst*-ridden Mahler of 'The Song of the Earth', but also Freud and the whole galloping harvest of psychology.

It is surely no accident that for his first completely original ballet, mounted there ten days ago, Rudolf Nureyev has delved into the uneasy caverns of the human psyche. *Tancredi* is a choreographic exploration of neurosis, a ballet for the Jung in heart.

This is no modest first-ballet suite of dances but, characteristically, a risky plunge into a dense and complicated piece of dance orchestration for a large company. The curtain rises on a weird scene. We are in a 'kingdom of the shades', but a very different one from the realm of *La Bayadère* which was the setting for Nureyev's first choreographic exercise. Barry Kay (the designer of *Images of Love*) has contrived, with riggings of curved network, to scoop out on stage a miraculous womblike shell: even the floor rises and falls unevenly. To one side stands a transparent spiral tower (umbilical?) with doors through which the characters come and go. It is a dissolving diaphanous world of skeleton and membrane, veined over, dark-cornered, fluid as a Rorschach blot.

Within this shifting ambience, Nureyev has set his tangle of split-personality tensions, set out in what he describes as 'a succession of images linked by poetic rather than by narrative logic'. Their unpunctuated stream-of-consciousness flow, and the continuous use of open counterpoint, with several loosely linked activities on the stage simultaneously, makes this a ballet almost impossible to grasp at a single viewing.

But the line of argument is roughly this: Tancredi (he is the only named character – all the others are archetypes, creations of the imagination) emerges into the world as an individual, only to find himself not a single creature but a complex of personalities; he is dogged by seven identical Reflections. In particular he is torn between Sacred and Profane Love. After a succession of hallucinatory experiences, his personality splits finally and fatally in two and, after a last struggle, he sinks back into the primordial chaos from which we saw him born.

This could have been heavy going, but it is conveyed in a fluent quick-moving style which gives plenty of scope for dancing. The idiom is mixed in the modern manner, rather than blended; classical technique alternates with suggestions of Modern Dance. The fantastic images flash ephemerally across the eye – a startling high-swinging entry for the bad girl; a stabbing Spanish-style solo for Tancredi; a beautiful group in which he struggles at the hub of a cross made by his *alter egos*; a Carnival procession of satirical ghosts mocking a bridal couple; a violent partner-changing *pas de quatre;* the hero's final dramatic fission – a series of visions as vivid but hard to recall as the sequences in a Fellini film.

The conception of the ballet is very much all of a piece – insubstantial, swirling, loosely edited – emphasised by the ten-year-old score on which Nureyev was invited to work, by Hans Werner Henze. In some ways the uniformity is too complete. The flowing choreography needs the support of a score with more guts and character. There is some excess of multiple dancing (it is noticeable that the most emotionally striking moment is during a simple *pas de deux* between Tancredi and the 'bad image'). In fact this is very much a young man's ballet, which rejects the virtues of spacing and economy in favour of a cornucopia of ideas, some of which jostle into each other.

How such an oblique and elaborate piece will stand up without its creator in the long and taxing pivotal part must remain to be seen. The Vienna company copes manfully, but it is not subtle enough in style to give the ballet the obsessive quality it needs. The 'good influence' (Lisl Maar), remains, like so many good girls, rather a nonentity, but her opposite number is splendidly danced by Ully Wührer – long, strong and elegant.

From a total experience which seems to be deliberately designed as slightly mystifying, one fact – hitherto undecided – emerges strongly, and that is that we have a real choreographer on our hands, with ideas that go far beyond mere classical dance-steps. It is rather sad that this continuously intriguing and often beautiful demonstration had to happen so far away.

29.5.66

# The Sleeping Beauty and Giselle, The Kirov at Covent Garden

But of course. This was the ballet which should have opened the Kirov season, as any of us wise guys could have foretold – *The Sleeping Beauty* with Kolpakova as the luminous Aurora and Soloviev doing his incomparable Bluebird, backed by a whole team of talent. It came at last on Tuesday, and made this a memorable date on several counts.

You can always tell what sort of an evening you are in for within seconds of Aurora's little run-on and solo in Act I. Kolpakova nipped out as light and sparkling as a jet of water and went on to give a rendering of this act which I have never seen equalled. It demands the spring-heeled bound of an antelope, the skimming speed of a swallow, the poise of a thrush effortlessly riding a treetop. Kolpakova has all these, and she has, too, a wonderful length of arm and leg which enables her to ornament the choreography without losing its form.

Fantastically gifted in technique, she carves out space with the precision of a razor-blade. Little angular accents break the flow like the dissonances in a piece of cool jazz and translate her delicate phrasing into subtlety of line. Her supporting leg may be straight as an arrow; the rest of her body is as ingeniously articulated as a cubist painting. Kolpakova is faithfully traditional and completely modern in a style which leads straight on to Balanchine. Her dancing has the temperature of sunshine reflected in an icicle. It is shaped with a cool, detached, Mozartian elegance which brings out that same element in the score (Tchaikovsky venerated Mozart) which so often gets blurred. The emotion is in the movement itself and nowhere else, and that is what classical dancing is about.

The last, more *à terre*, act does not bring out her qualities quite so well, but here we have the treat of Soloviev's dancing Bluebird to Makarova's Princess Florine. This is a pure interpretation mercifully stripped of those flutterings and flitterings which so often make the magic couple look like a pair of neurotic budgerigars. Soloviev is big for the part, but his soft, springy jumps, the plastic control which allows a movement to run slowly up his body into his arms, and his perfection of detail – watch those insteps in the air – made this a superb performance. I have never seen the celebrated *brisés volés* better done. Makarova was light as thistledown.

Of the rest of the performers in this bandbox of small treasures,

Fedicheva was a fine, free-moving Lilac Fairy without a trace of air–hostess graciousness, Semenov was a distinguished Prince in the old tradition and the various fairies were good without being outstanding. What was outstanding was Anatoli Gridin's Carabosse – terrifying but always elegant, like some mad duchess aunt of Danny La Rue – and the beautifully studied Court Chamberlain of Gennadi Selyutski.

The production as a whole is handsomely mounted (with a new white-pillared final scene) though some of the costumes jar. In the main, it is not far from the Royal Ballet version, but it feels a bit nearer to the original. The *Valse des Fleurs* is a perfect evocation of the nineties, children and all; the Vision scene – which wisely includes a solo for the Prince – is very convincing in detail; and the evening ends with that traditional of kinetic art, the fountain which damped the backs of generations of Maryinsky *coryphées*.

Between these ninety-ish delights and the 1840s lies a huge gulf. *Giselle* was born in the heyday of romanticism, all mist and melancholy, when sweet, unhealthy girls lured men to their doom by their Gothic pallor. To be the natural interpreter of that period demands very different qualities – though many ballerinas, including Kolpakova, have bridged the gap by pure art.

Anybody who had seen Natalia Makarova's touching *Cinderella* would guess that she would be ideal for the part, and so, on Friday, she turned out to be. She has a tender waif-like personality and a marvellous slow-dropping way of dancing which combines with a wispy grace and lightness to make her the very embodiment of the disembodied. In the long series of solos and *pas de deux* through the 'wili' act her feel for the drifting spidery line of the dance never faltered once. Gabriela Komleva's Myrtle (Myrtha) was quiet and good, and once again the *corps de ballet* were a collective marvel.

Albrecht was the redoubtable Soloviev, in whom dancing seems to run like a river. His solos (including an interpolated one in Act I) were as faultless as ever, and the two lovers were beautifully matched in their duets. His open, candid features and style are not, perhaps, the vehicle for the full dramatic depth the part contains and – maybe to suit his straightforward hero – the role of Hans (Hilarion) was given a brilliant new twist by Gridin. Contrary to the Bolshoi version, the Honest Woodcutter now appears as a shifty, embittered figure, the most interesting character on the stage.

It may have been this adjustment or it may have been indeterminate crowd work or lack of those tricks of production which keep

90

dramatic tension running through the dances, but in spite of excellent individual acting, the first scenes became slightly un-balanced. As a total experience this was not, in consequence, the most moving *Giselle* in the world; but it was certainly one of the most exquisitely danced.

18.9.66

*The [Kirov] corps de ballet was a continual joy – precise, stylish, musical, exactly matched yet retaining individual feminine charm ... Watching those seventy-two adorable little legs, you are watching, on this evidence, the best corps de ballet in the world.*

## The Kirov season at Covent Garden

The Kirov Ballet finished at Covent Garden yesterday, leaving in its wake – like any major company – a whole pile of relevant reflections about ballet in general. Here are just a few:

1 The season has not been a sell-out. The reason is obvious: the dancing is superlative, though not in the athletic show-off style of the Bolshoi, and a lot of the acting is good at close range. But the general production and *mise-en-scène* are weak. This raises in an acute form the question of Production versus Performance.

In the West, where for so long we made do with minor dancing talent, production has been enormously developed, and audiences find this ingredient of major importance. It is, of course. But the shadow of Diaghilev's late decline, when he had to substitute staging and décor for great dancing, hangs over the problem.

What *is* production? In ballet it is simply using every means of displaying the dancer's art to best advantage. Whenever it goes beyond this task it should be regarded with suspicion and made to justify itself. Glamorous sets and costumes, arresting stage effects, full-blooded accompaniment from the orchestra pit – in the long run they all revolve round those tiny figures on the stage. Once dancing standards slip into a secondary place, the decline of ballet is sure.

91

2 The Kirov's muted audience appeal seems to rise straight out of its approach to dancing, and is thus justified artistically. Its technique is remarkable, a yardstick for British critics; some of our kindly adjectives will have to be put away for more sparing use. It is in a pure classical style, a style the English have never managed to achieve in any art and which seems alien to our national temperament and sympathies.

In place of the 'coldness' and 'impersonality' which so many critics have found in so much Continental art, we tend to drift towards the cosier climate of the pantomime or a kind of delicate wistfulness which reflects the grey-green climate of our countryside – often very beautifully.

3 This spirit, so different from that of the Bolshoi, is what gives the Kirov its character. In today's conditions of international exchanges it is becoming more and more important for companies to hang on to their identity. Uniqueness should put an end to the absurd discussions about which is the 'best' company. In art there is good and bad, but there can never be best.

4 The Kirov's emphasis on correctitude produces fabulous performances from the stars (Kolpakova, Makarova, Soloviev) and from the *corps de ballet*. But instead of bringing out the personal qualities of the second line of soloists – maybe the very ones which prevent them from being stars – it seems to iron them out to an academic level which may delight the teacher but leaves the audience unmoved.

5 Finally – and final is the word – they are up against the oldest problem in the business, the scarcity of choreographers. In spite of isolated passages by Sergeyev, Jacobsen and Belsky (whose *Leningrad Symphony* I stupidly credited last week to Grigorovitch) it is clear that the supply is as short in Russia as elsewhere. The old Tchaikovsky classics are wilting from over-exposure. What is to replace them?

Of all companies the answer is easiest for the Kirov. They don't need even to look so far as Bournonville. With former pupils like Fokine and Nijinsky, Nijinska and Balanchine, composers like Rimsky-Korsakov, Borodin and Stravinsky, designers like Roerich and Benois and Bakst, a dip into their city's great inheritance could produce a vast hoard.

But, of course, this can only be the beginning. For a ballet company to limit itself to local creative talent is as illogical and suicidal as it would be for an opera company or an orchestra. This is one of the finest theatrical instruments in existence. It should claim the world's greatest collaborators as a right.

2.10.66

# Nureyev's production of *The Sleeping Beauty*, La Scala, Milan

If the Covent Garden *Sleeping Beauty* can be compared with a lively non-vintage claret (now slightly gone off) and the Kirov version to a dry white wine of superior quality, then the ultra-sumptuous version which Rudolf Nureyev has just mounted at La Scala, Milan, designed by Nicholas Georgiadis, is a deep, rich Burgundy – a trifle heavy on the palate but with the haunting bouquet of a great year.

There seems little doubt that this flavour of stately opulence is close to the Maryinsky original, which was criticised as 'much too serious'. Of all the versions I have seen (I missed the fantasies of the De Cuevas Company) Nureyev's is the most impressive, and also by far the most adult.

Roughly speaking, it is the Kirov version with giant gilded knobs on. The solos and *pas de deux* are identical, but the ensembles are new, and there are some additions – notably a long, typically wayward solo for the Prince in the Vision scene and a delightful 5/4 variation and a solemn sarabande for the King and his court in Act III.

The setting is no prettified fairyland but a substantial vision of some imaginary Versailles. The curtain rises to disclose a pair of enormous golden gates, through which we discern in the darkness a cataract of candelabra descending the stairs at the back of the vast stage. The servants are setting the table for a Veronese-type banquet, a feast to celebrate the infant princess's christening. The court pours down the steps – high-wigged, stiff with brocade and etiquette, a glimmering swarm with the dark lustre of a Renaissance mirror. Even the fairies, who troop on to do the royal occasion honour, have a plumed and courtly deportment.

The sense of imperial pomp and claustrophobia is maintained in a succession of scenes which mingle Le Roi Soleil with Lorenzo the

93

Magnificent (the sonorous Italian orchestra neatly echoes the interpretation). All traces of childishness and pantomime have vanished. The spirit of evil is no longer a hobbling witch but a sophisticated aristocrat of Beardsley-like glamour, and her opponent is a virginal beauty wielding the simple magic of innocence and youth. Both forces, Carabosse and the Lilac Fairy are arrayed in costumes of extravagant splendour; neither dances a step.

Apart from this revolutionary interpretation (which is also a near-reversion to the original) the Kirov story-line is pretty faithfully followed. There are a succession of inventive ideas – crowds of townspeople jostling to get a view of the royal birthday party; the court collapsing into sleep upon the staircase like a flock of birds settling on a tree; a fresh and witty approach to the hunting scene, with real coaches decanting a troupe of mincing courtiers, among whom the Prince bounds with a flash of royal mischief.

But what is most striking is the feel of a single vision which infuses both the style, the pace, the designs and the dancing and which is maintained up to the last bar. A production on this scale would have taxed the resources of the Maryinsky itself, and inevitably the large Milanese company proved no more than adequate, though the choreographer had coaxed miracles of style out of them.

The local principals, Vera Colombo and Roberto Fascilla, made a serviceable pair of Bluebirds. Carla Fracci, though lacking in authority, shone as Aurora like a pearl in a billowing sea of silk. And Nureyev himself – his dancing (rather to my surprise) in no way diminished by recent exposure to the Kirov, rather the reverse – gave a glittering reincarnation of the ardent, arrogant, half-cynical princeling who sailed through the Kirov production in Paris five years ago.

The majestically sombre tone and weight of Georgiadis's designs (even the fairies are in saffron and veridian) takes some adjusting to, and could do with a chromatic 'lift' in the last act, but they make a sumptuous setting for the palely clad stars and once seen, may make more sparkling interpretations look frivolous. If it is style and spectacle and ceremony you're after, this is your production.

9.10.66

# Merce Cunningham at the Saville Theatre

Theatre managers can't be too careful whom they let into their theatres: in the long run a regular audience dictates its own menu. One of the minor pleasures of going to see Merce Cunningham and his company (now at the Saville Theatre) is to find a whole new set of faces in the auditorium – many drawn from the world of painting and music. Properly nurtured, these can form the core of future ballet audiences. From the simple fare of this company they can be led on slowly to something like *Les Noces* and eventually, maybe, grapple with the rigorous disciplines of *The Sleeping Beauty*. For the truth is that what Cunningham offers is, to non-ballet addicts, much more direct and immediately appealing than what people enjoy at Covent Garden. The excitements and pleasures of his work (at its best) are open to anyone – surprise, dramatic strangeness, the basic mysterious joys of running, jumping and standing still. Inside all this, of course, the practised eye will find an immensely rich invention of new patterns, new attitudes to the art, new combinations, even new kinds of movement altogether – flopping, twitching, heaving – still unexploited by conventional choreographers. Above all, Cunningham has an acute sensibility to that indefinable 'awareness' which informs so much contemporary work by the young in all the arts.

17.11.66

# *Shadowplay*, The Royal Ballet, Covent Garden

Two exciting new ballets in one week – Antony Tudor's *Shadowplay* at Covent Garden and Glen Tetley's *Pierrot Lunaire* at Richmond. Such sudden richness is disconcerting, and certainly strains the capacities of this column. *Pierrot Lunaire*, which is the best thing the Rambert Company has offered us for a long time, will have to await discussion until next week.

Both ballets are basically American-inspired, and they reinforce the suspicion that modern ballet – like modern painting – is being born in New York. There is a kind of relaxed invention about them

95

which is wonderfully refreshing – an invention not of steps but of approach and physical dimension.

To suggest that Tudor is American may seem absurd. He was already well established before he left Britain in 1941 and his work is immensely English in style, stiffened by that taut English reserve which descends from the concept of the 'dandy'. But, quite apart from his openness to American-style movement in his early work, Tudor's new ballet could have been conceived only in a mind attuned to the mental climate of his adopted country. The smooth blend of oriental mysticism, literary allusion, sexuality and casual day-to-day realism appears in much good modern American art, music and writing. What European choreographer would plant his hero in a regal oriental posture and then let him swat a fly on his cheek?

In this rich, original and ambiguous work – like all good things it leaves a nagging doubt that several layers of interpretation remain hidden – Tudor has taken Kipling's basic Mowgli situation (an innocent human boy in the material world of animals), tinged it with the burnished oriental streak which colours Charles Koechlin's 'Bandarlog' music, and injected into it a stream of psychological undercurrents.

We are in the jungle – a mysterious arena outside normal human experience. A Boy with Matted Hair (Anthony Dowell) stands lost and doubting. He sets himself on a rock with proper manly authority, but suddenly he is invaded by the unruly animal world. He is half-repelled, half-fascinated. A highly charged encounter with a sinisterly beautiful male creature (perhaps a form of self-love?) shatters his innocence; he is due for his first experience of the Celestial female principle, half-creative, half-devouring (Merle Park).

After two long passages with her, first seductive then passionately struggling, he is a changed person. He takes his place almost resignedly on the seat of human responsibility. Round him the jungle creatures crouch like a solemn meeting of baboons. He takes the posture of authority; they awkwardly ape him, but soon one begins to pick his scalp, another nibbles something off the floor. They are still animals, while he is a Man. But as the curtain falls we see his hand go up to his ribs in a simian scratching gesture. He too is now part of the jungle of experience.

These are only the putative bones of a work of dense atmospheric texture which contains not only some marvellous moments – Merle Park floating away like a fading vision over Dowell's shoulder after an embrace: a grotesque Groucho Marx trio of gorilla-like heroes: the

96

Boy's final orgasmic dive below the Shiva-arched legs of the girl as though into the mouth of a dragon – but also a great variety of carefully disorganised movement, climbing, running, rolling. Though classically based (the girls are on points) it is all very unlike any other Royal Ballet work, and very unlike any other Tudor work. He could hardly have made a more felicitous return.

Though his costume is rather too balletic and tidy for a jungle boy, Dowell dances the long and taxing part of the adolescent hero with real sensitivity. The slow, twisting choreography makes full use of his long and supple line. Merle Park is splendidly assured in the very difficult role of the Celestial female, though the part really calls for a more Russian-type exoticism of neck and arms. Derek Rencher is a noble savage.

The company as a whole shows up well in unfamiliar manoeuvres (trapezes are not yet a normal part of ballet-school equipment) and look remarkably at home among the roots of Michael Annals's spreading banyan tree – a strange and alarming world vividly conjured up by Koechlin's beautiful score, which sounded both lively and seductive under John Lanchbery's baton.

29.1.67


## *Pierrot Lunaire*, Ballet Rambert, Richmond

A genuine American ballet has joined the Rambert repertoire. Glen Tetley's *Pierrot Lunaire* (created in New York in 1962) to Schoenberg's score of the same name was introduced at its recent Richmond season. It's a winner.

From the first moment it is clear that it embodies a great balletic virtue – the different elements are so intertwined as to be inseparable. The curtain rises on a stage bare except for an austere steel-scaffolding in the moonlight. At the top, perched like a watcher on a tower, sits Pierrot apostrophising the moon. He pours out his loneliness, then swings and loops down to the ground. His prayers seem answered in the appearance of Columbine, first in the guise of a simple servant, then as a sophisticated seductress.

But they are interrupted by the powerful Brighella (Pierrot's lower self?) who first eggs him on to change romance into sex, then joins with Columbine to torment and mock him. They strip him of his personality, his Pierrot's cap and clothes, and drag him back up the

97

tower. Finally, battered and broken, Pierrot hangs crucified between them. With a last gesture he seems to murmur: forgive them, for they know not what they do.

All this could be whimsy, corny and sentimental. It is not. The character of Pierrot is kept beautifully poised, so that his emotions – though moving – are those of an actor not of a soppy youth. It could be monotonous. Such a long work for only three dancers is potentially wearisome. But the range of movement clearly derived from 'modern' experimenters, is both wide and expressive: there is never a moment of mere music-matching embroidery. And the scaffolding lends a whole new vocabulary; it may be no coincidence that Tudor exploits a rather similar device in his new *Shadowplay*.

There are many exciting moments involving the decor – the entry of Columbine as a maid with an elastic clothes-line, complete with washing, which snaps out of sight when no longer wanted; the long intestinal scarf in which Brighella wraps himself; the puppet strings on which Pierrot suddenly finds himself dangled. The designer, Rouben Ter-Arutunian, is one of the stars of the show.

But obviously most depends on Pierrot. Christopher Bruce, a young dancer who has been doing small parts for some time, renders him so touchingly and tellingly that it is hard to believe the role was not written for him (actually Tetley used to do it himself). Lean and lithe, quick-moving and accurate, with a wonderful starved expression he is a living example of the way in which a choreographer can transform a dancer into a real artist.

5.2.67

# Fonteyn and Nureyev, *Paradise Lost* at Covent Garden

Launching a new ballet at a gala is a risky business; there is a danger that the venture may founder in billows of social celebration. But Thursday's performance at Covent Garden, in aid of the Royal Ballet Benevolent Fund, turned out to be a memorable and exciting evening.

The new work was Roland Petit's *Paradise Lost*. Petit is an experienced choreographer who built a formidable reputation after the war, but his mission here seemed a desperate one. He was faced with the problem of creating a completely modern work exploiting two stars rooted in nineteenth-century tradition. But with the aid of excellent designs by the Nouveau Réaliste painter Martial Raysse, in a restrained pop-art style, and a weird but melodious score by Marius Constant, he has succeeded on both counts. For the very first time the Sixties have broken into the opera house, in a tremendous vehicle for Fonteyn and Nureyev.

Some kind of extended *pas de deux* was obviously called for, and Adam and Eve provide an ideal theme. With a libretto by Prix Goncourt winner Jean Cau, Petit has devised a concentrated if rather gloomy résumé of our lifespan. In rapid succession we are taken through birth, adolescence, love, sex, disillusion, loneliness and sudden death – or, if you like, the creation of Adam, the birth of Eve, the Serpent, the Fall, the Expulsion, corruption and execution by the flaming sword of the Guardian Angel himself.

It is a profoundly serious work, but the cool and deceptively flip modern manner – a style which Petit understands completely, carrying it into the very shape of his movements – removes all trace of solemnity. The sexy, hotted-up idiom of the forties has given way to a new style which fits Petit like a glove.

The opening reveals the primal egg (or mandala). Within it flashing numerals mark a count-down; the rocket of humanity is going to take off. At zero, Adam materialises from flashing energy into flesh. He strides down a great ramp on to the stage and the action begins. It is traced in a long, richly inventive series of solos and duets which make the first half of the ballet one of the most stimulating dance experiences in a long time – Adam exploring his nature and powers; his first intimation of pain and the birth of Eve; their mutual suspicion thawing into complete harmony; the change wrought by the Serpent, Eve twisting into seduction and Adam into aggressive sexuality, ending in a denouement as theatrically breathtaking as Nijinsky's famous leap in *Spectre de la Rose*.

There is no nudity and the sex angle, though pervasive and powerful, is expressed rather than illustrated in a style much more subtle than in Petit's earlier ballets. We seem to be watching something genuinely primitive, a basic animal Adam and a quite inadvertently provocative Eve. When sex arrives, we can understand that lust is the most innocent of emotions.

It is hard to know which to salute more – the enterprise of Fonteyn in tackling so untypical a role and her complete mastery of it, or the astonishing range of Nureyev – dramatic, athletic and inimitably supple – in what must be one of the most taxing (and so rewarding) roles in modern ballet. Petit has exploited the harmony of phrasing between them, the gentle strength of Fonteyn and the

99

full range of Nureyev's vocabulary – leaps, spins, beats, velocity, slow undulations, shivers and twists and that solid earth-conscious spring which is the Russian secret. The result is that rarest of phenomena, contemporary choreography which gives full rein to the performers' capacities.

If only its second half were of the same quality this ballet would be a masterpiece. Unfortunately Petit's weakness at ensembles emerges, and the decor and score here let him down. The *corps de ballet* has some interesting movements, but they are done in a mechanical music-hall unison. Some loosening up is urgently called for.

But the reappearance of our noble ancestors – she slim and firm as a plant, he Michelangelesque and wild – soon re-ignites the imagination. The sense of breaking-up is immanent. A flashing sign indicates the victim and descends on him like a thunderbolt. Eternal Eve is left to mourn, and an upside down *pietà* makes a beautiful, eloquent and somehow natural conclusion.

26.2.67

## Dance in New York

For six solid weeks recently 8,000 people sat every evening in one small corner of New York watching classical ballet. This triumph, in a tough city renowned as the home of modern dance, has not been quick and easy. Credit must go above all to three figures now reaping their just rewards – to George Balanchine, that elegant Mies van der Rohe of the dance, to Lucia Chase, long-time supporter of American Ballet Theatre, and to Sol Hurok, the great international impresario.

There is probably more dancing – and more awareness of dancing – in America than in any country outside Russia. All over the country there are professional companies, amateur groups and schools – though their performances are intermittent. But New York is the acknowledged centre, and there the activity is bewildering.

At a rash guess I would say that there are about the same number of performances by professional companies as in London (seasons are short). But standards are surprisingly permissive and audiences exist for ventures which would quickly shrivel in London. Dance-hunger extends from the most vapid kitsch-in-synch school to the remotest corner of experimentation. On two successive nights last month,

100

equally well-filled houses applauded a tedious 'harlequinade' to saccharine Drigo melodies and an entertainment (strikingly beautiful, presented by Anna Halprin of San Francisco) in which four young girls and four young men danced stark naked for twenty minutes, entangling themselves with yards of brown paper.

There may be a lack of discrimination in New York, but what is immediately noticeable is the stimulating atmosphere of day-to-day invention, variety, improvisation and competition. In this respect the situation is totally unlike London, or indeed any European city. It is a condition of total anarchy in which different outfits (and their backers) stake out rival claims with the old pioneer spirit. The market is much more open than might at first appear, and it would be a clever man who could spot the eventual winner – assuming that one day a single organisation will dominate the national scene, something which still seems remotely unlikely.

The strongest contender is Balanchine's New York City Ballet, which not only enjoys a solid Ford Foundation grant but has founded a regular school, developed a style, and, above all, enjoys first rights to the handsome new State Theatre which forms the ballet counterpart to the new Metropolitan Opera House. There can be no doubt that this is by far the most polished classical company in the country, and its repertoire of Balanchine works gives it a unique character. But seen against the international backcloth it appears to be in some danger of developing into a specialist team, perfectly tailored for a particular repertory but not very suited for wider application – a kind of Moscow Arts Theatre of ballet.

This company seems to be having to make some concessions to its new audiences – the six-week summer season contained few of those modern works for which it is famous here, and the season's novelty, a Fauré-Stravinsky-Tchaikovsky confection called *The Jewels*, is very much a rehash of Balanchine's old achievements. (Like the film of his *Midsummer Night's Dream*, it has a startling visual affinity with modern Soviet creations.) The company contains some stunning dancers but the ensemble is a bit uneven, and a curious hint of Cellophane has crept into some performances.

If the New York City Ballet is at present slightly out of the main stream, there is no alternative sailing confidently down the international current. American Ballet Theatre has made a striking comeback with its impressive repertoire, which includes revivals of Antony Tudor's powerful *Pillar of Fire* and *Undertow*, Jerome Robbins's version of *Les Noces* (excellently theatrical but, like the

101

musical accompaniment, a trifle soft-edged), David Blair's production of *Swan Lake* (an honest but unpoetic adaptation of the old Sadler's Wells version, hideously designed) and two old classics to show off two eminent guest artists, Carla Fracci and Erik Bruhn. But although Ballet Theatre is certainly a mainstream troupe, it lacks a proper school; it is a mere guest at the State Theatre; and it lacks the continuity and leisure which are essential if it is going to compete in the 'grand classics' stakes.

A smaller newish troupe, the Joffrey Ballet, has made a big impression in the quaint old City Centre theatre, where Balanchine's company was born. I saw this 40-strong company only in rehearsal, but it clearly includes some accomplished dancers based on a sound classical school. The repertoire seems wide-based but is necessarily limited at this stage. With several grants behind it and an intelligent and ambitious young director, this could well develop into a serious contender.

An even more unknown quantity is the Harkness Ballet. This has a school (a fantastic one with chandeliers in the classrooms and Dalis on the stairs), a company which – to judge by a run-through – includes first-rate material, but as yet no public performances by which it can be judged. With ample resources and an open-minded policy, this could conceivably develop into a potential pace-setter.

Besides these conventional ballet troupes there are, of course, modern-dance companies like Martha Graham, Paul Taylor, Merce Cunningham, Alvin Ailey, and plenty of smaller ones. In fact the variety is overwhelming. New York is teeming with contrasting styles, aims and experiments conducted with endearing enthusiasm.

However, in art you cannot have your bread buttered on both sides, and the handicaps of this lively free-for-all are evident in a certain lack of artistic finish – the nuances of style, technique, musicality, production and expressiveness which give depth to a performance and change it from good to great. The convincing success of the recent Royal Ballet season was due to these advantages, which come from its established status and security – the very qualities which make it so hard to use for experiment. The present system – or lack of system – in America is certainly paying good dividends. But to an outsider two things seem eventually desirable. First an alternative, probably on the West Coast, to New York as a dance centre (on the analogy of Leningrad and Moscow). And second, some kind of security, common training and overall planning to make the best use of the great supplies of native talent. In the end every country gets the ballet, like the Government, it deserves; few nations, in this light, hold greater promise than America.

18.6.67

## The re-formed Ballet Rambert at the Phoenix Theatre

By a happy coincidence Dame Marie Rambert, who will be eighty on Tuesday, can, at the same time, celebrate the first West End season of her restyled company, whose two weeks at the Phoenix Theatre have established it firmly as a brave, healthy and useful member of theatrical society. Mme Rambert is a kind of Fairy Grandmother. Her first troupe was a suddenly dazzling flower which bore the seeds of the future; the second, post-war generation was banished to the provinces and necessarily became more conventional; the new baby is a lusty, awkward child who has kicked off the classical counterpane and thrashes out its bare limbs in unashamed freedom. The programmes were boldly chosen to establish its new personality. No classics (not even Tudor); this company has opted for the post of flag-bearer for the Modern Dance. In so doing it has dropped into a slot which was yawningly empty. No company more neatly complements the noble classicism of the Royal Ballet. The decision carries deep consequences. It is fairly evident that for sheer physical reasons it is impossible to excel simultaneously as a classical and modern dancer. This will mean eventually shedding all the classically-based works in the repertoire. To do them fairly well (as they are done now) will not be well enough.

As for the dancers, there is already a good team of men led by two nicely contrasted artists, Jonathan Taylor and Christopher Bruce. In Bruce, indeed, they have star material; his uncannily expressive and sensitive work, with its faintly exotic overtones, is unique in the British ballet scene. The girls are far less striking – capable, elegant but not femininely stunning. This may not be their fault. The company's new director, Norman Morrice, has found in Glen Tetley a splendidly solid choreographer to build on, but he seems to write mainly for men and even Morrice's *Hazard* gives few chances to the girls. There is certainly something in the modern style which favours the boys, and this is a problem to be sorted out.

18.2.68

103

## Fonteyn in *Giselle, Swan Lake* and *Romeo* at Covent Garden

The great are the critic's bane. It's ridiculous to keep repeating the virtues of Bach and Rembrandt; yet to ignore them may imply that young Mr So-and-so is in the same bracket. It's easiest to give them a regular passing touch of the forelock - but that's not always fair or wise, or helpful either. There are occasions for the 21-gun salute.

The return of Margot Fonteyn to Covent Garden after a long absence is one of them. We have had some fine performances while she has been away, but seeing her back puts them immediately into perspective. With her we are no longer in the canary-fancier's corner, rating one artist against another. We seem to move out into an altogether larger, calmer, freer world. It's not that she brings any qualities we don't know already. She doesn't jump any higher, spin any faster, balance any longer, have more elegant legs. The reason she astonishes is simply the truth of her dancing. It strikes home with a quiet finality, like a great painting seen after a long, anxious time. Yes, you feel, that's how it is. Everything is all right.

Of her three interpretations in the past two weeks, her *Giselle* was perhaps a shade more beautiful than her *Swan Lake*, where the virtuoso requirements now and then revealed the prodigious technical work which she normally hides under those movements which seem to flow so naturally and limpidly. But to both she brought her special gifts – economy, tact, harmony, the purest of lines and a kind of inner dramatic sense which informs her every step and phrase, lending conviction to the total role. She never forces or woos: why should she? We are all up there with her already. Her pauses are a wonder; she dances as eloquently when she is standing as when she runs and flies. There is a stillness at the heart of her every movement.

Watching her now and remembering her career, you can see how she has not only broadened her attack and style in recent years, but immeasurably developed her interpretative gifts. Maybe it's because of this that she now excels in *Giselle*, a ballet in which she never used to look quite happy; and why the best of all her new performances was in *Romeo and Juliet*.

Here another element enters – Nureyev. He, too, must usually be content with a brief note of appreciation, or even (for it is the fate of all master-figures to set their own standards and then be judged by them) of disappointment. But now that we are discussing Fonteyn we can discuss him, too, and acknowledge the enormous debt she owes to his consistently tactful and positive partnering, and also his own pre-eminence. Singly, they are irreplaceable; together they are incomparable.

The extraordinary harmony of their styles was never better revealed than it was last Tuesday – and here we should also salute Kenneth Mac-Millan, who devised the rich and subtle roles for them to fill. Fonteyn's Juliet, which was once uncertain, has acquired complete conviction. She is a reserved, aristocratic girl (astonishingly, she managed the difficult nursery scene better than ever) who, once committed, follows her star with a quiet, almost resigned, firmness from which nothing can shake her, as no emotion will shake her from her classical control.

Nureyev's Romeo, which also lacked consistency in the early days (the roles were originally written for two very different dancers, Lynn Seymour and Christopher Gable) has jelled into an interpretation in which dance and character blend with blazing vividness. He turned the rather niminy-piminy ballroom solo into a mating-display with an Elizabethan richness of vocabulary; he rocketed round the market-place as though his high spirits were bursting their buttons; and in the big balcony duet they came together with passionate abandon.

It was a revelation to watch, as the tragedy rolled forward, the purity of her style, the power and richness of his. She moved like a girl holding fast to a vision; he danced like a young man in love, a torch to her steady taper.

25.2.68

# Nureyev's production of *The Nutcracker* at Covent Garden

To those who take ballet seriously *The Nutcracker* has always been a bit of an embarrassment. Tchaikovsky himself was never keen on the rather infantile subject, and subsequent productions of the work (which must, initially at least, have had a kind of imperial splendour) have reduced it to a sugary piece of millinery, which only avuncular Christmas goodwill and the presence of two or three eye-catching numbers can render tolerable to an adult palate.

All the same it has survived as a popular favourite. What is the secret

105

of its attraction? The original story, a pawky children's tale by
E. T. A. ('Tales of') Hoffmann – which, incidentally, reveals how the
Prince got changed improbably into a nutcracker in the first place –
had the Grimm-like sadistic overtones which children love. But the
Dumas version, on which the ballet is based, became hopelessly prettified and shallow. The construction, with its inconsistent story-line
and lack of a single ballerina part, is disastrous (Petipa's original
suggestion was much better). The choreography has always been
decidedly mixed; Ivanov's version was clearly not successful and
little if any of it is left. Even the famous *pas de deux* is of disputed
ancestry.

There remains the music – and it, too, raises doubts. This was the
last of Tchaikovsky's ballet scores, written in 1892. It was largely
conceived while he was in Paris and he seems to have fallen a victim to
the fatal allure of that city. In place of the deep-chested romantic
overtones and the majestic flow of 'Swan Lake' or 'The Sleeping
Beauty' with their generous baroque line, he fell back on 'fine filigree
work' whose rococo charms won it a place in every palm court in the
world.

Daintiness, cosiness, prettiness and charm – these seem to be the
amiable breezes which have wafted *The Nutcracker* down the years.
How could they possibly be associated with Nureyev, whose qualities are almost exactly the reverse? As those familiar with his other
Tchaikovsky productions will know, his particular strength lies in
his grasp of the deep romantic pulse of Tchaikovsky and his ability to
bind the ballets together with a single psychological theme. In
dancing terms Tchaikovsky is a composer with a deep *plié*. The
surface brilliance is like the shimmer on a Russian river; what count
are the depths below. How would Nureyev cope with the shallow
sparkle of *The Nutcracker*?

He hasn't. Instead, he has done something quite different. He has
simply taken its innocent nursery romps and spun-sugar attractions
and turned them into a grand-opera-house spectacular, an entertainment in which fantasy, feeling and grotesque comedy blend within a
framework of adult splendour. The children's annual Christmas
outing has been elevated into a kind of classic.

He seems to have done it by a process which comes easier to a
Russian than to a Westerner – by taking the work seriously. Instead of
the kindly-uncle-handing-out-sweets approach he gives us the opposite, the grown-up world as it might be seen through the eyes of a
child; a vision marvellously abetted by Georgiadis's designs, whose

restrained, sombre and exotic richness gives a kind of dignity to the whole evening. The whole paraphernalia of confectionery has been abandoned; playfulness and thistledown daintiness give way to more enduring pleasures.

There has been a lot of basic rethinking. As in several recent productions, the little heroine, Clara, is identified with her own wish-fulfilling Princess (an obvious improvement). The 'mechanical dolls' of the opening scene turn out to be Clara and her brother and sister in disguise – a cunning interpretation. Her arrival in Never Never Land is barred at first by malignant bats (an echo of the rats in act one) who, as her nightmare fades, turn back into her friends and family, while the evil magician bearing the features of Drosselmeyer is revealed as the Prince. This last suggestion – that her old godfather can, with the aid of his magic toy, become the hero of her dreams – is a fancy with disconcerting Freudian implications.

The animals are quite frightening – no longer dear little furry mice but horrible bald-stomached rats who surround Clara and (Freud again) tear off her dress. The ensuing fight is as ferocious as the Battle of Poltava and leads into a flowing, super-romantic *pas de deux*, which lifts the emotion on to the plane of genuine tenderness and gives a real Tchaikovskian heart to what is often a rather synthetic romance. The music lends itself perfectly to this interpretation. Through the whole evening the score comes up fresh and sensitive.

This is partly due to the playing (which, on the opening night, was very good under John Lanchbery) and partly to the actual choreography, which is in a style fascinatingly different from the English tradition. It is very Russian – that is to say, that it is open and unhurried, replacing charm and detailed ingenuity with big rangy movements which involve slow control and a plastic deployment of back and shoulders. In particular it emphasises that awareness of the stage, of its weight and space and presence, which is the backbone of Russian dancing. There must have been some aching knees around Covent Garden during the last few weeks.

These qualities are most evident in the big showpiece – the Snowflake dance, which suggests the pure wide curves of drifts and snowscapes rather than the usual whirling flurry, which is not, in fact, suggested by the peaceful music; the Rose Waltz, which demands also some curious and difficult phrasing; and the two *pas de deux*. The first is all melting and drifting; the second is a bravura piece which stopped the show with some terrifying inventions, such as a kind of vertical 'fish-dive' which ends within an inch of the floor.

107

Production-wise the rather clumsy ending of the ballet is its least successful feature.

A hitherto unexplored side of his choreography emerges in the grotesque numbers, for instance, the excellent little doll-dances and the Chinese variation in act two. These final divertissements, presented from a little stage-within-the-stage, are unevenly successful.

One great merit of the production is that it provides not only some taxing (and therefore rewarding) dancing for the *corps de ballet* but juicy roles for both the Prince – who also has the character part of Drosselmeyer – and Clara. This is obviously going to be a ballet to make or break, a gorgeous Roman Holiday affair for the fans. The opening pair were just about ideal; Antoinette Sibley, all elegant frailty blossoming into genuine authority, and Anthony Dowell, cool and poised with an unshakable perfection of line and smooth technique. When they danced in parallel, as Nureyev likes to make them, they were like the two wings of an invisible soaring bird.

10.3.68

## *Enigma Variations*, The Royal Ballet, Covent Garden

The curtain rises on a misty sepia-tinted tableau. A youngish Edwardian-type gentleman stands in a garden reading, while his friends sit around. Trees frame the view and a modest house opens up to show a mock Tudor staircase. There is a suggestion of croquet and bees and cucumber sandwiches. It might be the beginning of a rather conventional production of *The Importance of Being Earnest*, but the light is too warm. It is the opening of Frederick Ashton's interpretation of Elgar's *Enigma Variations* which was launched at Covent Garden on Friday and it sets the tone of the piece – elegiac, autumnal and a bit claustrophobic, an evocation of the golden (or some might say gilt-edged) days before the cataclysm of 1914.

The approach exactly fits the familiar score, which is a suite of portraits of the composer's friends in a characteristic style which mingles sentiment and jokiness. It provides a perfect opening for Ashton's delicate water-colour talent and his inimitable gift for inventing short flowing variations, and it is a fine vehicle for the smooth, soft Royal Ballet style. If you enjoy leafing through an album of old photographs this is your ballet.

Anatomically, it consists of fifteen short variations – solos, duets, and *pas de trois* linked by unobtrusive background movement and an occasional suggestion of a 'situation'. The numbers are too short for more than the most encapsulated characterisation and it would be vain to look for Chekhovian subtleties. The girls are mostly tender and graceful and the men either formal or eccentrically droll: the young-love episode seems rather swamped by the costumes. There are four somewhat over-similar but superbly done comic solos (Stanley Holden, Brian Shaw, Wayne Sleep and Alexander Grant); Antoinette Sibley has an enchanting little-girl dance, Svetlana Beriosova is a beautiful, adoring Lady Elgar and Anthony Dowell does a dazzling scherzo dazzlingly. Elgar himself (Derek Rencher) is ill-defined. You just have to accept that he is an important and interesting figure.

The ballet is inevitably haunted by the ghost of two others set in the same period – there are strong echoes of *Lilac Garden* and *The Invitation*. It was rash to mix the realism of Julia Trevelyan Oman's pretty sets and costumes with the artifice of ballet – two stiff-collared gentlemen arabesquing together with their watch-chains flying are uncomfortably near to the comical, and it is disconcerting to see stage steam issuing from a doorway which you expect to frame a parlour-maid with a tray of muffins. But such flaws are acceptable within such a cunningly wrought whole. It is a trifle low-definition perhaps, but unmistakably Ashtonian, a charming album of memories in the wispy poetic-nostalgic-romantic style of the thirties.

27.10.68

## *Lilac Garden*, The Royal Ballet, Covent Garden

A hot night. No wind and a full moon, so that the shadows from the shrubbery lie black across the grass. Figures come and go, grouping and circling and parting again like moths. Something is afoot; a sense of aching disaster hangs in the air. This is the atmosphere of Antony Tudor's *Lilac Garden*, which was mounted by the choreographer at Covent Garden last Tuesday. Thirty-two years have passed since its original presentation by the Rambert company, and many ballets have derived from it. For this was a seminal work. There is a difference between a novelty ballet and a source ballet. *Lilac Garden* is decidedly the second. To exert an influence a ballet must first succeed.

Tudor's new idea was, to paraphrase Dubcek, 'ballet with a human face'. The characters here are no mythical or allegorical figures, but flesh-and-blood men and women, caught at the climax of a tight romantic tangle. The ballet has remained a Rambert favourite, and several other companies have proved that it can keep its impact in an extended version. The interest of last week's production was to see how it would sit on the Royal Ballet. The verdict so far is indecisive.

Its style is idiosyncratic. Flow is all and tension is all – the opposing qualities which blend so movingly in the violin in Chausson's score. In practice this means for the dancers a sustained current of movement in which every eddy, every pause or thrust of acceleration is charged with emotion. The famous 'freeze' near the end when the world seems to hold its breath for a moment, while the despairing theme breaks out in the orchestra, hearts crack, and four lovers brace themselves to go their separate ways, must be felt as immanent from the first bar. Tuesday's performance, led by Svetlana Beriosova, Donald MacLeary, Georgina Parkinson and Desmond Doyle, was smooth, distinguished and visually beautiful. But the split-second timing and phrasing and the absolute accuracy of position needed to screw the deceptively simple choreography into eloquence is so far missing. Both on stage and in the orchestra pit grace and delicacy replaced passion and anguish. Neither the private agonies nor the public decorum emerged fully; Georgina Parkinson and Desmond Doyle came nearest to conveying them.

17.11.68

*Tudor's special gift [is] for investing the particular with overtones of eternal ritual.*

## The Nutcracker and Sleeping Beauty at Covent Garden

I believe we are in the presence today of those two implacable spirits Ping and Pong. They have been offended and the sky darkens. They hang balefully over Covent Garden, where two Tchaikovsky classics running have produced vibrant critical explosions. Audiences may be permissive; there is no proof yet that the new *Sleeping Beauty* will be a box office disaster and *The Nutcracker* has proved pretty popular here

110

and extremely so in New York. But the high priests of taste have been seeing omens and rending their garments (not to mention Lila de Nobili's). The demons of disapproval are abroad.

Ping and Pong were first conjured up out of the deep by the eminent aesthetic necromancer E. H. Gombrich. In his book *Art and Illusion* he proposed a devilish scheme whereby the whole universe, and all that therein is, should be cleft down the middle and allotted to one or other of them. In other words, whenever we are confronted with an alternative – white wine or red, Mozart or Beethoven, cricket or football, Harold Wilson or George Brown – we should ask ourselves whether they belong to the kingdom of Ping or to the kingdom of Pong.

The decision is usually easy, which is all the more surprising because the categories have no real character at all. They carry no suggestion whatever of superiority or inferiority, of pleasure or pain, of male Yin or female Yang, no hint even of the familiar smooth-rough, left-right, tender-tough antithesis. Just the unmistakable quality of pingness or pongness.

The amazingly wide general agreement about what falls into which slot – an agreement which you can test by experiment (it makes an excellent parlour game) – suggests that there is some hidden device in the human mechanism which invariably makes one instant and unconscious judgment, which we afterwards expand and rationalise. We brutally divide into two what has been called 'semantic space'. And once we have allocated a concept to one side of this territory, we are led by association and by synesthesia (short-circuiting of the senses so that, for instance, hearing is confused with seeing) to pile into the same category a whole jumble of others. An American professor, Charles Osgood, has even worked out, in his book *The Measurement of Meaning*, a whole map which charts out the areas.

Roughly speaking it is obvious – though difficult to explain rationally – that qualities like shrill, shallow, high, dry, thin, hard and gay belong to the Ping area, while booming, low, deep, wet, massive, soft and solemn tend towards Pong. What is remarkable is that apparently irrelevant objects can be classified just as sharply. Try it on food (mutton and beef, bread and butter), on animals (dogs and cats) and even on whole species (birds and mammals).

You can extend it to historical periods (eighteenth century and nineteenth century) or places (Paris and London), to cultures (Greek and Roman), or people. Happy marriages and famous partnerships

111

are apt to combine the two, though not always with the same sex playing the same role (how would you place Olivier and Vivien Leigh, Burton and Taylor, Fonteyn and Nureyev?). Try it on cars and cutlery, on colours, shops or film directors. Try it on your friends. Ping and Pong are very real presences, and the root cause of the Royal Ballet's troubles is that they have been confused, even defied. Given that ballet is already a ping art compared to opera, *The Sleeping Beauty* is clearly a pong ballet compared to *The Nutcracker*. Its new Christmas card staging, which tries to twist it into the gentle English pastoral-lyrical tradition, runs diametrically against the inherent character both of the music and of Petipa's formal choreography.

In the same way the allocation of *The Nutcracker* to the excessively pong Nureyev (with an equally pong designer, Georgiadis) goes right against the natural grain. It has proved less shocking because there is much pong Tchaikovsky in the score, especially in the first act (and in the big *pas de deux*). But the passionately pursed lips with which some critics have greeted it reveals a deep subconscious disturbance about the whole treatment.

29.12.68


# Rolf de Maré exhibition, Museum of Modern Art, Stockholm

Who in 1920 got Bonnard to design Debussy's *Jeux*? Who first commissioned ballet music from Poulenc, Auric, Milhaud and Honegger? Who put on a Negro ballet designed by Léger with a score by Cole Porter, orchestrated by Charles (*Shadowplay*) Koechlin? Who mounted a ballet by Jean Cocteau with costumes by Jean Hugo? Who first used Chirico as a ballet designer? Who created a Paris scandal with a Dada ballet devised and designed by Picabia including a crazy 'underground' film by René Clair to music by Satie?

No marks to all those clever dicks who answer Diaghilev. A special prize for the few who know that it was Rolf de Maré and his Ballets Suédois. This extraordinary Swede who at a crucial moment challenged the great Russian on his own ground, and in some ways surpassed him, has remained too little known. Understandably he has been overshadowed by the more massive and lasting achievements of his great rival. But now a major exhibition in his honour has been mounted in the Museum of Modern Art in Stockholm. It would be a shame if at least a part of it did not travel abroad. It would increase our respect for Swedish artistic enterprise and it would put the records straight for many of us woolly minded ballet-goers.

In many ways the Ballets Suédois were a chip off the block of the Ballets Russes. They were a direct result of a visit to Stockholm by Fokine after one of his rows with Diaghilev. He became ballet-master at the Opera, mounted several of his own ballets and danced in them with his wife. One of his keenest supporters, with whom he sometimes stayed, was a rich young landowner, Rolf de Maré.

This sophisticated art-lover – he had a house in Paris and another in Africa and had travelled extensively in Asia and America – was so fired with enthusiasm that he decided to form a company of his own. It was to be Paris-based and to be led by a 20-year-old Swedish dancer who was burning to try his hand at modern choreography, Jean Börlin. The troupe was duly launched in Paris at the Théâtre des Champs Elysées in October 1920.

The sample quoted above gives a fair idea of its repertoire which was uncompromisingly modern, laced with a sprinkling of Swedish folk tradition. Its weakness was the limitation of its dancers to relatively inexpert Scandinavians and its reliance on a single choreo-grapher, Börlin. After five years of avant garde success in Paris, London and America (not Sweden) the harassed young man, who was principal dancer as well as choreographer, had a nervous breakdown on the eve of what was to be his most legendary work, the Dadaist *Relâche* of Picabia. With his disappearance the company folded.

The relatively weak dance-talent threw the emphasis on design. De Maré was a keen and enlightened collector – the museum already owes many works to his taste – and the full-size re-creation of Léger's magnificent sets for *La Création du Monde* and *Skating Rink* are in themselves a monument to a notable contribution to the experimental phase in ballet which is now rightly being reassessed in the light of modern theatre.

None of Börlin's ballets has survived and the pendulum has swung back against his approach. It was curious to go from the exhibition to see Erik Bruhn's new production of *Giselle* at the Opera House – a straightforward, dramatically sound affair entirely in the traditional style with a pretty and sumptuous setting by the British designer Desmond Heeley.

6.4.69

# Fonteyn, on her fiftieth birthday

Margot Fonteyn (the Dame part seems almost irrelevant in her case) is a name familiar to thousands who have never been within a mile of a ballet performance. She is irrefutably a star – but very much not a shooting or a lucky star. She did not wake up one morning to find herself famous after some sensational role or a stroke of fortune. She is of the steady lasting kind, increasing each year in radiance to reach her present dazzling lustre – star of a world of stars.

'Dazzling' is not really the right word to describe her as either a dancer or a person. Some cooler, less explosive adjective is needed. She seems never to have had any doubts and her career has been almost humdrum.

Her quiet, confident progress owes much to her physical gifts – beauty, ideal proportions, uncanny healthiness – but almost more to her temperament. She is unflappable, realistic, cheerful, intelligent, self-critical, and fanatically hard-working. Few people in any walk of life could have coped so resiliently with what she had to face – the tragic crippling of her Panamanian diplomat husband.

She is not only intuitively musical; she can phrase a movement to show you exactly why the choreographer inserted it, and by that sheer theatrical power we call 'glamour' she can hypnotise an audience without seeming to notice them and without departing an inch from her pure classical style.

This kind of quiet, restrained, but scrupulous excellence is something we like to think of as especially English. You could call her the Rolls-Royce of the dance – but if you did she would laugh and say she preferred her little Mini.

15.5.69


# *Knight Errant*, The Royal Ballet, Covent Garden

A strong personal accent is as rare in ballet as in any art. Antony Tudor has it – but would those who know only his recent *Shadowplay* recognise it in *Knight Errant* which finally reached Covent Garden on Friday? Probably not. Yet this is just as intensely a Tudor

114

work – subtle and calculated, laced with a detached and dandified mockery of human endeavours. It emerged as a rare small treasure, probably not destined for mass appeal but likely to become a cult with the connoisseur. Its success owed much to David Wall, who had been prevented by injury from taking part in the première in Manchester last autumn. Now he slips into the key role of the profligate eighteenth-century anti-hero with a relish which can be felt in the farthest corner of the theatre. The ballet's icy lasciviousness conveys with marvellous precision the flavour of the period – age of the periwig, the patch and the pox – and Wall knows exactly how to indicate false sentiment and affected virility with a glance or a tilt of the head without losing our sympathy. This was a performance to remember, though he could make it still more witty if his footwork were more finished. The complacently deflowered heroines were danced with just the right coy ardour by Alfreda Thoroughgood, Sandra Conley and Elizabeth Anderton and the complicated story emerged with extraordinary adroitness. Stefanos Lazaridis's austere set and costumes provide a spacious setting which echoes the economy that is the keynote of the ballet's style, while Richard Strauss's delicate score gave a polished veneer to it all. Altogether a cabinet of curious and elegant delights.

25.5.69

## *Spartacus*, The Bolshoi, Covent Garden

Grigorovitch's new version of *Spartacus* is an archetypal company production – one of those blockbusters nobody else could or would attempt; it is bulging with audience-appeal, and it is controversial, stirring the strongest enthusiasms and dislikes. My own reactions include both. What I am against is the easy middle course, a patronising attitude of enjoying it as a huge bit of camp. It is both better and worse than that. The story fits the Bolshoi's style perfectly. There is an obvious affinity between the tramp of the Roman legions and the thunder of the Bolshoi battalions and – as shrewd impresarios have known from Commodus down to Cinecittá – a bunch of gladiators makes irresistible theatre. The plot of the tragic Slaves Revolt has just the right ingredient of underdog heroism and social comment.

Grigorovitch has stuck pretty closely to traditional silent-film treatment, with big production numbers alternating with close-ups, or 'monologues' as he calls them. The pace is unrelenting. For three and a half hours the stage shakes to soldiers pounding, leaping and brandishing their swords; the rest of their time is taken up with orgies. It's a man's world. Apart from courtesans and a few shepherds and shepherdesses there are no civilians except for Spartacus's faithful wife. This is a long hymn to militant virility and the girls shrink almost to invisibility in the cloud of manly dust. Bessmertnova is not quite at home in the symphonic style and Timofeyeva's role as the tyrant's mistress, though danced with total identification, is too vulgar to be attractive. The ballet is a gift to the male dancers and they accept it magnificently. As the cruel, flamboyant Crassus, Maris Liepa creates a richly drawn character, and the Spartacus of Lavrovsky drives like a sword through the whole evening. This is a dazzling performance – true, intense, blazingly vital yet impeccably controlled. You could hardly believe it when he sprang out with yet another series of urgent, ardent leaps and turns.

Knockout performance; decent design; stunning impact – yet queasy doubts persist. Barrel-chested heroics, a combination of the spotlight and the parade ground, have won quick victories before. A streak of Hollywood pasteboard runs through the evening, exaggerated by the *kitsch* music of Khatchaturian. The theme is swallowed up in spectacle (there is not much sense of conflict until the last act) and the choreography is patchy. This is an evening of glorious sound and fury; but artistically its significance is small. Revolution has been turned into a mammoth revue.

20.7.69

*Ballet – which in the west carries associations of a sophisticated, almost scented, minority art – means something quite different in Russia. It is a pop art. People go to it as they go to the opera in Germany, as a normal form of family entertainment. And they not only look. There are several million Russians regularly taking part in amateur dance performance, besides thirty full-scale ballet companies.*

116

# Cell, Contemporary Dance Company, The Place

The last item in the last programme of the Contemporary Dance Company at The Place was called *Cell*: choreography by Robert Cohan, score specially composed by Ronald Lloyd, designed by Norberto Chiesa. The prospect was a trifle bleak; we had already had a rich diet of monks, coffins, stained glass, mourners, penitents and other echoes of Martha Graham's puritanical turn of mind (if frivolity is the bane of ballet, solemnity is the curse of modern dance).

It was great to be disabused. This final piece was not only outstanding in the programme, it was outstanding in the season. In fact, it is outstanding, period; one of those works in which conception, collaboration and execution come together in what seems inevitable conjunction. Together with Graham's *El penitente* (they can be seen together on Wednesday) it fully justifies the season. While the Graham ballet is a notable survival from an earlier generation, this one – perhaps alone of all the works presented – fully deserves the adjective 'contemporary'. In a white space six dancers act out what seem to be three stages in Sartre's vision of Others as Hell (and Heaven, of course), everyday, idealised, transcendental turning into nightmare. There is not a cliché in sight. Every move seems motivated by the strange vision; unkinky, non-uptight, humane yet not emotional, the action held the audience like a rivet. The finale, always so difficult in the non-spectacular modern idiom, is sensational – limbs and bricks flying in flashing stroboscopic light as the central figure (brilliantly danced by Robert Powell, the finest artist in the company) struggles to rebuild the shattered walls of his own prison.

Excellently designed and lit, admirably danced to an effective score of whispering taps and pings and creakings. This is a winner.

14.9.69

# Dutch National Ballet season at Sadler's Wells

The Dutch National Ballet, which has just finished its absurdly short season at Sadler's Wells, turned out to be one of the most interesting companies to visit London lately – far better than I had been led to expect. That a country of 12 million should be able to develop and support both it and the admirable modern-style Nederlands Dance Theatre is astonishing. This company is, in aims and character, a kind of echo of our own Royal Ballet – though a mere baby by comparison. It was founded only eight years ago. Under its first director, Russian-born Sonia Gaskell, it made extraordinary progress. The dance standard is high and the repertoire phenomenal, stretching from the nineteenth-century classics to avant-garde pieces which would not look out of place at The Place. It is a large company (not more than half of it appeared in London); it has enjoyed both Russian and American teachers; its repertoire has a strong Balanchine backbone; and at least one of its new young directors has important choreographic talent. Clearly it is a company with a future and the Dutch Government will be mad if it does not set up a school to consolidate it.

One of the juiciest plums in its varied programmes came on the opening night with a ballet that I thought I knew well. The first cast I ever saw in Balanchine's *Apollo* was Eglevsky, Danilova, Alonso and Kaye. I was totally bowled over, so much so that I have never since seen a cast which entirely satisfied me. I never dreamed that it would be a Dutch company which would restore my conviction – which had lately been wavering – that the ballet is a masterpiece.

I think there were three contributing elements. The size of the theatre, so much more apt that the large, tasteful, gilded presentation at Covent Garden; the participation of a perfectly matched Balanchine-type trio of Muses (Olga de Haas, Helene Pex and Sonja Marchiolli), long-legged, athletic, coolly detached; and Nureyev as Apollo. He starts with the essential gift of dominance. To this he has added, over his natural suppleness, a kind of divine ferocity of movement. When he slides his foot along the floor he seems to be tracing out a celestial geometry: he stamps and freezes, not decoratively, but with an inhuman detachment. Precision becomes a power-tool to carve out the real Apollo – god of fire and discipline as well as of purity, courtesy and art.

The company had already established itself in another Balanchine ballet, *The Four Temperaments*. I had never seen it before and again I was gripped by the conviction, which I have occasionally dared to doubt, that Balanchine is a genius. The arrangements to Hindemith's score are so strange, so individual, so difficult, so right. And they were done by excellently rehearsed dancers obviously steeped in the style – and no wonder, with nine of his ballets in the repertoire.

118

The same understanding of his idiom – so different from the Fokine flow from which the English style ultimately derives – could be seen also in his *Concerto Barocco*, though this could have done with more freedom and attack. There was a generous ration of *pas de deux*, including the graceful writhing-in-coils by Oscar Araiz which we saw done by his own troupe recently, and some classical numbers for the ballerinas (who concealed admirable virtuosity under almost prim control) and for Sylvester Campbell, who has a beautiful soft *ballon*; besides an athletic piece by Brian Macdonald pitched too high for comfort.

But the main interest was in the contributions by van Dantzig. The weakest was the earliest. *Jungle* (1961) evokes semi-human life in semi-tropical anarchy. Both the style and also the electronic score (by Henk Badings) have dated, but already it revealed his rare sense for theatrical timing and flow and the harmonious collaboration between him and his designer, Toer van Schayk. *Moments* is a fascinating but difficult piece, a kaleidoscope of abstract movement to a remote spider's-web score by Webern. Classical technique is used in a very modern, personal way to construct a ballet which cries out for a second viewing. I was gripped all right, but slightly baffled.

His other two ballets were immediate and obvious successes. *Monument for a Dead Boy*, to a dramatic electronic tape by Jan Boerman, could be described as a kind of Dutch version of MacMillan's *The Invitation*. It, too, is about adolescent sex-horrors, though the flashback tale of parental misunderstanding, gang-rape in the school changing-room and furtive affairs with young girl and older woman is interrupted, characteristically, by a vignette of terrifying mime (mum and dad at it on the carpet in pink slip and braces) whereas the Briton, on the contrary, interposes charming classical interludes. It too has the ingredients of a popular classic, and a star central role. On the opening night this offered Nureyev a chance to dive for the first time into modern electronics – a chance he seized voraciously to create a character of desperate anguish, his plastic style adapting easily to modern movement. In later performances Toer van Schayk gave a gentle, sensitive rendering which was equally valid.

Finally, the most recent and the best of all van Dantzig ballets, *Epitaph*. This seems to be a long meditation on death, explored in a series of vivid but non-rational images. Figures come and go; huddle in coffins; are lost, comforted and mourned; greet and part; are visited by mysterious bride-mothers. The music – crashing organ-noises by Gyorgy Ligeti – is tremendous, van Schayk's

119

movable designs appropriate and beautiful, the dancing excellent. The flow of visual happenings is as smooth and evasive and haunting as a Berlioz melody, ending in a solemn but alarming tableau as the two brides gently close the doors round the piled-up figures and sink down on prie-dieus which clamp death fast like gilded locks. This is an exciting, moving and completely original ballet.

7.12.69

# The Seventies

# Nureyev in *The Ropes of Time*, Covènt Garden

The curtain rises on pitch darkness, total silence. Gradually we make out a figure straddling a huge globe. He twists, curves in and out as if drawing first life-giving breaths; there is a crash like the breaking of a thousand dishes and he is down, crouched for action. The bang marks the Royal Ballet breaking the tradition-barrier at last. We are away into the 1970s.

The event took place at Covent Garden last Monday at the première of *The Ropes of Time*, a new ballet by the Dutch choreographer Rudi van Dantzig. With its electronic-tape score, its wiry constructivist designs, modern choreography, free structure and ambiguous theme, it adds up to a giant leap forward for our national company in terms of style. What is immediately striking, almost disconcerting, about the new work is its sustained intensity. We sometimes forget that Van Gogh sprang from the same culture as the serene Vermeer. Anybody familiar with Dutch art today knows that a streak of expressionist anguish races through the national character. This sense of desperation emerged in the ballets by Van Dantzig which his own company recently performed at Sadler's Wells. His new ballet is charged with the same dark energy.

Van Dantzig is not the man to trace a direct narrative path, but we can take it that the curtain rises on a birth and falls on a death. What happens between is not the steady curve from youth to maturity, still less a reflection of any individual experience, but more a kind of canvas on which areas of feeling are laid out freely in strong colours. Even these allusions have been drastically rendered down and translated. There are no surrealist real-life references as there were in his beautiful *Epitaphs*. This is entirely a dance ballet. He makes us aware of an underlying feeling about the inseparability of Life and Death by the way these two characters (the only ones besides the central Traveller) link together, share movements or jointly enwrap the hero; and we can grasp his hopes and fears. But nothing is expressed literally. We are presented with a flow of dancing which only reveals its content slowly.

This dancing is devised in a style which manages to combine classical with modern movement and yet maintains a personal character (no body-beautiful posing, easy jiving or score-interpretations). Van Dantzig has a gift for animating the stage with unexpected groupings and for dramatic strokes; the giant hemisphere at the start opens like an oyster to give birth to the Traveller's companions and the three protagonists are linked at one point by tapes which echo the ribbon-dances of tradition.

The electronic score, by Jan Boerman, consists of weird hissings and wails and thumps which suggest the bowels of some gigantic ship and add greatly to the emotional tension. The lack of any rhythmic framework (there are even long passages done in silence) makes the dancers work with extra concentration and this communicates itself to the audience. The urgency is unremitting; in fact, a moment of relaxation somewhere at the heart of the dense choreography would help some of us frailer spirits.

It is clear from the start that Van Dantzig and his designer Toer van Schayk are in total harmony. The austere cat's cradle of wires and flats which hangs over the dancers, moving occasionally to take on new shapes, mirrors the cunningly simple but becoming costumes and the criss-cross patterns of the dance. The total effect is a fine, serious sculptural design which could stand up to gallery presentation.

The ballet is designed as a vehicle for a special talent, shaped in concerto form round a single dancer, Nureyev as the Traveller. It is a stupendous role – thirty-five minutes on stage as the focus of the whole ballet and filled with athletics of every kind, culminating with a wild solo demanding the furious control of one of those dances in *Spartacus*. It is a major challenge to the dancer – for whom it was custom-built – defying him to show us what he can offer in the way of range, virtuosity, plastic dynamics, dramatic projection, eye-compelling magnetism and sheer physical stamina. He seizes it with both hands, not to mention the rest of his anatomy, to give a blazingly sincere performance which at the same time stretches his powers to the limit.

8.3.70

# Sir Frederick Ashton

People who are not quite what they seem to be, or even what they think they are, have a special fascination. They arouse the detective instinct. A fine example of the species is Sir Frederick Ashton, CH, CBE, Director for the last seven years – and until last night – of the Royal Ballet.

Everybody in the dance world knows him by sight – smallish,

quick-moving, quietly nervous, one of those figures in which a slender sharp-featured youth still lurks inside the solid composure of maturity. You will find him in the corner of the room, not the centre, gossiping, not holding court. Can this diffident, evasive, soft-voiced, almost stealthy individual be the man who has launched eighty ballets into the spotlight, directed stars in their courses and set his seal on one of the great theatrical companies of the world?

It can be, and it is. Clearly Ashton is something more than a bundle of supersensitive nerve-ends bound together with taste and intelligence. Where is the key to the mystery? Luckily, Ashton is an artistic creator and there is a lot of truth in the saying that all works of art, without exception, are self-portraits. He has left clues all over the place in his ballets, and perhaps the most significant are the roles he has written for himself.

There are not a great many of these. In his youth Ashton was an expressive and elegant dancer, but he never had the physique nor the plain physical drive to make a career as a performer (his finely tuned temperament is held steady by a touch of healthy English laziness). The first parts he created for himself were curiously prophetic. In his very first ballet he played an amorous couturier, simultaneously worshipping and controlling with his delicate scissors. In a work based on Degas drawings called *Foyer de Danse* that he arranged for the Rambert Ballet at the beginning of his career he cast himself as the ballet-master. Authoritative, witty and nimble, maliciously sharp but pitted with soft spots, he had to conjure up a kind of orderly lyricism out of the scruffiness of the studio. Not a bad likeness of his later career.

Another role takes us a bit deeper into his personality. This was in a piece for the Sadler's Wells Ballet called *Nocturne*, done when he was thirty to dreamy music by Delius in a dreamy setting by his friend Sophie Fedorovitch. It was a poetic vision of Paris, seen as a city of light and lyricism filled with lovers – meeting, quarrelling, parting and finding each other again in a perpetual masquerade. Through the eddies of passion and fashion, Ashton moved as a mysterious stranger. As the curtain fell he was left alone, wrapped in a romantic cloak, watching the sun rise over the rooftops. He had given us a glimpse of the melancholy detachment which lies behind the quick repartee and the watchful eyes.

Recently he has offered another prospect of himself, ludicrously caparisoned in false nose and pounds of grotesque padding as one of the Ugly Sisters in *Cinderella*. To stuff himself into such a rig at this dignified stage in his career points to a steely moral nerve, and the character itself is revealing. This is the put-upon sister, the shy, untalented, trusting one, resigned to her role as one of nature's doormats. Lovable, pathetic and deprecatory, she looks, as she patters about on her little feet beneath an enormous bonnet, like a character from a child's animal story – a relative perhaps of Beatrix Potter's Mrs Tittlemouse, all quivering whiskers as she ventures out from the wainscoting.

He presents a triple portrait – theatrical wizard, poet, insecure individual. What is interesting, of course, is what it leaves out. The fastidious ballet master is true all right and combined with the visionary to create those stage adventures that have moved (and doubtless will continue to move) so many audiences to that ecstatic state of mind which hovers between pain and rapture. It is even true that he sees himself as a mildly imposed-on character who survives in a brutal world only by extreme cunning, always ready to beat a retreat to his little house in Chelsea as snugly fashioned as a nest.

But the historians will have other facets to record. They will comment on his luck. With typically perfect timing he appeared on the scene just as British ballet was coming to birth after the death of Diaghilev; and he found, first in Marie Rambert, then in Ninette de Valois, ideal, totally different Directors under whom to develop his talents, and in Margot Fonteyn the perfect instrument to embody his ideals. Mention will be made of his extraordinary gifts as teacher and guide, gratefully acknowledged by everybody who has worked with him, from Nureyev down to the youngest recruit in the corps de ballet. There may be a passage about his Englishness (he was actually born, in 1906, in Ecuador) with his instinct for restrained elegance, his love of gardens and his distaste for violence, soulfulness and foreign parts. A place must be found for his incredible fecundity and tenacity when he gets going – felicitous but never facile – and for his shrewd theatrical know-how. His famous delicate touch has survived all kinds of work in films, musicals and opera and he is a professional to his fingertips beneath the casual coolness. Perhaps he will be called the Beau Brummell of the dance, changing a nation's habits by the passionate tying of a knot.

26.7.70

# American Ballet Theatre at Covent Garden, the Kirov at the Festival Hall

The latest temptations dangled before the dwindling purse of the London ballet-lover are offered by the American Ballet Theatre at Covent Garden. The company is an old favourite here, but it is fourteen years, no less, since we last saw it. It interests us especially because – unlike the New York City Ballet – it is based on the same formula as that of our own companies, a catholic mixture from many hands and lands. The only difference – a serious one – is that it lacks the continuity line provided by a steady subsidy and a school. This gives it a slightly improvisatory quality which can be a positive advantage in short new works, but presents difficulties in the classics. It was bold to open the season in London with two of them. The fact that both were newly restaged by the ex-Royal Ballet David Blair must have been one reason for the choice; another was probably the simple desire to show off the dancers in the most searching of tests.

The company, as a whole, emerged with credit. It is tough on any dancer to tackle Petipa with the Kirov over the road, and these may lose a few marks for technical polish; but they compensate by an enviable dramatic punch and dancing verve. A fine example of this in the opening ballet, *Swan Lake*, was Bruce Marks's Prince – manly, positive, acted with conviction and danced with dash, a boldly outlined performance which exactly suited the simple line of the production. His ballerina, Cynthia Gregory, gave total confidence technically but looked somewhat unmoved, and for whatever reason the romantic fire never broke into flames. They were not fanned by the Disney-type designing or by some notably insensitive conducting.

Blair leans towards the naturalistic Stanislavsky school of production, which paid off in the first act but may have contributed to the low emotional temperatures of the performance. His is basically a re-touched version of the old Sadler's Wells edition. His approach fitted more aptly into *Giselle*, which also benefited from better costumes and playing. It came across as a very clear and convincing drama, though perhaps not the ideal setting for Carla Fracci's rather mannered interpretation. Her first scenes were well acted, ending in a fine and touching madness, but she was more soft than springy as a Wili and had some rather idiosyncratic arm movements. Ted Kivitt made an honest but anonymous Albrecht.

127

After these traditional offerings, the bread and salt of ballet so to speak, the company began to pour out some examples of its extraordinarily rich repertoire. José Limón's *Moor's Pavane* (an encapsulated *Othello*) looked a little lost in the Opera House spaces and I missed the sheer density of the choreographer's Moor as he showed it here a few years back. Completely new was Dennis Nahat's *Brahms Quintet*, a pleasant abstract arrangement which gave an opening for some beautiful dancing by Cynthia Gregory, Mimi Paul and Ivan Nagy. Agnes de Mille's twenty-year-old *Fall River Legend* has become a period piece, a sex frustration melodrama full of good passages and offering a plum role to the ballerina. Sally Wilson absolutely devours it but the ballet sags a little in the middle and is handicapped by its trivial score. It was followed by the wonderfully intelligent choreography of Balanchine's Tchaikovsky *Theme and Variations*, creditably danced.

Meanwhile at the Festival Hall the Kirov Company continues to demonstrate the triumph of craft over art. What it offers is a scrumptious helping of plum pudding with the pudding left out. This week's goodies included *Chopiniana* (*Les Sylphides*), beautifully danced by Komleva, Makarova and Zagurskaya under lighting which at least solved the mystery of what sylphs wear under their gossamer. We also had the meaty *Leningrad Symphony*, a strip-cartoon version of the siege of the city by the Nazis which precariously explores the frontier between the sublime and the ridiculous, with Soloviev as a heroically bounding superman and Alla Sizova athletically symbolising suffering womanhood, and the campy splendours of *Walpurgis Night* with Osipenko flying with the greatest of ease into the muscular arms of Jonny Markovsky above a wriggling litter of over-excited fauns. The string of short numbers was especially distinguished by Natalia Makarova in a Délibes *pas de deux*, Leonid Jacobsen's ingenious and brilliantly danced *Baba Yaga* grotesquerie, and the amazingly clean, smooth dash of Mikhail Baryshnikov in *Flames of Paris*. Here is a pure knight of the dance, *sans peur et sans reproche*.

2.8.70

*The good is destroyed by the better, says the French proverb – a cruel truth much in the minds of ballet-goers recently. The American Ballet Theatre, which has just finished its season at Covent Garden, had the bad luck to clash with the Kirov Company at the Festival Hall: when it comes to dancing, particularly to classical dancing which Londoners love most, there was no doubt which would excel. The Makarova-Soloviev Giselle, with Gridin's Hilarion and a pas de deux from Bolshakova and Baryshnikov, was of the kind momentarily to remove all comparisons.*

## *Dances at a Gathering*, The Royal Ballet, Covent Garden

The first new offering of the new Royal Ballet management, which it presented at Covent Garden last Monday, was a resounding success, as could have been foretold. In fact, Jerome Robbins's *Dances at a Gathering* arrived trailing such clouds of encomium that it was hard to bring an objective eye to bear on it. Through the thicket of praise a work of genuine stature emerged triumphantly. Perhaps its most attractive quality is its feeling of organic growth. There is no sense of rigid structure or agonised obsession; it starts tenderly, develops, branches out this way and that, and tapers off to a quiet finish as natural as a tree-top resting on the wind. Reputedly it was expanded bit by bit from a single *pas de deux*. Its form, wayward but persistent, certainly suggests just such a happy birth.

Its shape is riskily long and slim, consisting as it does of no fewer than eighteen short dances for ten dancers, arranged to Chopin piano pieces, mainly waltzes and mazurkas. It is inimitably rewarding from the dancers' point of view – each one gets the chance to make a clear individual impact. The variety and invention never flag but are never forced. In the same way the mood varies from the lyrical to the satirical, from fun and virtuosity to the slightly mysterious; but the points are never rubbed in. A cool detachment reigns. We are fascinated and entertained but seldom moved or involved.

As with many good ballets the inspiration seems to come straight from the score. Robbins has found in Chopin a vivid thread to hold his numbers together. The curtain rises on a single figure. He walks almost absentmindedly across the stage, seems to become infused with the music, pulls up, sways, and gradually swings into a solo. He is wearing calf-boots and the music is a mazurka, and the melancholy fire of that Polish dance illuminates the whole ballet. The boots save what are often straight classical movements from all classical

129

daintiness; a turn of the body, a flash of toe and heel or a flourish of the elbow give a touch of virile mischief to the most graceful manœuvre. The idiom controls the range of movement, preserving it both from classical camp and from folksy bumptiousness.

There are too many inventions to be enumerated. From that simple but theatrical opening ideas flow in a stream, each new bit of dancing seeming to rise from a human situation. Inevitably not all are equally striking (there is a *pas de six* near the middle which flags a bit), but the mixture is beautifully calculated. Though originally written for the New York City Ballet it fits like a glove the nearly all-star cast of the Royal Ballet, led by Antoinette Sibley, sunny and lyrical, Lynn Seymour, seductive and witty, and Monica Mason, breathtakingly speedy. Robbins is that real rarity, a choreographer who writes for men as well as he does for girls, and the boys have a ball. Nureyev, relaxed and lithe and powerful, cheerfully contends with Anthony Dowell's stylish vitality, while David Wall bounds with ease and Michael Coleman spins and darts like a bird.

It must be admitted that a full hour of short Chopin pieces, at least half of them in three-four time, is a bit hard on the ear of anybody not addicted to that composer, especially when played forcefully enough to fill an opera house with a single piano (Anthony Twiner gave a fine rendering in the circumstances). Chopin's music has been compared to 'the fluttering of a humming bird over an abyss', and Robbins – deliberately – never strays very near to the edge of the precipice; his choreography remains inside the music instead of straying beyond it as Fokine did in *Les Sylphides*. If this keeps the ballet from making the most intense of impacts, it gives it the great merit of integrity. It feels like the honest reflection of a contemporary mind, caught in a pattern of consummate craftsmanship. I only wish the costumes and design were worthy of it. The dresses are innocuous, but clouds moving across a cyclorama suggest exactly the kind of phoney blue-sky lyricism which the choreographer has so skilfully avoided.

25.10.70

## *Mutations*, Nederlands Dans Theater, Sadler's Wells

Let's face it fully and frontally, we are in the autumn of modesty. Fig leaves flutter down all around, scattered by the wind of change.

Thirty years ago Ninette de Valois was showing the formidable founder of the Sadler's Wells Theatre, Lilian Baylis, the backcloth for a new ballet. It was promptly censored on the grounds that the stomach of a female statue depicted on it was too large. 'But it's no bigger than mine,' protested de Valois untruthfully. 'Ah, my dear, but you have had an operation,' replied Miss Baylis.

What would she have said last week? In her own theatre, in *Mutations*, a new ballet by Glen Tetley (with films by Hans van Manen), four young men and one young girl of the Nederlands Dans Theater danced naked for minutes in full spotlight, not to mention long film sequences in which one of the performers appeared enormously magnified and slow-motioned as if to prove that he was every inch a genitalman.

It has been widely reported that the effect was perfectly unremarkable and indeed irrelevant. Certainly dancers' slim bodies suggest Bosch's 'Terrestrial Paradise' rather than a Rubens orgy. But I must make an embarrassing confession. In the nudity field I am an outsider, a freak, perhaps even that ghoul which haunts the law courts where learned men fulminate on sex and censorship. Not only am I likely to be depraved; I probably am depraved already, for I find the spectacle of beautiful naked bodies exciting. Their introduction in this ballet induced a glow of added interest which it was painfully easy to analyse.

I comforted myself afterwards by reflecting that respectable authorities in other fields have admitted similar sensations. Lord Clark has even written that all good nude painting and sculpture is sexually stimulating. Sex assumes many disguises. On the stage we readily admit arousal by crafty costumes, lighting or posture, and I tried hard to think that the lack of all disguise was no more sinful than they. Exactly what is contributed – or lost – by the final fall of brassiere or jock-strap varies a great deal. Apart from the fact that some naked people look more naked than others, nudity can obviously be employed either innocently (as it was here) or for hard-core sensuality. The simple shock of seeing it on the stage at all comes largely from the surprise of finding it out of normal context. In my sheltered life it is still usually confined to bath or bed, but the probable spread of its use in the theatre will soon, alas, deaden its impact. What will be left will be more visual than psychological. From the formal point of view the costumed figure presents an image with a single focal point – the head. By adding a dark patch in the centre of the image a second visual accent is introduced, and this is something choreographers will have to take into account.

These minor questions apart, nudity is used in this ballet as a stimulating but serious ingredient which completely justifies itself artistically. The scene is a kind of arena (by Nadine Baylis) into which white-clad figures gradually fight their way. Once arrived, the mood changes. A nude figure appears dancing on film, and this is followed by a nice trio for girls, a typical Tetley wrestling match, and some all-in applications of red paint suggesting violence. A couple dance, clad and unclad on screen and stage, to gently variegated electronic sounds by Stockhausen; more join in and the film triplicates, until some mysterious figures in transparent suits sweep the action off stage, leaving the couple – naked and strangely vulnerable – alone as the lights fade.

It is not perhaps the most completely successful ballet in the repertoire – the start is slow and the films not very imaginative – but it is sincere, shapely, rich in those plastic movements in which Tetley excels and works up to a fine climax. It was never trivial or titillating and was extremely well danced by the finely trained and good-looking company.

8.11.70

## Béjart's *Wayfarer* and *Sacre* in Brussels

The vast sports arena was packed, 5,000 people in row above row and clustered on the gangways in solid ranks which would give British safety officers a nightmare. Red seats, usherettes in red space-helmets, huge red hero-medallions hanging from the girders. Jutting out from one wall, a gigantic platform marked out with a white circle like a circus ring. As the lights faded, tiny torch-beams showed where two figures were taking their place in the darkened ring, and immediately the clapping and whistling began, even before we could see who they were. Suddenly the lights came up; silence fell like a curtain and the action began. Not a sound from the audience, not a breath until the pair made their last slow exit behind the arena. Then pandemonium. Clapping, rhythmic stamping, shouts and counter-shouts as the couple ran from side to side of the auditorium, and that shrill metallic yell you hear at a school prize giving. Twenty minutes of action and thirteen minutes of applause. 'It's my ninth visit!' exclaimed my neighbour ecstatically.

Yet this was not a sports match. It was a dance-event Belgian style,

132

a performance by the Béjart company in Brussels, and those heroes under the roof were Bach, Mahler and Stravinsky. The atmosphere was so strange, so far removed from the devout refinement of most ballet performances, that it seemed to set the whole problem of the dance theatre, and its place in our society, in urgent agitation.

The ballet which had packed the arena for a week was by no means sensational; in fact, it would obviously gain enormously from a normal closed-stage presentation. It was another melancholy setting of a Mahler song-cycle – this time his 'Wayfarer' suite, of which the text, written by the composer himself, gave the clue to the dances. These came out strangely like an extract from Kenneth MacMillan's *Song of the Earth*, showing a young man with his only true travelling companion, his destiny. At first he greets it, then resists it, until at last – with doubting reluctance – he resigns himself to his final lot.

It is a quiet, sincere piece, very different from other Béjart ballets I have seen; near-classical in style, with some well-designed, even moving, passages. A *pas de deux* for two men (for this is what it amounts to) sounds embarrassing; but the relationship, though tense, was never faintly amorous or awkward, even allowing for the overblown emotions needed to project it into the cavernous auditorium.

The ballet was created – and this, of course, was what most of the hullabaloo was about – for a guest-star, Nureyev, whose personality easily filled out the part of the angst-ridden hero to the necessary dominating proportion, while his plasticity underlined the expressiveness of the choreography. His 'opponent' and friend – whichever way you look at him – was ideally cast in Paolo Bortoluzzi, a regular member of the company. With his crisp, firm movement and statuesque appearance he made a perfect foil for Nureyev, and I doubt if the ballet could be better danced.

This duet was followed by another piece extraordinarily unlikely for an arena production – a long and uneventful neo-classical *pas de deux* to a Bach sonata, in which the ex-Balanchine ballerina Suzanne Farrell was partnered by Jorge Donn. Béjart has not succeeded in fully exploiting her icy elegance – but who could fail to respond to those gazelle-like legs?

The evening – which had begun with a rather rambling but strongly danced collage of traditional and modern dance – ended with Béjart's *Sacre du Printemps*. As it will be returning to London soon, this is no place to comment on it, except to say that – as done here in arena style by the powerful Angèle Albrecht and a blazingly aggressive Nureyev

133

as the chosen victims (for a fate worse than death, in this version) – it became a kind of sex-demo in which we all seemed involved.

As the shouts and stamping died away and the audience (mostly young) struggled out into the rain, I found myself thinking of Meyerhold's dreams of a circus-theatre fusing experiment with popular tradition, and his dread of prissy élitism. Just how can our own ballet break out of its minority prison? Maybe this was no satisfactory answer; but the question was thunderously posed.

28.3.71

*Béjart has the vast merit of a bubbling creative drive, but the simultaneous affliction of a self-lacerating tendency to exaggerate. It is always agreeable for a British critic to find himself, for a change, urging the snaffle instead of the spur; but it is exasperating to see genuine invention take on an air of falsehood through inflated presentation.*

## *Anastasia*, The Royal Ballet, Covent Garden

The touching awkwardness of a split personality has always hung about the story of *Anastasia*, the lady from Germany who claims to be the daughter of the last Tsar. It has passed into the new ballet which Kenneth MacMillan has devised on the subject and which had its première at Covent Garden on Thursday. He has rightly sensed that the real-life story contains the stuff of legend. It concerns the whole mystery of individual identity. A ripe theme for a ballet, then, and four years ago he made a one-act version in Berlin revolving round the bemused pretender in her mental ward – a modern nightmare conveyed through expressionist movement, a contemporary score (Martinu's 'Fantaisies Symphoniques') and a set by Barry Kay symbolising the vortex of memories and hallucinations swirling round her. It seems to have been a valid piece in its own right. Now he has made a full evening's work of it by adding two preliminary classical acts spent in her childhood and youth. To solve the problem of extra music he has used what were roughly contemporary scores, two symphonies by Tchaikovsky (1 and 3).

The first scene is a childhood idyll, a picnic in the woods with some

134

naval cadets to liven up the afternoon. The second act is Anastasia's coming-out ball in St Petersburg and includes a balletic entertainment by two luminaries from the Maryinsky. The celebrations are suddenly invaded by armed revolutionaries. The party is over. When the curtain rises again we are in a hospital ward with a crop-headed young woman who may or may not be the same delicious girl who skipped and waltzed through the previous scenes. The final blackout brings no solution. Pale and proud on her iron bed, Anastasia confronts her past, her present and her future – alone, but defiantly surviving.

There is no doubt that the structure of the ballet is very awkward. It is the classical dog which now wags the dramatic tail. Two Tchaikovsky symphonies in a row make a big mouthful, stuffed though they are with dancing. We start straight away with a set of men's solos (brilliantly danced by officers Dowell, Wall and Coleman) and these are followed up by a stream of numbers strung as closely as in a Petipa divertissement. The ballroom scene adds some ravishingly costumed ensembles for the whole company, with a virtuoso *pas de deux* for the Maryinsky couple (Sibley and Dowell) thrown in for good measure.

The narrative thread is leisurely and tenuous, but no more so than in many nineteenth-century classics. The picnic sounds an echo of the *Sleeping Beauty* hunting scene (we half expect some Blind Man's Buff) and – owing to period and casting – of Ashton's *Enigma Variations*. The ballroom act is straight pastiche Petipa and the switch to the modernistic last scene is disconcerting. But such style-mixtures are now a commonplace in modern art and no doubt we shall get used to it.

Continuity is supplied by Lynn Seymour as the historical and then the putative princess, a switch which she manages with magnificent ease – the liquid and lyrical warmth of her first scenes (for instance, in the glorious solo in act one) is as convincing as are her confused contortions in the finale; and by Kay's beautiful and ingenious sets in which the spiral motif haunting the first acts finally becomes a twisted, imprisoning shell.

MacMillan has brought off several major feats. He has provided an evening packed with classical dancing which is always distinguished and inventive in that quiet way which rewards repeated viewings; he has created a bunch of roles which show the company to great advantage – the irresolute Tsar (Derek Rencher) and his enveloping wife (Svetlana Beriosova), the hypnotic Rasputin (Adrian Grater), and the

135

frail Tsarevitch (Marilyn Trounson); and he has created a plum part for a ballerina who – as in *Giselle* – can encompass both lyricism and dramatic hysterics.

On the debit side is a lack of masculine weight to counter-balance the feminine flutterings; the officers' dances are too much a mere display of neat spit and polish and the revolutionaries have no time (or space) to display their virility. A far more serious handicap is the choice of music. The Petipa-type pattern of successive numbers sits uncomfortably on the meandering symphonies, which are not only much too long but lack the fizzing climaxes and artful contrasts of which Tchaikovsky was such a master in his real ballet scores. This can be felt everywhere, notably in the virtuoso *pas de deux* in the ballroom whose technical feats, though done well enough (but without much sense of period style), made less impact than they deserved; an insertion of good old Minkus would have been entirely appropriate here and much more effective.

The final handicap lies in the theme. The choice of a story which we must take seriously makes us expect to be moved in a way which we are not, and shows up the frequent inadequacy of the traditional classical idiom; a *pas de cinq* involving the Tsar, the Tsarina, Rasputin and a couple of ballet dancers strains credulity to the limit, and a *jeté* and a pirouette seem an odd way of greeting a declaration of war. Moreover, the story itself lacks that most reliable of theatrical standbys – romantic love. We are shown the Tsar's absent-minded affection for his family, the Tsarina's mother-instincts, a glimpse of Anastasia's anonymous ravisher-cum-husband. But whom is Anastasia interested in? Herself. There is compassion in plenty; but that is no rival to passion in a three-hour ballet.

25.7.71

## Alwin Nikolais at Sadler's Wells

Abstract art has a reputation for inaccessibility, but sometimes it is a relief not to have to worry about meaning. The dance company of Alwin Nikolais is a good example. The absence of undertones in his work is what gives it its special overtone. The only adjectives you could apply to it are non-emotive ones – ingenious, original, enjoyable. His programmes are a long *capriccio*.

136

When he first appeared with his 'dance theatre' in London (from America) two years ago, he rightly bowled us over with his style and images. He is one of the few real masters of theatrical trickery, a man who not only invents new effects but knows how to develop them, thus becoming a goldmine for his dramatic colleagues. 'Much of his ["Performance Theatre"] is simply modern ballet performed by people without professional ballet training. And to anyone who has seen the real thing it is pretty hard to stomach.' The words are not those of a dance addict, but of theatre critic Ronald Bryden, and it will not surprise me to find some of our brighter young directors crouching in the darkness of Sadler's Wells watching Nikolais unfold his latest wonders. For he is a maestro of theatrical impurity, throwing off mixed media ideas like fireworks. For him movement, colour, light and sound are all one: he not only creates a unity out of them, but invents them all himself, and it must be admitted that the electric tapes which he devises as accompaniments are much the weakest links in this crochet-work. I hope one day he will call on an outside composer for one of his pieces.

His opening programme contained one of his most brilliant diversions, *Tent*. To say it consists of ten dancers and a parachute is to say all and to say nothing. With this scanty material, colour projections, lighting and a sound track, he has constructed a series of metamorphoses of startling imaginative variety ranging from comedy to ritual solemnity. The silken sheet becomes a flower, a floor, a roof, a multiple shroud, a skein of iridescent cobweb. The dancers change from panic to pathos. It is as variegated as a pack of cards, but it never feels uncontrolled or indulgent. The 'tent' holds it together and it makes its own sort of sense.

The other substantial ballet, *Echoes*, is much less convincing – in fact it shows up the main weakness of Nikolais's approach, which is too much invention contained in too frail a formal structure. It is hard to build up a climax in this style and the ballet runs on and on like a brightly lit avenue leading to nowhere in particular. This may be partly due to the company, which this year seems to lack outstanding performers.

There are no sensations in the opening piece, a set of short divertissements, but it clearly illustrated Nikolais's wit and sense of proportion. His dancers do extraordinary things with elastic tapes or turn themselves into gliding tops or concertinas. Like kinetic art, its impact is sharp rather than penetrating. But it would be a dull

137

dog who did not gasp at the expert surprises, and a blind bat who did not relish the kaleidoscopic stage-pictures.

4.9.71

*Over his long career – he produced his first ballet in 1939 – Nikolais has created enough major pieces to earn him a secure place in dance history.*

## Nureyev's production of *Raymonda*, Zurich

Ballet tradition notoriously rests on a perilously narrow base. *Giselle, Coppélia, Swan Lake, The Sleeping Beauty, The Nutcracker, Don Quixote* and *La Sylphide* – that is all we have in the West (the Royal Ballet ignores the last two) – and they are visibly being worn into the ground. Several others survive in Russia in one form or another. We have a scrap of *La Bayadère* (when will the Russians bring us the rest?), and *Raymonda* has lain hibernating, a sleeping beauty waiting for the final kiss of revival.

Nureyev has already given her two pecks, once for the Royal Ballet Touring Company and once for the Australians. Neither quite restored the colour to her cheeks, and last weekend in Zurich he made a more vigorous onslaught. In true fairy-tale fashion the third try proved lucky and she has emerged at last in her true full-blown spendour, a lavish addition to the meagre nineteenth-century menu.

*Raymonda* only just squeezes into that category. It was born in 1898 and represents the final phase of the Romantic movement in which classical ballet is grounded. We are familiar enough with the early phase of disembodied sylphs and wilis; but the other face of Romanticism, the warm-blooded sex-and-violence exoticism celebrated by men like Sir Walter Scott or Delacroix, has so far been missing from dance-drama. Here it is at last, and a brave show it makes – a splendiferous dish for the groundlings sprinkled with the choicest choreographic plums for the connoisseur.

Of course it has its odd conventions, but what romantic work does not? To the sceptical eye the flapping owl-man in *Swan Lake* is pretty ridiculous; but we are used to him and doubtless we shall soon adjust to this new swashbuckling convention. Fashion is on its side, as a visit to any youth-orientated supermarket shows. The Pre-Raphaelites with their brocades and battlements and knights in shining armour are back, while Asiatic savagery is positively trendy. Switching from *Giselle* to *Raymonda* is rather like trading in your black-and-white TV for a colour set – a bit of a shock but richly rewarding when you get used to it.

Zurich, with its neat Swiss personality, may seem an odd place for such an exotic reincarnation. But after all it was the birthplace of Dada and the home of Jung, and its modest little opera house by the lake has seen some notable performances. The new production must have strained its capacities to bursting-point but it has coped splendidly. The ballet is built like a Bolshoi blockbuster – sumptuous, confident, planned in bold strokes, a gigantic piece of costume jewellery designed to show off stars of superhuman panache and virtuosity. How it would fare with lesser lights I cannot say, but with Marcia Haydée from Stuttgart, revelling in one of the most demanding roles in all ballet, and Nureyev himself as her chivalrous lover-knight, the opening performance gave off an opulent effulgence shot through with flashes of clear brilliance.

The diamond glints come mainly from the Petipa variations, some of the most beautiful he devised, which are artfully scattered through the evening. They are set in a production which Nureyev has reworked to give it more coherence, and to lubricate the unfamiliar period conventions without betraying the driving conception which set them in motion. In this new version Raymonda becomes so excited at her imminent marriage to Jean de Brienne, freshly back from the Crusades, that she begins to confuse him in a dream with one of his dark and sensual Saracen enemies (we are reminded of Odette and Odile). The period fantasies – dusky warriors, jousting, oriental orgies and hand-to-hand duels – become figments of a period imagination. With this small twist the whole pasteboard edifice becomes believable, without the faintest retreat from the original.

Raymonda, too, is more interesting. The technical demands of the role are formidable, requiring speed, balance, the strength to maintain the Petipa style through three almost uninterrupted hours and now dramatic subtlety as well. I doubt if there is any ballerina anywhere who could carry it off better than Haydée. She accepted each challenge head on, and fully deserved the ovation she received.

Nureyev has not greatly built up his own part. A straightforward young knight on leave from the East (it is the gift of an oriental tapestry which sets off Raymonda's amorous dreaming) offers few dramatic

139

openings. His chances came as an ardent lover and a bonny fighter and especially in four new solos. The small stage inhibits broad movement and he has mainly concentrated on close-knit steps of alarming difficulty – all surmounted with his usual verve on the opening night.

The other main role, the Saracen Abderachman (Gabriel Popescu), is primarily an acting part but includes an athletic Golden-Slave-type dance; and there are some exquisite solos for Raymonda's friends, done with foreseeable style by Eva Evdokimova and very creditably by the local dancer Irena Milovan. Chinko Rafique (ex-Royal Ballet) and Roberto Dimitrievitch were an agile pair of troubadours. Some of the Petipa point-work was a bit much for the *corps de ballet* but they did the many character numbers with spirit. Edith Muller and Norbert Schmucki were especially good in a Spanish dance.

The ballet has been mounted by Nicholas Georgiadis in a setting which manages to combine mobility with nobility, successions of rich and varied costumes in free-moving sets suggesting the heavy sheen of Cordoba leather – a style which exactly matches the splendid but rather ponderous swing of Glazunov's tuneful score. The whole production moves like a well-oiled chariot bearing bushels of choreographic invention, many of them Nureyev's own. The most striking are a long, flowing *pas de deux* to match Glazunov's haunting melody in the visionary Garden scene, a *pas de sept* in Act II which wonderfully explores the relationships between the characters, and some successfully maintained long climaxes. For diversion we range from pounding pig-tailed Hungarian knights to ferocious slaves released from a cage, not to mention a Hollywood-style tournament in which arrows fly at golden shields and jousters charge one another on golden hobbyhorses.

This is clearly a production which would benefit greatly by magnification. Ideally I should like to see it danced with these two stars by the Kirov on the stage of the Bolshoi. This being unlikely, one can only congratulate Zurich on hatching in its modest theatre a chimera of such gorgeous plumage.

30.1.72

## Nureyev at Covent Garden, ten years on

It was exactly ten years ago last Sunday that this column – under the prescient editorial heading 'Comet over Covent Garden' – saluted the first appearance with the Royal Ballet of Rudolf Nureyev. He had just danced in *Giselle* with Margot Fonteyn, launching what was to become a legendary partnership. Last night he was performing the same ballet in the same theatre – with a different partner, the superlative Merle Park – thus neatly rounding off a notable decade.

He was hailed that day as a great romantic and this he certainly turned out to be, an artist who can breathe passion into the dry bones of a classic and set modern heart-machines like *Romeo and Juliet* or *Marguerite and Armand* humming. But it seemed then as if temperament, training and appearance might typecast him as a permanently prancing prince, that the momentum of his dramatic lift-off could peter out into a predictable orbit. The last two weeks have proved us beautifully wrong.

He may still be a peer among princes, but his famous 'leap to freedom' was, as he always maintained, a dash towards a wider field of experience and expression. His range is now phenomenal. The farthest removed from his Kirov schooling is undoubtedly Tetley's *Field Figures* in which, to the skeined structure of Stockhausen's electronic tape, the central male dancer crouches and leaps and writhes without a trace of classical virtuosity. It was remarkable to see in his latest rendering how he had finally mastered the style, making it not only one of his own best roles, but helping to turn this performance (with Deanne Bergsma at her unmatched peak and Michael Coleman giving breadth to the part of the 'stranger') into the most gripping I have yet seen.

Early Ashton is not a natural but he fizzed through *Les Rendezvous* at the Sadler's Wells Gala agreeably enough. Early Balanchine is another matter, and in *Apollo* last week he showed us again how a masterpiece apparently frozen by familiarity can be melted by burning commitment. The whole ballet is now moulded round his very individual conception, which reflects his stage personality. The special mark of this is the human warmth he breathes into his roles. There is a touch of Dionysius inside this Apollo. He is a god made in the likeness of man, and the ice-cool classical drama takes on a fresh sharpness. With choreography, music, design and interpretation now seamlessly integrated, this was a totally convincing performance of one of ballet's most flawless works, both by Nureyev himself and by his three Muses – Georgina Parkinson, Monica Mason and Diana Vere.

5.3.72

# Nederlands Dans Theater at Sadler's Wells

Who would have guessed, ten years ago, that Holland, a country with virtually no dance tradition, would today boast both a large classical company and a modern-dance troupe of international repute, and that Dutch choreography would become an export business? Of the fifteen works presented by the Nederlands Dans Theater in its current season at Sadler's Wells Theatre, three have already been imported into British repertoires – and still the invention keeps flowing. No less than eight ballets are new to London and two successes in the opening programme were by yet another new choreographer, Louis Falco.

Falco (who is American) seems to have both a strong feeling for the theatre and a genuine thrust towards new dance territory. His dramatic flair showed in *Huescope*, an extended trio which depicts, without disguise, a girl trying – successfully – to come between a man and a boy. It is fluently worked out (a shade less explicitness might have given it even more power) to a rather all-sorts musical collage, with a striking setting of rainbow stripes by William Katz, and was expressively danced.

The intersex harmony was rather unusual. I don't know what is going on in Holland, but in Dutch ballet as soon as boy meets girl a stand-up fight seems to break out. Falco's other piece, *Journal*, is a riotous sample of this pastime. Cleverly combining Pinterish dialogue with athletic dancing, music of a sort and a brilliant set, also by Katz, which steadily pours dry-ice – presumably in lieu of cold water – over the bickering parties from a set of tall poles, the entire cast engages in a running battle in which every tactic is explored. There are verbal sparrings (in English), slaps, bangs, tumbling and writhings which add up to a non-stop display of all-in sexual wrestling. Continually inventive, and often funny in a sad New Yorkerish way, this is a piece of multi-media theatre which really works.

13.5.73

142

# Makarova in *Romeo and Juliet* at Covent Garden

The question whether Natalia Makarova could fit into a modern British ballet was settled decisively at Covent Garden last week, when she tackled MacMillan's *Romeo and Juliet* with Nureyev. She was superb, and – perhaps just as important – she will almost certainly become better still with experience. Her physique is in her favour for the part. Almost excessively slender, she looks like a real adolescent and she plays the role with a feverish, childlike excitement which passes instantly from fun to infatuation to frenzy. It is taken with whirlwind speed. She skims round the nursery like a swallow; her ingenue début at the ball is as light as a breeze; her balcony duet is ecstatic, her sulks with Paris suitably exasperating. In the long mime scene in the bedroom she flutters like a bird beating against the bars. This is a girl whose thoughts react instantly into movement. You could tell beforehand that when she awoke in the tomb to find Romeo dead her first instinct would be to try to pummel him back to life. She died as quickly as she had lived, falling back towards her lover (it is tempting to say 'boy-friend') like a wisp of vitality suddenly burnt out. Technically she is faultless; without changing a step she makes the choreography look freshly minted. At this first try she tends to play the whole ballet in top gear, and she will surely learn to vary her intensity and attack, as Nureyev now does so tellingly. He responds magnificently to her interpretation, emphasising youth and impetuosity with a hundred small variations of acting and dynamics. The frisking colt turns before our eyes into a fiery young stallion galloping headlong towards the precipice.

24.6.73

# The Paul Taylor Company at Sadler's Wells

That un-British phenomenon, the personalised dance troupe, may have its limitations, but the Paul Taylor Company, which has just had a season at Sadler's Wells Theatre, starts with the advantage that its leader has a personality which is both strong and elusive. His own dance style is an individual mixture of loose-limbed suppleness and

143

quick movements which turn from mischief into menace. He exploits casualness with deliberation and uses charm as a weapon. He is the easy rider of the dance, a Petrushka disguised as the Moor. This dual personality appears at its best in *Big Bertha*, a scarey piece about a fairground organ with an automaton which takes control of a family, with gruesome results. As in a Kafka story, the symbolism is held at arm's length, and the tale unfolds with its own horrific momentum. The performers – Bettie DeJong as the bespangled fate-figure and Taylor, Eileen Cropley and Carolyn Adams as her victims – are perfect.

The other 'black' ballet this season was *Scudorama*, which we have seen before. It is a strange piece in which Taylor seems to be both a damned and a demoniac figure moving through a sea of suffering. This time the atmosphere was a trifle untroubled; too much light, perhaps?

8.7.73

# Dance in Britain

One of the most unforeseeable phenomena in the British arts scene since the war has been the sudden emergence of theatrical dance, or ballet, as a flourishing and popular entertainment.

Surprisingly, in view of our staid morals and undemonstrative lifestyle, we have always been a nation of dancers. London was an important date for the stars of the nineteenth century; the back rows of Diaghilev's and Pavlova's troupes were full of (re-christened) Britons; and it is typical that one of the few genuine contemporary folk arts (characteristically middle class) is British-born – ballroom dancing.

So we provided fertile soil for the scatter of seeds that followed the death of Diaghilev in 1929 and the break-up of his company. First came what can now be seen as a period of germination, during which two powerfully creative women, Marie Rambert and Ninette de Valois, founded and nurtured companies here. These were still of interest to only a small minority. But de Valois's creation, the Sadler's Wells Ballet, was to become the keystone of a structure spanning the whole country. Ballet became popular as an escapist art during the war, and when her company moved in 1946 to Covent Garden (and changed its title to the Royal Ballet in 1956) it found a

144

large audience that has continued to grow. It has now sprouted a smaller company for touring and lives in healthy competition with the rival Festival Ballet, another classical touring company using point-shoes and mounting the old classics with a repertoire to match. Meanwhile, two companies – primarily classical – established themselves in the regions: the Scottish National Ballet in Glasgow and the Northern Dance Theatre in Manchester.

London is now one of the world's main dance capitals (rivalled only by Moscow and New York) with a very large and experienced audience. The Royal Ballet tends to dominate the British dance scene (its danger is that, with its semi-official standing and honours-list officials, it may become overtly tied to the establishment, a fate which has proved fatal to more than one opera-house ballet). Much of its character and power is due to the happy emergence out of the Rambert Company of a choreographer, Frederick Ashton, gifted with a rare flow of invention and a personal style – lyrical and elegant – into which he moulded the company's dancers, notably its first international star, Margot Fonteyn. He took over the directorship after the retirement of de Valois in 1963, and was in turn succeeded by another talented choreographer, Kenneth MacMillan.

The changes in the national company mirror pretty accurately the trends in the national ballet scene. An obvious, but nonetheless important development is the inexorable rise in the costs of productions and performance. Full-scale ballet employs a large and highly-skilled personnel – perhaps 150 dancers, musicians and stage staff for a single performance – whose salaries keep rising without any hope of increased productivity. This means increasing Arts Council support (all our dance companies are now state-aided) and less elbow-room for experiment, while higher admission charges lead back to social exclusivity. Television seems to be the only way out of the dilemma, but haggling between the TV companies and the theatre union, Equity, continues to deprive the general public of a share in an art that it helps to pay for.

From the artistic angle, British ballet has been exposed to two strong but opposite influences. The first wind of change blew from the east, from Russia. Russians have always played a big part in ballet in the West (Balanchine in America, Lifar in France, Gsovsky in Germany, Sonia Gaskell in Holland) and visits by the Soviet companies in the late 1950s provided shock therapy to British dancers, setting new standards of technique and attack – Russian stages are mostly bigger than ours and encourage a broader, bolder style – particularly for the men. The arrival of a Kirov-trained dancer, Rudolf Nureyev, as a regular guest-artist from 1962 onwards, further stimulated the dancing, while his reconstructions of some of the old Russian classics tipped the repertoire towards tradition. His partnership with Fonteyn meanwhile produced a peak in ballet popularity.

But a new breeze soon blew in from the West, bringing the American style of dance and choreography known as 'modern dance'. Adopting the hallowed battle-cry of 'Back to nature!', its champions reject the ballerina's point-shoe and the traditional poses and steps for a new set of conventions slightly more naturalistic, devised mainly by Martha Graham from Central European dance movements. The new experimental technique, with its break from the past, offers a whole new vocabulary into which jazz-based steps fit naturally (as can be seen from television dance teams).

It took time to catch on in Britain, but the visit of Graham's company and other troupes spread its popularity and it now has a considerable following, particularly with young audiences. Like many minority arts it tends at present to make a virtue of necessity by clinging somewhat puritanically to arcane subjects and advanced electronic music. But it provides a healthy and stimulating alternative approach, still so fluid that other experimental arts – film, painting or sculpture – fit into it more easily than into the fully codified classical style.

Its adoption – in an individual form – by the Ballet Rambert, after Madame Rambert handed over to Norman Morrice in 1970, and the birth of the London Contemporary Dance Company under the direction of a former Graham dancer, Robert Cohan, has established 'modern dance' firmly, with schools to turn out dancers trained in the new style. Already the effect can be seen at Covent Garden, where ballets by the two foremost American choreographers, Balanchine and Jerome Robbins, have been joined by works by another American, Glen Tetley, entirely in the modern style – unclassical and plastic, to electronic scores. The Russian emphasis on classical technique and tradition has been counterbalanced by American pioneering.

The net result, when added to some fine revivals of Diaghilev ballets by both our big classical companies, is as rich a mixture as can be found anywhere in the world, and a good augury for the future. With a wide and watchful public interest, sustained standards of performance and flexible administrations, the road seems clear. It is unlikely that the next twenty years will surpass the last twenty. But it seems certain that dance is here to stay as a sizable ingredient in our national theatre repertoire.

30.9.73

## The Australian Ballet in Nureyev's *Don Quixote* at the Coliseum

'The story of a lean, shrivelled, whimsical child, full of varied fancies that no one else has ever imagined' – so Cervantes described his *Adventures of Don Quixote*. He published it in 1604, a long and complicated satire on the tales of romantic chivalry currently in fashion, in which the dreams of the conventional hero were translated into the hallucinations of a gaga old gentleman. But by the nineteenth century the story had been turned completely on its head, so that the crazy knight became exactly the romantic, suffering symbol he had been intended to send up. This sentimental version persisted right into this century (in Massenet's opera of 1910, for instance). A more robust approach seems to have been in the air in Russia in 1869, when Petipa devised his ballet from the story, and now Nureyev has redressed the balance completely. He presents us, not with a high-minded fable about spiritual purity, but with a cheerful comedy-spectacle entertainment of the kind we get today from musicals. His *Don Quixote* re-creates the 100-year-old ancestor of *The Man of La Mancha*.

The old genre has largely been replaced by the new (though it lingers on in some of Massine's ballets and in early Cranko) and it is not easy to recapture its style. It needs a certain extrovert toughness and physical drive. These are exactly the qualities the Australian Ballet is rich in, and *Don Quixote* made a splendid vehicle for its return to London at the Coliseum, in a production designed by Barry Kay with a gusto which conceals some ravishing details and accompanied by Minkus's unpretentious tunes, spruced up by John Lanchbery.

The hero being manifestly past his dancing years, Petipa used him as a rickety peg for colourful and exotic diversions concocted round the cheerful love affair between the beautiful Kitri and Basilio, a young barber in the style of Figaro. Nureyev's new arrangement of

147

the old ballet (oddly there is no hint of its chequered history in the programme) makes sense of the story, which unfolds at whirlwind speed with comedy and spectacle succeeding each other in a multi-coloured stream of invention. To relieve the rather numbing hail of Spanish rhythms, Petipa inserted a classical interlude in his usual 'vision' style, which contains some ravishing and characteristic solos. Nureyev has added among other things a romantic *pas de deux* in the moon-shadow of the windmills, besides building up a charming little episode for child actors – whom the Don mistakes, of course, for real characters.

We begin with Don Quixote, bemused by too much balladry, appointing himself champion of the downtrodden, assisted by the paunchy little Sancho Panza (Ray Powell). We end with him walking off into the sunset, like all good picaresque heroes, in search of further adventure. In between we have Gypsies and toreadors, a comic grandee (Colin Peasley) and a puffed-up innkeeper (Francis Croese), a fight with a windmill, a reluctant duel, tossings in a blanket, a hilarious mock suicide and, of course, a cascade of dancing, which ranges from dashing ensembles to bravura solos and duets.

The company has just the right vitality – not over-elegant, but showing a fine open style and power. But this is frankly a vehicle for three stars. Robert Helpmann is the eponymous pseudo-knight – aloof and super-dignified. Lucette Aldous seems tailor-made for Kitri, tiny and dynamic, racy but never coarse, and sailing over the fearsome technical passages with ease.

Nureyev as Basilio holds the confection together with a perform-ance of tingling vitality, a supple high-voltage Harlequin (to Help-mann's Pierrot), a spring-heeled Jack slipping effortlessly from mischief to virtuoso fireworks. Among such pyrotechnics the famous *pas de deux*, which can look vulgar when performed alone, falls natur-ally and elegantly into place. Cervantes might be surprised, but he would smile, I think, to see the fun restored to his fantasies.

7.10.73

## *Manon*, The Royal Ballet, Covent Garden

Reversing, as every motorist knows, is the riskiest of all manœu-vres. In going back to old-fashioned *ballet d'action* style for his new *Manon* at Covent Garden, Kenneth MacMillan has taken a big chance. He emerges with more credit as a choreographer than as a producer.

*Manon* was a ballet (with a score by Halévy) fifty years before Massenet turned it into an opera and it has one big advantage in this form. The frankly odious characters of the faithless little heroine and her besotted lover are forgivable if they are seen as the result of exposing adolescents to the cruelty of a grown-up world. Dancers can convey this teenage frailty in a way with which no middle-aged singer can hope to compete.

The background to the Abbé Prévost's original novel offers vivid parallels with the rapacious metropolitan society of today. But that was written when the Romantic Movement was putting out its first tender shoots into the hard, sophisticated eighteenth-century soil, while Massenet lived in its soft-cored aftermath. By sticking to the nineteenth-century composer (though he has avoided the opera score, replacing it with a patchwork compiled by Leighton Lucas), MacMillan has interposed between two strikingly similar hard-boiled cultures a veil of perfumed Victorian sentiment. The obsession with sex and money is lost in clouds of sugary salon melody and a sense of wistful anaemia runs through scenes where blood and passion would be more appropriate. The production seems too bulky for its engine – a handsome bulldozer fuelled by lavender water.

The lack of rhythmic drive in the score – much of which was not designed for the theatre and virtually none for dancing – slows down the action and makes the dance episodes seem desultory. This is a pity because they are often very well arranged. Most of the *pas de deux* would look good out of context, there are some excellent solos, especially in Act II (a dazzling one for Monica Mason), and an acrobatic arrangement for Manon and her admirers which could bring the house down. But MacMillan seems deliberately to have avoided blood-stirring ensembles or dramatic climax. He opts each time for the off-beat finish; many of the numbers end with the dancers on the floor, effectively muffling our applause.

While the drama needs a good deal of tightening up, the fun and games in the elegant brothel scene in Act II provide some fine entertainment. A bit of comedy, some exciting solos and a decent ration of roistering, scuffling and sudden death makes lively fare and we have time to enjoy at our leisure the rich and beautiful costumes and ingenious settings of Nicholas Georgiadis. The last act, in the penal colony in New Orleans to which Manon has been transported, is less theatrically effective; the opening scene seems irrelevant and the heroine's dying vision, which brings the whole cast on again, is corny and unconvincing. But we end with all stops out – a full-blooded deathbed duet *à la* Romeo and Juliet or Marguerite and Armand to a succulent excerpt from *La Vierge*. It makes a fine, florid finale – but it comes too late to raise the temperature of a long, mild evening.

What has made Manon a French folk-heroine is the feminine charm of her character, in which appetites for fun, cash and sex chase one another irresistibly. It is not a natural role for Antoinette Sibley, with her light lyrical English style. She has flashes of real conviction and dances throughout like a feather; but a whiff of chastity clings to her. As her student lover, Des Grieux, Anthony Dowell has the least well worked out part in the ballet. His dancing is impeccably easy and graceful and when called upon, he partners with conviction; but he spends an inordinate amount of time standing or sitting about and has little chance to assert himself. He must envy the rumbustious warmth of Manon's brother, Lescaut, an overwhelming charmer as played by David Wall, whose tipsy villainy threatens at every moment (and especially when he is matched by Monica Mason) to stop the show.

10.3.74


## *Parade*, Festival Ballet, Coliseum

The prominence of the different elements in ballet varies. Sometimes it's the music which counts (e.g., *Sacre du Printemps*); occasionally it's the story (e.g., *Rake's Progress*); often, especially these days, it's the pure dance, as in *Agon*. *Parade*, which was revived by the Festival Ballet at the Coliseum on Tuesday, is a rare example of a final category – not danced theatre nor music-as-movement but painting in action. I am not sure that it should not have been subsidised out of the art budget of the Arts Council.

The score now sounds sweet, the colours are pretty, and it needs an effort to recapture the shock it caused when it was first produced in Paris in 1917. This tongue-in-cheek version of popular entertainment was inserted into Diaghilev's programme at the Châtelet Theatre in a critical week in World War I, when French troops were threatening to mutiny after the disaster of Verdun. But in place of heroic gestures or the escapist glamour for which the company was famous, the public was offered a confection as cheeky and frivolous as a paper hat.

It was a dazzling snook cocked at the whole Establishment, and its originator was Jean Cocteau. Harking back (according to Douglas Cooper's classic account in *Picasso: Theatre*) to *Petrushka* and a circus-ballet project he had offered to Diaghilev as early as 1914 (it was turned down) he asked his friend Satie to provide the score, Massine to choreograph and Picasso to design the settings. But hardly had the Spanish genius (unfamiliar with ballet) taken on the commission than the whole character of the work changed. Not a trace of the whimsical mystery of Cocteau's original conception remains. It is Picasso's accent which survives – dynamic, caricatural, demotic and a bit rough.

Picasso simply transferred his current pictorial problems straight into the theatre. He translated the shallow overlapping planes and multiple view points of his Cubist pictures into stage flats and cloths; and he also introduced his new preoccupation with mixed styles. The celebrated drop-curtain (surely reduced here in size?) is in a picturesque manner very different from the towering townscape on stage, and – just as he stuck bits of real newspaper on to his painted canvases – he mixed genuine dancers with sculptured figures who were as artificial as the scenery.

From the art, stage-design and theatre-production angle, *Parade* was a pregnant event, and the moment when the curtain rises and the Manager enters – an eerie, ramshackle incarnation of Cubist principles – is still stunning. But the ensuing action is almost non-existent, even in the revised version which Massine has devised for this revival. There are only five characters and one of those is a horse; they simply do their send-up numbers (very capably though without much personality) and exit.

The handicaps of the whole genre of painting-ballet emerge clearly. Unlike music-ballet, it is deficient in the time element – maybe it needs words to carry it forward – and it can succeed only if it is short and designed by a genius. Fortunately, *Parade* fulfils both these demands. It could never be a popular favourite, which makes its revival after nearly fifty years' absence from London all the more to the Festival Ballet's credit; but it is not to be missed by anybody with a sensitive eye, a feel for the past or a liking for sophisticatedly simple fun.

26.5.74

*Massine has a uniquely observant eye for idiosyncratic gesture, and his ballets are stuffed full with miniature character sketches built up by the*

151

*caricaturist's device of exaggeration and formalisation. He is a kind of Dr Coppelius in reverse, to whom all men are not only players but puppets. He sets them in motion in an antic whirl in which mime and posture are magically transmuted into dance.*


## The Stuttgart Ballet at Covent Garden

Even Shakespeare might have been surprised to know how many of his exceedingly articulate plays would be turned into dumb show. The latest is *The Taming of the Shrew*, which John Cranko devised for the Stuttgart Ballet in 1969 and which came into the company's all-too-short season at Covent Garden last Monday. Comedy is risky in the theatre and to have brought off a full-length version of this male-chauvinist exercise was a real feat. Cranko brilliantly translated the verbal karate between Petruchio, the debonair hero, and Kate, the reluctant heroine, into choreographic argument. The fun was put across with the zest we have come to expect from the company.

The snag is that the story revolves round a single situation and the second half of the evening can only extend and repeat the first. Moreover, Cranko's determination to retain a lusty Elizabethan flavour often seduced him from comedy into farce and, in Act II, into full string-of-sausages slapstick. This fatally undermines the would-be lyrical ending and is at odds with the rather refined Scarlatti-based score. This is always a handicap. In many episodes Minkus would have been preferable; a touch of vulgarity in the music would have permitted less mugging on stage.

But what carried the evening triumphantly was the performance of the two principals. The versatile Marcia Haydée transformed herself into a furiously and uproariously protesting little whirlwind in petticoats, and Richard Cragun – bounding and spinning like an escapee from *Seven Brides for Seven Brothers* – not only carried her off her feet but bounced her into surrender. Simply as a vehicle for these two gifted dancers, and for Egon Madsen's extravagantly ridiculous Gremio, the ballet is a winner.

*The Shrew* is a rich legacy from the company's late director, Cranko. It is, paradoxically, the brightest portent that his contributions to the final programme were quite overshadowed by a work by its new director, Glen Tetley. This was *Voluntaries*, one of those moody, near-abstract pieces which include both episodes of pure movement and passages of emotion, arranged to the melodramatic Concerto for Organ, Strings and Percussion of Poulenc.

Written as a tribute to Cranko, it carries still further the move away from 'modern dance' suggested in Tetley's recent work for the Australian Ballet. It is almost purely neo-classical in idiom, but with the geometry broken into subtle free-running and cross-rhythmed patterns. There are fairly conventional movements for the *corps de ballet*; flowing *pas de trois* for Reid Anderson, Jan Stripling and Birgit Keil, who has developed into a dancer with not only a strong technique, but also a beautifully sensitive line; and long elegiac duets for Haydée and Cragun, which give a mysterious core to the work. Cragun's sinewy leaps and turns were used to great effect, and Haydée added her inimitable dark intensity to a role which perfectly displays her control and speed. As an expressive artist there is surely no ballerina today to match her.

4.8.74

## *Letter for Queen Victoria*, Bob Wilson, Paris

Dance can be interpreted freely these days and I have no hesitation in classing under this label an extraordinary show which, if and when it reaches London, is likely to make as big an impact as the first appearance of Merce Cunningham. It is called *Letter for Queen Victoria*, devised, directed and partially performed by a young New Yorker called Bob Wilson. I caught it as it passed through Paris on an extensive European tour.

Reverberations of his productions have been rumbling in the theatrical air for some time. In 1971 he rocked the Shiraz Festival in Iran with a performance lasting seven days and seven nights: this was followed by *The Deaf Man's Glance*, in which the only dialogue was three loud screams. It was a huge success in Paris and was followed by *Overture*, a compendium of irrational exercises. He now runs a studio in New York, where he works out his extra-ordinary routines and gives occasional performances.

The new offering runs for normal length in a proscenium theatre and is labelled an 'opera'. But it could equally be described as a 'ballet with words and songs'. It is staged with brilliance and per-formed with dedicated professionalism: for once a multi-media show adds up to more than its parts and amounts to a genuinely original genre.

*Victoria* is as strictly structured as a Petipa ballet, divided into sections and measured out against a (very pleasant) collage of music. The opening seems to owe something to Martha Graham, with a towering black goddess and a wax-effigy Queen, played by Wilson's 88-year-old grandmother, who also delivers a 'scream song' with true Southern generosity. There are episodes which smack of Gertrude Stein (especially, perhaps, Ashton's production of *Four Saints in Three Acts*), with dialogue shuffled like random typescripts. There are passages reminiscent of frozen-frame film technique and a Japanese episode as stiff as paper sculpture. There are chunks of music-hall routine, an oddly touching scene of speech-therapy and a slice of mime theatre. The whole confection is fused together as deftly as a combine painting by Rauschenberg.

The 'abstract' use of the English dialogue (we have seen the device in some modern dance pieces) seemed to make it totally acceptable to a French audience. In one scene Wilson repeats the action at a faster speed with the emotional volume turned up to match, the tempo marked by two dancers on each side of the stage who gyrate like the spools of a tape-recorder. In another scene what seem to be spacemen shuffle and posture in ankle-deep sand under a cold light streaming through a window frame in the sky. A dreamlike feeling of emotional weightlessness hangs over their stiff gestures and near-rational talk, which reached the audience as though through the effect of some drug.

What Our Dear Queen would have made of it all perhaps only that screaming grandmother could tell. To me it appeared strange, sometimes moving and consistently beautiful. It seems sad – and uncomfortably significant of the new provincialism that is settling over London, which until recently could count itself a vital part of the world's cultural scene – that such an original offering, which has been widely discussed in America and the rest of Europe, should not yet have appeared here.

3.11.74


## Nureyev's production of *The Sleeping Beauty* for Festival Ballet, Coliseum

Nureyev's *The Sleeping Beauty* rolled on to the Coliseum stage last week like an imperial juggernaut, a vehicle celebrating the Festival

Ballet's twenty-fifth anniversary which overwhelms not only with its opulent magnificence – it offers the finest spectacle since Bakst – but with the scale of its conception. It seems to have more of everything – more drama, more dancing, more mime, more verity and more resonance of meaning. It gives the feeling of reaching far back into ballet history, and at the same time it is disconcertingly radical.

London has known this ballet for thirty-five years, ever since the Russian *régisseur*, Nicholas Sergeyev, mounted it on our national company. Since then it has had many revivals and countless additions from our own choreographers until, today, the Covent Garden production (which previous Festival Ballet versions have followed) is almost as British as God Save The Queen. This is as it should be; but, as recent attempts to renew it have shown, artistic loyalties have their dangers. Nureyev's production is no patched-up version of an original; he has taken the ballet by the throat and given it a completely new character. The light, lyrical fairytale romanticism which is a natural part of the English artistic genius has gone; in its place is a sumptuous page of history presented with the authority which springs from control by a single mind.

The mind is Nureyev's and not surprisingly the flavour is strongly Russian – majestic and slightly operatic. This is not just the tale of dawning love in a young girl, but the more deeply reverberating myth of youth versus age, experiment versus tradition – even (very suitably, for this new approach is bound to offend the guardians of protocol) the outsider against the Establishment. The magic kiss seems to symbolise the breathing of new life into old forms.

Taking as their starting-point the resemblance between the Tsarist court of the 1890s and the regime of Louis XIV, Nureyev and his designer, Georgiadis – their achievements are so closely linked as to be inseparable – have set the action in a palace as grand and power-heavy as Versailles; silks and plumes and jewellery fill the stage with a sombre glow like old gold. The only 'fairies' – and these are rather symbols of good and evil – are Carabosse and the Lilac Fairy (the rest are court entertainers dressed as sprites). Reverting to pre-Diaghilev tradition they are non-dancing roles, two beautiful women, the one hard and sophisticated, the other gentle and innocent. The 'witch' element is transferred to three 'knitting women', who recall *Macbeth*, the guillotine hags and the fatal spinning women of Greek legend.

The production's highlights range from a splendid Act II curtain, with the whole company sinking into sleep up the palace staircase like a great wave subsiding, to fine details of etiquette, character and make-up – the King could have walked out of a painting by Rigaud. Apart from the main Petipa numbers, Nureyev has devised his own choreography throughout, sometimes following Kirov custom, more often inventing anew. Aurora has her usual share of the dancing, but the Prince has extra solos in the hunting scene, including one of fascinating but rather distracting complexity which will surely be a hurdle for other interpreters.

Some of the ensemble numbers look crowded on this stage, which is much smaller than that of the Scala, Milan, or the Metropolitan, New York, where they were developed. Throughout, the style is unrelentingly classical, with fussy steps for the older set contrasting with fluidity for the young invaders. Outstanding are the deployment of the four cavalier suitors round the Rose Adagio and the formal saraband which surprisingly starts the last act.

Evdokimova, with her pure line and deer-like jump, needs only warmth and confidence in the last act to make a very distinguished Aurora, while Nureyev displays his whole vocabulary of virtuosity, subtlety and style as the Prince. The Blue Birds – Dagmar Kessler and the previously little-known Paul de Masson – were good; Patricia Ruanne, as the leading entertainer, has never looked better; and the whole company carried off the aristocratic manœuvres with an air, managing their magnificent costumes with conviction.

20.4.75


# Martha Graham Fiftieth Anniversary Gala, New York

The fiftieth anniversary of the Martha Graham dance company was celebrated in New York last Thursday with a gala that fulfilled almost every romantic dream. The little troupe, which in its first years had struggled fitfully from date to date in tiny halls on a shoe-string budget, was presented with full magnificence on the large stage of a Broadway theatre and filled its near-Covent Garden sized auditorium with a celebrity-studded audience, most of whom had paid £50 for their seats. The President's wife (an ex-Graham pupil) led the homage – one first lady saluting another.

It was an evening of many moving ingredients. Not only did we have Graham herself – aged eighty-two, tiny, upright and as imperial as ever – as *commère*, watching and commenting as though from a

156

niche in history; we were given shrewd and generous excerpts from the past, including the famous very early solo *Lamentation*, first performed in 1930, an excerpt from *Clytemnestra, Seraphic Dialogue*, with its holy victim, St Joan, and its glorious Noguchi setting, and the lyrical *Diversion of Angels*. All these were superbly danced, with Takako Asakawa leading the girls, and an athletic team of men. Our own Robert Irving was conducting.

We were also witnesses of a momentous coming-together of the worlds of modern and classical dance, for the arch-rebel herself welcomed as guest stars the very symbols of classical ballet, Fonteyn and Nureyev, in the most balletic of dances, the 'white' duet from *Swan Lake*. The marriage produced, moreover, a striking offspring – a brand new ballet. *Lucifer* (to a score by the composer of *Clytemnestra*, Halim El-Dabh, and designs by Leandro Locsin and Halston) is explicitly a vehicle for Nureyev and shows that Graham has lost none of her theatrical flair. She saw her character 'not as Satan but as the bringer of light' (did she know that Nureyev means 'son of the sun'?), a fallen angel who becomes half-man and half-god, with Fonteyn as a dark lady who tempts him on earth with her wiles and snares.

The ballet opens with the hero spreadeagled, nearly naked, on the rocks on to which he has been cast out from heaven – a Prometheus figure with the Devil as his devouring eagle. Thereafter, torn between his two worlds, Lucifer rages and writhes in a succession of Dionysiac dances, tossed and half-strangled by attendants with enormous cloaks or flourishing them in displays of his fatal pride.

With his flying hair and muscular plasticity, Nureyev gave the role his unique demonic urgency and arrogance – you could see why God had to get rid of him. It is a piece of master-casting, to which Fonteyn made a serene but almost over-gentle foil. The ballet is written in the high Graham style: a more austere setting would be an enormous gain if it is to enter the normal repertory. But on this extravagant occasion it seemed the only possible ending to what the programme rightly called 'a historic night for dance.'

22.6.75

# Dance in New York

New York is the home of the hyperbole, and the arts come in for their share of excess. Currently it is dance which is the mania of Manhattan. The Lincoln Centre has replaced the Museum of Modern Art as the rendezvous of the trendies; businessmen debate *batterie* and *port de bras*; and the recipe for popular success in the theatre seems to be that it should be by, with, or about dancers. Risking a few swingeing generalisations after a short visit, I would say that New York is now unquestionably the dance emporium of the world, with an unmatched wealth and variety of choice; that Balanchine's revolutionary emphasis on dance-for-dance's-sake has produced incredibly high technical standards but some loss of feeling and a penchant for music-hall virtuosity; that American training emphasises legs and feet at the expense of torsoes and arms; and that the native love of the digest hangs on with a preference for the potted quickie 'in excerpt form'. Musical standards are high but local ballet design is abysmal. The competition is ferocious. The modern dance season was over when I arrived but in five feverish weeks I saw ballets by over twenty choreographers. An astonishing array of stars revolved before my eyes – Suzanne Farrell, Patricia McBride and Edward Villella with the New York City Ballet; Marcia Haydée and Richard Cragun with the Stuttgart company; Fonteyn and Paolo Bortoluzzi with Nureyev's concert group in Washington; Bessmertnova, Vassiliev, Lavrovsky and Liepa with the Bolshoi; Karen Kain with the Canadians; Makarova, Cynthia Gregory, Gelsey Kirkland, Erik Bruhn, Mikhail Baryshnikov and Fernando Bujones with American Ballet Theatre; and Nureyev, as usual just about everywhere.

27.7.75

# Baryshnikov as Romeo at Covent Garden

The part of Romeo in Kenneth MacMillan's ballet offers rich possibilities to a dancer, but its complexity and close intermesh with the rest of the cast make it a tough starter. Mikhail Baryshnikov was bold to choose it for his first appearance in London since he joined us in the West (I avoid the word defection, as that would mean applying it equally to dancers like Nijinsky and Balanchine, or – in reverse – even Petipa himself). The venture paid off last Wednesday at Covent Garden. A more simply virtuoso part would have made a bigger sensation, but instead he proved that he is a genuine artist who understands how to express emotion through movement and to follow a dramatic line to which technical feats are incidental.

Baryshnikov gave the role a new twist to accord with his own style and appearance. He is small and compact, with the face of Sir Galahad on the body of a centre-forward, and he turns this to advantage by playing the character as a young tearaway, hardly old enough to grasp the serious passions and preoccupations of his elders. He stands out among the rest by his immaturity. The impetuous ease with which he switches from Rosaline to Juliet is entirely convincing, and he is carried through the whole ballet by a straightforward ardour which is touchingly simple.

The interpretation exactly fits Baryshnikov's style of dancing, which is exceptionally quick and light, with springy feet that seem to carry him perpetually half an inch above the stage. He does not 'feel the floor', as some Russians do, but he has a typically Russian drive to his movements very different from our smooth native flow. He uses a sharper and more varied punctuation; our own dancers are inclined to articulate only with commas. His clean, fast jumps and turns were a delight, and he threw in an occasional firework, such as an extraordinary step in which he seems to fling both legs in the air, glue them together, and then corkscrew round them. Occasionally, as in the big balcony scene solo, the emotion was blurred by the impression of extra spins and beats, and the romanticism of the last acts did not pierce very deep; but for a first attempt this was a remarkably complete reading.

Merle Park's Juliet is pretty familiar by now. She was dancing in top form – rather more restrained than Makarova the previous week, but technically just as sure and sharp; both these Juliets suggest that Verona has had some lean harvests. If Baryshnikov was already among the best Romeos, Dowell was the finest-ever Mercutio. He always excels in roles with a glint of aggression (Death in *The Song of the Earth*, Oberon, the Joker in *Card Game*) which give extra attack and a cutting edge to his dancing. Here he seemed to be letting go the curb and, as we horsemen say, riding the part on a loose snaffle. You could understand why it was he who first attacked Tybalt, and he died emphatically but unsoppily – the victim of a stab in the back which still seems to me a misguided flouting of Shakespeare, revealing a woeful misunderstanding of the honour-code of the Renaissance nobility.

Whatever may be said against guest performers, they certainly put a company on its mettle, and the whole Royal Ballet troupe (except perhaps Juliet's companions) were showing the cleanest pairs of heels and toes. Wayne Sleep nearly stopped the show with his Wedding variation, Desmond Doyle made a chillingly brutal Tybalt and Gerd Larsen wobbled delightedly as the Nurse – if her hat gets any bigger she will turn into a kinetic bundle.

26.10.75

## Fonteyn and Nureyev in *Romeo and Juliet* at Covent Garden

It is the mark of great dancers that they leave an indelible impression on a role; their interpretation haunts it long after they have gone. MacMillan did not create his *Romeo and Juliet* for Fonteyn and Nureyev, yet their rendering of it has stamped the ballet permanently. There will always be two alternative ways of playing the heroine – the way of Lynn Seymour, whom the choreographer first had in mind (headstrong, rebellious, the prime mover in the tragedy) and the Fonteyn way, gentle and resigned, the unyielding victim of larger events.

It is rumoured that this is not how MacMillan had seen the character, but it is certainly a valid reading of Shakespeare's text. If exaggerated it can lead to sentimentality, just as the alternative approach can turn to hysterical neurosis. But when interpreted with judgement and sincerity it can plumb the full depths of the story, and this image – a lamb going open-eyed to the slaughter – is what Fonteyn uniquely conjures up.

There must have been many apprehensions at Covent Garden last Monday when the curtain went up on the return of the legendary pair in this legendary role after a very long absence. Does the famous magic still work and would this tender Juliet touch us as much as she used to? It does and she did. To say this is not to pretend that we were seeing the same performance as on the ballet's opening night ten years ago. But criticism can easily go astray through facile comparisons. In

160

the same way that it is misleading to try to judge by the same yardstick an early and a late painting by Renoir or opera by Verdi, it is a mistake to equate interpretations by artists at different stages in their career. Each performance should ideally be assessed as if it were unique. When, for instance, Ulanova first appeared at Covent Garden as the Bolshoi Juliet she was already forty-six, and I have no doubt that many Russians were pointing out that she was not giving the same interpretation as she had when she created the part sixteen years earlier. But we lucky Londoners had no such preconceptions or memories; we saw her afresh and found her – rightly, I feel sure – wonderfully moving, though she was clearly no longer young.

It is hard for us to regain a completely innocent eye with which to watch Fonteyn's performance. I think a newcomer would have been unconvinced, as almost always, by the nursery scene; found the ballroom dancing only adequate, though the acting was fine; and then surrendered completely in the balcony duet. The serenity of Fonteyn's presence in front of the moonlit window – a joy after some recent writhings and wrigglings – and the delicate whole-heartedness, far short of sensual abandon, with which she gave herself to Nureyev's Romeo in the garden took on a touching reality. Some extraordinary harmony of musical timing and expression between these two makes the choreography ring like poetry. A girl sitting behind me was sobbing into her handkerchief before the long spiral of disaster had even taken its first turn, and you could understand why.

Fonteyn's dancing in the later scenes was muted, but she contrived to make this seem the expression of an inner reserve. She flinched from the fateful draught with a hopeful timidity, fell asleep without undue convulsions, and died with unhurried determination. The quietness which is her greatest theatrical attribute served her well.

Nureyev's Romeo is familiar but equally unforgettable – a mixture of fire and fun and open-hearted passion expressed in movement which ranges from mercurial flexibility to big swinging rhythms. The perfect foil to her restraint, his vitality lapped round her like a flame and he partnered with a care which conveyed genuine affection. When they bid their last unsynchronised goodbyes an elegiac sadness hung in the air. We mourned the fragile ephemerality not only of love and lovers, but of artists and partnerships, foretasting the sorrow of the inevitable and final parting of a great pair.

11.1.76

# Festival Ballet and Plissetskaya, in Paris

All good dance addicts know that for 200 years Paris was the centre of the ballet world, and that in our own century its artistic vitality was Diaghilev's inspiration. But latterly the impression has got around that Paris is no longer much interested in dance. A brief visit last weekend suggested just the opposite. The Opera House was packed, the gigantic Palais des Congrès was overflowing for a Béjart season and – a boost for national pride – the even bigger Palais des Sports (seating nearly 4,000) was crammed with a vociferous audience for the London Festival Ballet's *The Sleeping Beauty*. The milling crowds and high prices make ventures like the Royal Ballet's tent look puny. In many ways it is London which has become a rarefied backwater.

The Opéra programme was a spin-off from New York and Moscow – Plissetskaya guesting in a selection from the New York City Ballet's Ravel Festival. The five works did not, to be honest, add up to anything very substantial. Without *Daphnis and Chloe* (not, it seems, one of the successes of the New York occasion) Ravel's contribution to dance is distinctly lightweight. The most solid offering was the Balanchine *La Valse*. It is a marvellously period piece. To symbolise death by exchanging long white gloves for long black ones is a bit of high Cocteau camp, which is carried off with total elegance and conviction. Wilfride Piollet was exquisitely doomed, with Michael Denard as her helpless, handsome lover.

The big draw of the evening was Plissetskaya in Béjart's *Bolero*. This apotheosis of randiness is a bit of cabaret kitsch. The Russian ballerina has nowadays more authority than eroticism, and she performed the table-top routines with a cold, angular menace which invited a masochistic response. I have seen Pastoria Imperio at seventy shake her hips more seductively – but then she wore a sexily swirling skirt while poor Plissetskaya had only a skimpy T-shirt and tights. The number suffered from following immediately on Balanchine's *Tzigane*, another gipsy turn, performed rather tensely by Ghislaine Thesmar.

Of the two new pieces Jerome Robbins's *En Sol*, to Ravel's Piano Concerto in G (*en sol*) was delightfully fresh and exhilarating – a seaside frolic set in the early thirties when the piece was written, broken by a sentimental interlude to the long adagio. Piollet was as light as ozone, with Jean Guizerix splendidly plastic and athletic, though rather lacking in humour, as her lover. Erté's spare and witty decor is bang on.

Balanchine's *Le Tombeau de Couperin* proved disappointingly slight. It is a characteristic piece of dance embroidery. The formations are complex while the steps are kept to daisy-chain and oranges-and-lemons simplicity. As done here by very young dancers, it looked rather like a work for students. Maybe some seventeenth-century costumes instead of the fortyish-looking Balanchine uniforms would have given it more character. The company looked in good shape, though, with some strong soloists and plenty of promise in the ranks.

Maurice Béjart is a magic name in Paris, and a frequent visitor with his Ballets du XXe Siècle. Clashing engagements allowed me to see only a rehearsal of some of his works with which I was already familiar. By far the strongest of them was his *Le Sacre du Printemps* which showed the troupe to be in bounding athletic shape as usual, with Jorge Donn (disconcertingly limp-wristed in *The Wayfarer*) supple and moving as the chosen victim.

British ballet is virtually unknown in Paris. The Royal Ballet has not appeared there since 1963 (and then only the touring company) and the Festival Ballet not since 1969. That it can fill the Palais des Sports to the roof night after night is, admittedly, due to the presence of Nureyev as both choreographer and dancer. He is just the kind of star personality to draw the Paris crowds and he gave them their money's worth – careering through his own *Sleeping Beauty* with inimitable dash and stylish brilliance.

But the rest of the company has also been very well received. Evdokimova now makes an exciting Aurora – always technically exceptional, she has a new dynamism under her cool but springy poise – while Patricia Ruanne is consistently sure and well-placed.

1.2.76

## *A Month in the Country*, The Royal Ballet, Covent Garden

The Royal Ballet has been waiting impatiently for a new ballet from Frederick Ashton ever since he retired as its director in 1970. He has

163

bided his time, but last week he finally relented. On Thursday *A Month in the Country* was launched to an obviously delighted audience.

Sir Frederick is seventy and hardly likely to spring surprises. This is a completely Ashtonian work. To say that it is a compound of *Marguerite and Armand* and *Enigma Variations* would be too facile to be true, but there are certainly elements of both in it. It is 'freely adapted from Turgenev's play', and the adaptation is necessarily fairly drastic. There is no strong drama in the plot; a young tutor arrives in a provincial household, causes feminine heartbreak all round and departs. Turgenev's art lay in his building up of the suffocating atmosphere of bourgeois domesticity with all its attendant emotions – a basic theme in nineteenth-century fiction. The listless *ennui* of provincial Russia hangs over the story like a summer thunderstorm.

This background is shared by another Russian tale, *Eugen Onegin*, but Ashton has transformed it. Tchaikovsky has been replaced by Chopin, and Repin by something nearer to Watteau; in fact the mood is that of a Mozart opera – airy, feathery, melodious and delicately embroidered, with self-contained numbers strung on the narrative like beads and the sentiment laid on as lightly as silk.

The dance invention is continuous and detailed but it is not so closely meshed into the story as in, say, *The Dream*, and the succession of individual numbers prevents the passionate build-up of *Marguerite and Armand*. This is a deliberately superficial image, in which the deep reactions of the human heart must be guessed from the ripples on the surface. Only now and then does real feeling break through, and these rather melodramatic moments are the least satisfactory; the silent-film idiom seems out of place in the sophisticated context.

The 'Enigma' side of the work shows in the first section, in which the characters are introduced in a series of separate dances. The most striking is perhaps by the most marginal figure, Wayne Sleep, as the small boy who necessitates the employment of the tutor. These are fitted very cunningly to Chopin's 'La ci darem' variations.

The emotional tensions when the hostess, Natalya, finds that she is a rival of her own ward for the innocent tutor's attention is set to the 'Fantasia on Polish Airs', which permits some nice ethnic touches in the choreography, and develops to the 'Grand Polonaise in E flat for Piano and Orchestra', which leads to a suitably dying fall. Skilfully built up orchestrally by John Lanchbery, the score provides a shimmery framework which Ashton has used throughout with characteristic sensitivity. There are even suggestions of a sudden fresh breeze when the tutor arrives, and of a passing thunderstorm.

The Mozartian approach is not without its handicaps. A more elaborate and extended treatment would have been necessary to convey all the niceties of the original play – for instance, the key moment in which Natalia craftily extorts a confession of love from her still-immature ward; the 'recitative' passage seems unduly simplified. And the marginal characters such as the husband and the platonically adoring house guest Rakitin are reduced to shadows so that we are left with a slightly conventional triangle.

A more serious alteration is to the social setting. The whole action has been upgraded so that a footman stalks round the gigantic salon with a distinction worthy of Buckingham Palace, the husband looks flustered rather than bucolic, and the tutor – symbol of healthy red blood in an over-sheltered hothouse – is as elegantly dapper as Rakitin. I could not help remembering the house party in *Les Biches* with its stylised, poetic setting. Julia Oman has devised some enchanting costumes and carried out her commission with taste and restraint; but the choice of a completely literal set, fit for any drawing-room comedy, seems a fundamental mistake.

As Natalia, Lynn Seymour looks ravishing – almost too young to make the ideal foil to her rival – dances with her inimitable melting grace and flirts enchantingly. When the whole production has pulled together, she will surely find temperamental depths in a characterisation which is still rather sketchy. Dowell is irresistibly handsome as the tutor and puts all his polish into his difficult and plastic movements; as yet the touchingly unthinking *gaucherie* which attracts Natasha is vestigial.

More performances (or maybe more viewing on my part – this is necessarily only an instant impression) may yield emotional riches in a ballet which is visibly a mine of dance gems.

15.2.76

*Ashton is a one-man distillery. Few choreographers, if any, have his gift for the reductive approach to ballet – squeezing a mood, a period, a situation, or a character down to its minimum.*

## *The Sleeping Beauty*, Festival Ballet, Coliseum

You have to go back to the days of the Vestris (to see whom, in 1781, Parliament suspended a sitting) or of Nijinsky (who totally monopolised the billing for his 1914 appearances in London) to find a male dancer dominating a season in the manner of the current Nureyev Festival at the Coliseum. Probably only Fonteyn could today wear the mantle once comfortably borne by Pavlova and Isadora Duncan. So the pendulum swings. The opening programme is by the London Festival Ballet in Nureyev's own majestic vision of *The Sleeping Beauty* – a controversially new conception which is likely to prove, like the once equally novel 'Diaghilev' and 'Oliver Messel' productions, the focal interpretation for a generation. The clue to its character is the opening of the last act – no glittering ballroom entertainment, but a stately royal sarabande, led by the haughty monarch himself (Donald Barclay) and his queen (Linda Darrell). This is no fairyland occasion, but a glimpse of the corrupting splendour of power.

Nureyev has shifted the design of the ballet, not by subtraction but by addition. The old lay-out gave Act I to Aurora, divided Act II between her and the Prince, and shared Act III between them – an arrangement which limited the Prince to a single solo in the last scene. Nureyev has somewhat equalised the roles by inserting dances for the Prince in the Vision scene of Act II, principally in a long introductory solo – a strange, intricate skein of weaving and wayward movement which marks his hesitations before setting out for the Enchanted Castle.

It is in a strongly personal style, adding what amounts to a new wing to the old structure. But the original fabric remains, leaving to the ballerina still the larger share of the dancing – a huge role. In the absence through illness of Eva Evdokimova, the Canadian star Karen Kain stepped in on the opening night to show herself an enchanting Aurora. She does not dazzle technically in any particular department, but her overall style is as clear and clean as spring water and her fresh, intelligent personality is just right for the part; to watch her is like sitting under a sun lamp. A shade nervous at first, she melted and softened as the evening went on, ending by joining Nureyev – who was in fine form earlier, with characteristically quick and vivid

166

changes of mood – in a last act *pas de deux* where her feminine charm perfectly complemented his breathtaking blend of fire and fluidity.

The whole company now wear Georgiadis's sumptuous costumes with natural ease, and the second cast was just as strong as the first. Patricia Ruanne and Manola Asensio both made very distinguished Principal Dancers, Freya Dominic glittered as the new-style glamorous Carabosse, and if Nicholas Johnson was a light, crisp Bluebird on the opening night, two days later Frank Augustyn (also from Canada) was outstanding – poetic and stylish, he restored stature to a role which has fallen into poor repute.

6.6.76


## *Nympheas*, London Contemporary Dance Theatre, Sadler's Wells

Now that modern-dance companies can, and indeed must, appeal to a broad public, some way of devising contemporary pieces as easily accessible as romantic-style ballet has become a necessity. Few choreographers have succeeded in breaking through the élitist barrier more successfully than Robert Cohan, with his strong theatrical sense. His new work for the London Contemporary Dance Theatre, presented at Sadler's Wells last week, is called *Nympheas* and was inspired by Monet's famous waterlily paintings. Boldly seizing the cliché by the horns, Cohan has gone to the obvious composer, Debussy, for the score. Classical ballet would have completed the Impressionist picture with fluttering chiffon and delicate *brisés*; Cohan has eschewed these and found fascinating equivalents in the modern style. He reflects the feeling of iridescence and ephemerality without imitating its appearance and has produced a ballet which is seductive but not sentimental, elusive but firm. The constantly shifting groups and gently plastic solos set up a shimmer which is echoed in Norberto Chiesa's ingenious set, with pale ledges across which Cohan spreads his dancers to make dappled networks of limbs. They tackle the unfamiliar style of movement with uneven success, but the total effect is continuously interesting and pleasing.

5.12.76

*While the eventual mingling of the two styles can be taken as inevitable, some paradoxical differences persist. Historically, it is the 'modern' style which is the more traditional; the bare foot came before the shoe. But on the other hand, the apparently artificial classical ballet is, humanly speaking, the more natural: virtually every movement in its vocabulary is derived from ordinary social dancing, whether aristocratic or rustic. Modern dance, by contrast, is almost completely artificial, unrelated to normal movement. Like classical ballet, it is constructed like a game, with strict rules of its own; an actual naturalistic gesture looks as out of place in it as a speaking voice would sound in a Verdi opera.*

## Revival of *La Fille Mal Gardée*, The Royal Ballet, Covent Garden

I have not looked up the article, but I am fairly sure that I under-estimated *La Fille Mal Gardée* when I first saw it. I remember being bowled over by the happy comedy – who could not be? But, frankly, I was put off by the pink ribbons. Since then I have learnt to appreciate better the cunning with which Ashton has balanced sentiment and prettiness against jollity and some quite difficult dancing; but now and then I still have qualms.

Any student of aesthetics knows that good taste has been the curse of British art for generations. (When did it creep in? Nobody could accuse Shakespeare and Marlowe of it, nor Hogarth, nor the Restoration dramatists, nor Blake and Turner.) Vitality, God's greatest gift to an artist, arouses suspicion among the pinstripe brigade. We – and here I refer, alas, to us critics and not to the public – tend to put conformity before inspiration, discipline above passion. Above all, we cling hopefully to what we call 'English lyricism', a quality for which foreigners often use a different and less flattering name.

Not even *Fille* is immune to this dangerous influence. The dancers chosen by Ashton to create the ballet, Nadia Nerina and David Blair, were both blessed with a kind of down-to-earth substantiality which sailed triumphantly through the ribbons and petticoats; but there have been performances lately in which daintiness got out of hand. Charm – the kiss of death to art – seemed to be claiming another victim.

Last week's revival at Covent Garden restored my faith. Once

168

again the lovers, the farmer's boy and the country lass, had the natural vigour from which all good eighteenth-century art sprang. Warmth and spontaneity spread out from the stage and communicated itself to the audience. Lesley Collier comes nearest to Nerina in the role than any dancer I have seen so far and added some extra touches of apple-cheeked rustic vitality of her own, stumping and pouting with delightful determination when she was not performing her variations with a dash and precision which never thinned out into ballerina brilliance.

Nureyev was exactly right as her lover, a Rowlandson lad with a gallant eye and more in his breeches than a promise of marriage, who melts into tender gentleness (and style) at the first breath of a *pas de deux*. It was good to see him almost right back on form and dancing his solos with exciting expertise, though he had to adapt some of the steps for his injured leg. But it was above all as a pair that they worked. This was a haystack romance you could really believe in, with an evident understanding and harmony which bodes well for the future.

The bucolic sentiment – something the period understood – made sense of Osbert Lancaster's designs and also of the near-caricature minor characters. Wayne Sleep was making his debut as a diminutive Alain (the costume was designed to make the sturdy Alexander Grant look smaller); he has not yet put the different elements of the role together, but they are all there. Ronald Emblen is unbeatable as the Widow Simone, tyrant of the kitchen, queen of the cloggies. The poultry pranced, the harvesters danced and the pony seemed to have bought a new fur coat. Once again red corpuscles were running through this most lovable of ballets. If it doesn't get blown off course by us well-meaning critics it should last for ever.

30.1.77


## Scottish Ballet's season in Paris

The love affair between France and Scotland goes back into history, and for the last two weeks the romance has been revived. As part of a Nureyev Festival in Paris, Scottish Ballet has been bringing a touch of the Highlands to the Porte de Versailles. You could almost hear the bagpipes in the Metro, where posters showed the young maestro himself resplendent in kilt and sporran. It could have brought its

*Mary Queen of Scots*, which is set on both sides of the Channel; but instead it presented two ballets of unmistakably Parisian origin. The shrewd first choice was *La Sylphide*, France's charming nineteenth-century salute to the spell which Scotland cast over the cradle of the Romantic Movement.

The company is small and the theatre in which it has been appearing is enormous; the Palais des Sports holds about 5,000 people in a stadium adaptable to provide a proscenium stage when required. But *La Sylphide* was born in 1832, a time when the public demanded stars above all, with the company mainly providing support. No numerous array of talent was needed. The stars on this occasion were of the largest magnitude – Makarova and Nureyev, resealing a partnership which had come unstuck rather sensationally on their last appearance together in Paris. This was the happiest of reconciliations. I doubt if the ballet has ever had two more luminously apt interpreters.

Makarova was in her element as the sprite – feather-like, seductive, almost transparent as she darted across the stage like a beam of northern sunlight. Nureyev, the embodiment of gallant romanticism, was in bounding form as the over-impressionable hero, blending charm and vigour with a *batterie* crisp enough to curl the hair of every girl in the glen. It was touching to see these two Russians so much at home in the Franco-Scottish story; already the local wits have christened them MacKarova and MacRoody. Their genuinely Hibernian companions emerged with credit from the international test. Kit Lethby made a dashing Gurn and Gordon Aitken was a scary witch. The corps de ballet were more convincing as villagers than as sylphs. The ultra-realistic production was a bit modest for the auditorium, but it was wise not to compete with the celebrated setting of the ballet at the Opéra.

The company scored a definite hit on its own with Jack Carter's *Three Dances to Japanese Music*, whose exotic glamour appealed greatly to the French public. Hans van Manen's meditative *Four Schumann Pieces* hardly held its own in the stadium environment, but it was a reassuring sign of Nureyev's determination not to let the programmes slide into gaudiness.

The second week brought *Giselle*, another Paris-born work, although here it was given a decidedly un-French flavour in Peter Darrell's production. With Lynn Seymour and Nureyev as the principals, the quality of the performance could hardly go wrong; they both made a miraculous blend of the dancing and the acting, and

Elaine McDonald's big jumps showed up well in her rendering of Myrthe, but the production fell to pieces on this stage. In a small theatre the novel village-square look of Act I lends it a certain veracity, but when it is opened up, as it was here, and under poor lighting, its merits disappear; while Act II, with its rows of blonde-wigged ghosts in modern frocks, made less sense than ever.

13.2.77

## *A Month in the Country*, The Royal Ballet, Covent Garden

'The great dancer is not the one who makes a difficult step look easy, but the one who makes an easy step look interesting.' So suggested Nureyev to me one day when we were discussing Fonteyn – and her example surely proves the accuracy of the definition. It reminded me of Matisse's reply to a visitor who sarcastically asked him how long it had taken him to draw one of his egg-shaped faces. 'Fifty years,' replied the painter. To pack into a simple statement the full power of an artist's skill, intelligence and personality is the supreme achievement. In dance it involves many ingredients – timing, presentation, definition and above all a unity of the whole body. A few dancers – Isadora Duncan must have been one of them – are born with the gift and end by relying on it too much, neglecting the effort to extend their range. Others advance from the opposite end; born with technical facility, they may take years to turn it into an instrument of expression. Last week-end we had glimpses at Covent Garden of both types.

Few contemporary dancers have been as blessed as Lynn Seymour is with that instinct for physical harmony which makes a movement tell on the stage, but for a period she seemed unable to penetrate into the technical areas which would give it full rein. Recently she broke through the barrier; though still no pyrotechnician, she can now ride a difficult passage with the assurance needed to subdue it into a general interpretation. As Natalia in Ashton's *A Month in the Country*, she delighted us with the flow of delicate choreography, but never at the expense of the characterisation. This was a beautifully judged piece of dramatic dancing.

Wayne Eagling is probably the most interesting young male dancer produced by the Royal Ballet in recent years, with a combination of

171

speed, elevation and musicality which is continually arresting and completely individual. Yet the roles in which he seems completely fulfilled have been few; he remains the company's least exploited asset. The difficulty lies partly in the mainly classical-romantic repertoire: Eagling is not physically a pure classical dancer nor temperamentally a romantic one. Criticisms of his acting seem to me misplaced; what is still inexpressive is his dancing. The technical feats (and sometimes the limbs) are unco-ordinated, lacking the build-up of controlled power which can give simplicity more substance than any complex virtuosity. He is an artist of exciting promise and he deserves careful coaching or – better – a choreographer who can turn to advantage his special idiosyncracies. I suspect it will be one working in a modern idiom, for Eagling is unmistakably a dancer of our time.

13.3.77

## Baryshnikov as Romeo at Covent Garden

In 1975, Mikhail Baryshnikov made his debut with the Royal Ballet in *Romeo and Juliet*. Last Tuesday he was back at Covent Garden – again in *Romeo and Juliet*. It was not very imaginative programming, but any excuse for seeing him is welcome and it gave us a chance to find out if and how he had developed meanwhile. The answer is – a lot. He is in peak dancing form and he has gained considerably in stagecraft – more at ease and well able to hold the eye, even when not performing one of his amazing *tours de force*. He has also built up the dramatic side of the role. He stressed the youthful element much less and has worked out an interpretation which is refreshingly simple and consistent. He presented Romeo as an engaging, spunky young man, a bit pugnacious in a friendly way (he faced up cockily to Tybalt) and always ready for some fun with a rapier or a girl. It is a straightforward approach, completely in sympathy with the choreography. Where he differed from most interpreters was that he did not change gear when he met Juliet, but drove right on to the end. There was no sign of thunderbolt conversion from youth to manhood, from playboy hedonism to total commitment.

Following his marriage to Juliet, he improvised a skipping step down the stairs, which expressed cheerful delight rather than dedication, as though she were a crowning feather in his amorist's cap.

172

For him the big change came when he lost his temper at the death of his friend Mercutio.

This masculine interpretation misses one of Shakespeare's points, but worked perfectly with his whole style and enabled him to throw off his brilliant technical embellishments without interrupting the dramatic flow. It paid its biggest dividends in the earlier acts (he seemed hardly the type to die for love), which moved by with a marvellous urgency, propelled by that extra vitality the Russians seem able to draw on. It became an adventure story in which almost impeccable execution became an expression of clean narrative – an exhilarating performance which did not close the door to further explorations in depth.

The double-work has sometimes gone more easily, but Baryshnikov's innocent directness made a fine foil to Lynn Seymour's Juliet, which took on the dominating element that MacMillan has planted in it. While Romeo rushed heedless to his fate, this Juliet – danced with Seymour's usual eloquence – seemed aware of, and indeed directing, every fatal twist in the story. Michael Coleman's Mercutio took on an extra sophisticated eloquence and Michael Batchelor (replacing the injured Wayne Eagling) made a promising debut as Benvolio. Wayne Sleep – perhaps the nearest we have to the Baryshnikov type of virtuoso – stood up dashingly to the competition in his wedding solo.

20.3.77

*Of the three roles which Baryshnikov has danced with the Royal Ballet, that of Colas in Ashton's* La Fille Mal Gardée, *which he performed at a matinee last weekend, suits him far the most naturally. It is surely no accident that he first made his mark here in another eighteenth-century role – an evocation of Vestris with the Kirov. His neat, nimble, open style is exactly right for a period still untouched by the undertones of the romantic movement.*

## *Les Sylphides*, Festival Ballet, Coliseum

What the Kingdom of the Shades scene in *La Bayadère* stands for in the work of Petipa, *Les Sylphides* does for Fokine. Both portray a male vision of impalpable females and both originally formed a minor part of a larger ballet filled with character dances.

173

It was Petipa's practice – perhaps his invention – to insert a classical 'vision' episode at the heart of almost all his ballets (e.g., *The Sleeping Beauty, Swan Lake, The Nutcracker, Don Quixote*) and Fokine's masterpiece can be seen as an unconscious salute to Petipa as well as an evocation of Taglioni. What was new and rebellious was the fluid Art Nouveau form of the dances – an approach which was to revolutionise choreography. *Les Sylphides*, apparently so gentle and traditional, marked a watershed.

It was conceived in 1907 as part of a gala in St Petersburg in aid of the Society for the Prevention of Cruelty to Children, and in that version (called *Chopiniana*) it consisted of a ballroom polonaise, a Polish wedding and a tarantella into which a romantic *pas de deux* – added to the score by Glazunov at Fokine's request – was inserted. This waltz, danced by Pavlova and Obukhov, was so successful that a year later Fokine arranged a second version with new lyrical dances built around it and all else suppressed.

This, then, is a quintessence piece – the distillation and expansion of a single dance. Its purity has preserved it, but at the same time it sets extreme standards of authenticity. For some reason the Festival Ballet has always excelled at interpreting Fokine: its successes in *Les Sylphides* have evidently been simply due to the fact that they were produced by Alicia Markova. She has revived it again and the first performance last week proved that she is incomparable at catching its mood.

Fokine was never averse to changing his mind and purists may find minor deviations from his original Karsavina-Nijinsky version. But such details are unimportant beside the overall style and atmosphere, and these Markova has caught marvellously. In the mazurka and the vital *pas de deux* Evdokimova is a natural; her gentle lightness conveys the period without a trace of coyness and her hands – sometimes rather limp for Petipa – exactly suit the Fokine style.

Peter Schaufuss, though not a natural romantic, proved again that the taxing role of the Poet demands technical strength rather than graceful swooning. Manola Asensio and Vivien Loeber gave delicacy and sincerity to the Prelude and the Waltz and the corps were admirably uniform.

15.5.77

*[Fokine's] popular fame is, of course, partly due to the fact that it was with programmes entirely composed of his ballets that Diaghilev hit the Western*

*world like a bomb before the First World War. The brand of exotic romanticism enshrined in this unparalleled row of works imprinted itself indelibly on the public imagination and has never been replaced. His reputation with knowledgeable devotees rests on an even surer base. He is incontestably the father of all modern ballet.*

## Nureyev's production of *Romeo and Juliet*, Festival Ballet, Coliseum

'Most discussions of *Romeo and Juliet*, and most stage productions, give a simplified view of the play. It is "a play of young love", "a pæan of romantic love", "the great typical love tragedy of the world", and so on. Such remarks do an injustice to the complexity of *Romeo and Juliet*. . . . There is music and dancing, fantasy and bawdry, the heights of joy and the depths of misery.' So begins the introduction to the New Shakespeare edition of the play, and Nureyev might have taken the words as the motto for his new production, with which the Festival Ballet launched the Nureyev Festival at the Coliseum on Thursday.

It is an entirely new interpretation of the Prokofiev score, as different from the closely linked Cranko and MacMillan versions as from the Kirov-Bolshoi one. It is less smoothly homogeneous than these and has the curious quality of containing more dancing and yet being less balletic. It follows the current stage tendency to drain all traces of Victorian sentiment out of Shakespeare and replace it with a rougher, tougher approach. The flavour is nearer to the Aldwych Theatre than to Covent Garden. The changes from humour and squalor (we start with a cartload of plague-stricken corpses) to courtly splendour, from rioting to rhapsody, from spectacle to dramatics at an almost cinematic pace – facilitated by Ezio Frigerio's ingeniously simple setting – reveal the Shakespeare touch. The fights are alarmingly violent; Mercutio (Nicholas Johnson) is genuinely funny; and for Romeo and Juliet the natural expression of love is sex. We are confronted by a disaster which turns into a blessing – for, like Shakespeare, Nureyev leaves us with the feuding families reconciled, private tragedy becoming public joy.

The production is exceptionally fluid, a quality which invests every detail of the dancing (he is especially good at counterpointed groups). The binding theme is the power of chance. By hinging the

175

whole action on an accident – the interception of the Friar's message to the exiled Romeo – Shakespeare stressed the slender thread on which the fate of a whole city can hang. Nureyev has restored this scene (usually omitted in ballet) and retains the theme throughout.

The rich, complex production – we wander freely into Elizabethan allegories, visions and flights of fancy – is contained by Frigerio in ravishing Carpaccio-like sets and sumptuous costumes. It still had some rough edges on the opening night, but the company produced just the right gusto and the highlights stood out.

The most striking invention is the death of Mercutio as his mockery turns horrifyingly against him, followed by Juliet's moment of hysteria when confronted with her husband turned assassin – a vivid Act II curtain. The convincing Renaissance feeling is helped by red-blooded market ensembles and some charming finger-linked period dances; there is a spectacular number borrowed from Sienese acrobats and flag displays, some witty Mercutio solos, and a crisply classical choreographic canon round the sleeping Juliet. We see Death covering Juliet like a lascivious black eagle, a lithe and high-tempered Tybalt (Frederic Werner), a sexy young Nurse (Elizabeth Anderton), and an athletic Benvolio (Jonas Kage).

Patricia Ruanne acted Juliet with genuine power as a strong, positive girl for whom the luck runs out and tackled the difficult dancing without faltering. Nureyev has given himself a relatively modest part as Romeo, but it includes many of the sinuous, intertwining movements at which he excels and he traced the path from playboy to passion with total conviction. The 'balcony' *pas de deux* is arranged in swirling, flying movements (they need practice to make their full effect), while the bedroom duet is frankly erotic and the twin deaths horribly real. This is not picture-book romance, but a tale of sex and violence conveyed in vivid tragedy.

5.6.77

# American Ballet Theatre at the Coliseum

Florists around St Martin's Lane must have done well this summer. Seldom can so many bouquets have showered on to the Coliseum stage as during its twelve-week ballet season – most of them, it must be said, for the Russian dancers. With Nureyev, Baryshnikov and Makarova at the receiving end, it has been a little Kirov festival. The final one-week season of American Ballet Theatre (whose new offerings I discussed last week) showed the star system in full form, providing exhilarating helpings of Russian guests, even if it rather frustrated audiences eager to see how American dance is progressing.

From this point of view the most arresting performance was the last, when Gelsey Kirkland appeared in *Giselle* and proved herself in a single evening to be a dancer of world class – perhaps the first American girl of that calibre since Isadora Duncan. Born in Bethlehem, Pennsylvania, twenty-four years ago, she trained and began her career with the New York City Ballet, transferring to American Ballet Theatre in 1974. She became a big favourite but then retired for a period due to ill-health.

It was tempting to see traces of this experience in her reading of Giselle, whom she showed (as Markova used to) as an ultra-tender plant. From the start she moved with delicate caution making her lightest springs and highest arabesques – for she has a formidable technique – an expression of fragile sensibility. In Act I she was shy, remote and immature, a snowdrop doomed to a brief flowering; in the mad scene she retreated gently into her own mind; in Act II she was a mere presence. It is an interpretation which could become mannered, but on this occasion it was miraculously sustained.

That she could bring off such a success almost immediately after Makarova's famous interpretation – which I discussed when she danced it two weeks ago with Nureyev – was a real achievement. Cynthia Gregory, coming between them, is handicapped in the role by her tall and ultra-aristocratic physique; technically impeccable, she could make a wonderfully cool, crystalline Myrtha.

Owing to the illness of Ivan Nagy, both Makarova and Kirkland were partnered by Baryshnikov, who gave us a display of classical dance at its Kirov perfection. Every step in his variations was light and neat and clean and shining, the quintessence of the *danse d'école*. Quick and vital, he defies gravity through sheer velocity, not soaring but flying.

To fit this dynamic attack into the character of Albrecht is clearly a problem. Baryshnikov solved it intelligently by playing down the aristocratic overtones in Act I (except for some oddly unrustic white tights) and abandoning all suggestions of the upper-class cad; he portrayed a straightforward youth attracted by an impressionable

177

girl. This sturdy reading fitted well into David Blair's rather homespun (and miserably designed) production, though, with such a likeable Hilarion as Frank Smith and such a lovable Giselle, the stage seemed rather overloaded with virtue, and occasional snatches of old-fashioned romantic agonising such as Baryshnikov's curtain scenes (hysterics after Act I, showers of lilies after Act II) looked a bit out of place.

If Kirkland stood up with honours to the challenge of Makarova, so did the company's own Albrecht, Fernando Bujones, to that of Baryshnikov. He is, incredibly, only twenty-two and clearly a candidate for becoming the world equivalent of Kirkland. Exceptionally slight and slim, he gave a touchingly youthful, elegant impression – again not a cad, but a shy, sincere young man sinning through sheer immaturity.

His technique in Act II was dazzling, with incredibly high soft beats, but he still needs to get all his talents together. Already a phenomenon, it is exciting to look forward to his peak in, say, five years' time. Marianna Tcherkassky and George de la Pena were outstanding in the Peasant pas de deux.

Makarova's careful production of the Kingdom of the Shades scene from *La Bayadère* suffered somewhat from the gala atmosphere of the opening programme. It is, with one exception, a faithful replica of the Kirov version, slightly less pliant and romantic than the Royal Ballet production with which, apart from some changes of dance order, it is identical. She has done wonders with the corps de ballet, which (as in *Giselle*) was impeccably drilled, though the soloists were not strong – better on the second night.

The ballet is a typical Petipa 'vision' episode within a picturesque ballet and the introduction of a male solo into it requires – as in the separate version of *Swan Lake* Act II – great tact. Baryshnikov has jettisoned the Chabukiani solo and replaced it with a more showy dance, combining style with some breathtaking acrobatics, which rightly brought the house down but fractured the dream-like mood of the ballet. It ended up as a triumphant spectacle – heart-warming, but not, I think, quite what the choreographer intended. Makarova herself was brilliantly elusive as the ghostly Nikiya; on the second night Martine van Hamel added a serene remoteness, unluckily not much helped by the injured Nagy.

Gregory's tall distinction appeared to perfect advantage in Tudor's *Jardin aux Lilas*, in which her display of anguished despair encased within upper-class protocol was beautifully controlled (Makarova indulged in too much Russian emotionalising). She needed a more dynamic Lover and the big stage changed the quick film-style cuts between the episodes into 'dissolves', but the tense private drama (this must be the first ballet to exploit people *not* looking at each other) came over vividly, with van Hamel adding urgency to her smooth classicism as the Other Woman.

The main recommendations of Alvin Ailey's *The River* was that it offered chances to just about the whole company, which they took with zest. It was the men who impressed most. Led by dancers like Clark Tippet and Charles Ward, they have a masculine vigour and athletic virtuosity most European companies could envy. But there is plenty of talent among the girls, too, and it is frustrating that we had no time to see them deployed. Let's hope that the next visit of this exciting company will be longer, giving us the chance to look below its glittering surface.

31.7.77

## *The Sleeping Beauty*, The Royal Ballet, Covent Garden

Ballet has such a short history and so few masterpieces that authenticity is exciting. *The Sleeping Beauty*, which has just been revived by the Royal Ballet, furnishes special material for pedigree freaks. It was created by Petipa in St Petersburg in 1890. Nicholas Sergeyev became *régisseur* to the company and in 1909 he helped to revise the ballet, making a few changes. In 1921 he revised it again for Diaghilev in London, and in 1939 he revised it once more for Sadler's Wells; in 1946 de Valois and Ashton produced their own version of that revision for the Royal Ballet at Covent Garden. By ballet standards, this is pretty near to authenticity and the 1946 production became almost as sacred as the original. The new revival at Covent Garden is an overt attempt to revert to it.

Should it be judged as a revival or as a modern interpretation of a classic? It scores more on one count than on the other. The success of the 1946 production has proved an awkward legacy. Daringly different from earlier versions, Oliver Messel's airy rococo vision and de Valois's innocently beguiling production made the perfect setting for the Ashtonian elegance of the company and for the lyrical purity of Fonteyn as centrepiece. Recent changes having proved unsuccessful, the new version might seem an example of playing safe. In

179

fact it is a venture so bold as to approach foolhardiness – an attempt to reproduce a triumph of thirty years ago.

But the theatre is not like the cinema. Old films survive because they are complete, with the original cast, make-up, acting style and costumes coalescing into single experiences. Like paintings and music and architecture they are frozen essences of a single moment. But on the stage casts, alas, must change and with them a whole complex of taste and fashion. It is impossible to resurrect one part of a theatrical experience without the whole. De Valois and Ashton have heroically taken on a venture which is virtually impossible – particularly since, even if they succeeded, they would have to face the fact that subsequent samples of the Russian approach make us see the ballet differently today.

Given a certain carbon-copy element which is inherent in the operation, the restoration is remarkably faithful. The general tone of the 1946 production is well maintained – light, cheerful and pretty. There are no attempts at fresh interpretation, psychological overtones, social undertones or realistic credibility. We are faced with a simple pantomime fairy story. David Walker's pastiche designs lack individuality, but they are pretty and practical, and the tempi are brisk at the expense of breadth and drama. This is an exceptionally gentle production, with everything scaled down (the Prince meets no opposition on his way to the Enchanted Castle) and the acting reduced to cardboard gestures. Happy make-believe is unalloyed.

This unassuming lyrical-pastoral approach has its drawbacks. There is hardly a trace of St Petersburg grandeur. Charm has replaced style and this has a diminishing effect on the score and on some of the dancing; Petipa would, I think, have raised an eyebrow at the winsome fairies in the Prologue. But there is plenty of nostalgia-fodder around. The old sequence has been faithfully restored, with the last two acts run together and minimal stage effects for the Transformation and travelling scenes. Retained from later productions are MacMillan's Hop o' my Thumb solo for Wayne Sleep in Act III (with this rather Buttons-like number, the Three Ivans and the Cats, we are perilously near to music-hall here), and Ashton's variation for the Prince and his 'waking *pas de deux*' with its creamy, if rather un-Petipa romanticism in Act II.

Delightfully uncomplicated and evocative, the production can be seen best as an attractive setting for sparkling dancing. The opening Princess was Lesley Collier, new to the role but full of promise.

Experience has taught that – unlike *Swan Lake* or *Giselle* – this ballet can be a vehicle for a *demi-caractère* star, and Collier brings to the role musicality, warmth and vivacity. She has a strong technique and a winning personality. Understandably nervous on the first night, she brought off an accomplished Rose Adagio and will doubtless soon learn to relax her sharp dynamics into a little more ease and poetry.

She was lucky to have as partner Anthony Dowell, who rightly received an ovation on his return after a cruelly long absence through injury; it was good to see again his inimitable ease and grace and fluid elegance. As in some other recent productions, Carabosse is played by a woman. Lynn Seymour was an original choice for the role; she can be imagined as a malevolent Bette Davis-type spitfire, but this would need a colder, less agitated style than the one devised for her. Alfreda Thoroughgood brought a welcome touch of classical breeding to her Prologue solo and Stephen Beagley was at perfect ease in the *pas de trois*.

The *réchauffé* approach provoked inevitable comparisons with the company of thirty years ago; it may be nostalgia which tipped the balance against today. No doubt we shall have plenty of opportunities to correct our estimates, for the production is as English as a Savile Row dinner jacket – unostentatious, conventional, a bit old-fashioned, but made to last.

23.10.77

## Dame Marie Rambert at ninety

Ninety is a decent age and sometimes limits people's hours of alertness. I thought I should telephone Marie Rambert, who is to celebrate that birthday tomorrow, to find out what time I should best call to congratulate her. For the sake of tact, I rang early so as to talk to her faithful housekeeper first. 'Did you want to speak to Dame Marie? I'm afraid she's gone off to a rehearsal at Hammersmith. She won't be back till this afternoon.'

She did manage to fit me into her schedule a few days later, and I rang the bell of her house on Campden Hill. She opened the door herself and ushered me nimbly into the sitting-room. Before I had time to take off my coat, she was showing me some new treasures – sea-shells from Lincoln Kirstein, founder of the New York City

181

Ballet, and a little sculpture showing an elfin shop assistant pursuing a customer with a pair of scissors.

'Isn't it wonderful, how it catches Fred's elegant arms and the angle of my cigarette?' It was a sculpture done by a friend from a photograph of a *pas de deux* from Frederick Ashton's *A Tragedy of Fashion*, a ballet arranged in 1926 for a Hammersmith revue and danced by himself and the then thirty-nine-year-old Marie Rambert.

Ashton had been born in Ecuador and Rambert came from Poland, but this work was to be the ancestor of all modern British ballet, just as she was to become its godmother. This honorary post has not added an ounce of Englishness to her character, which remains almost absurdly Polish – fiery, romantic, impractical, poetic, martial. She is a pocket warrior who revels in pitting her tiny resources against the world.

As she sat, challenging the years with her clear grey eyes, perfect hearing and a spine like a ramrod, I accused her of inventing her own obstacles. She insists on regularly teaching herself new sonatas on her upright piano and not long ago she bought a typewriter to wrestle with. I hinted that her love of dance arose from the fact that she enjoyed fighting with her own body.

'Not at all – I just love to move. I couldn't talk to you unless I had done my practice. Look.' Jumping up from her chair, she held on to the marble mantlepiece and thrust at me an alarming, waist-high leg, un-folding it into a perfect knee-tight *développé*. 'See my deportment? You would say it was good? Well, watch!' Head erect, she dropped her shoulders about half an inch. 'There, that's the difference. Every day you learn something.' Chin up, her eyes blazed into a distance just above my head with the eagle glare of a hussar sighting the enemy. 'It is not a struggle, it is a need.'

It seems still to be this urge to move, to dance, which provides the power driving this extraordinary little artistic dynamo. She no longer directs the company, founded in 1930, which bears her name, the Ballet Rambert (she handed it over in 1970 to Norman Morrice, now director of the Royal Ballet), but she still plays an active part, watching and advising, and she has strong ideas – or rather feelings, for she is not an analyser by nature – about its future. 'Neo-classical,' she announced firmly as soon as I mentioned the company. 'Neo-classical, that's what I call it. A new way of using the old tradition. It's changed from what it was at the moment of transformation, when Norman took over; that was the time of throwing off all fetters. Now the old classical discipline is coming back. The point is, its roots are so strong you can direct them anywhere.'

She has lived in London for over sixty years, but her foreign accent is as strong as ever. She was born in Warsaw, where her father was a bookseller. Her memory goes back to, roughly, one and a half. 'I can remember quite clearly the songs our nurse sang to me. One day she was reading a story to us, something about three innocent boys, and I was so moved I just slipped down under the table – perhaps I didn't want her to see my tears.'

Poland was still part of Russia when she was at school and even the lessons on Polish literature were conducted in Russian. She soaked up yards of Pushkin and Lermontov which she can still reel off today, besides long passages of Corneille and Racine. Goethe and Schiller. Shakespeare and Byron came later, an added solace during the long nights; Dame Marie is an irrepressible insomniac.

One evening she saw Isadora Duncan dance in a Warsaw concert hall, and the experience left a permanent impression. Soon afterwards she was sent off to a doctor aunt in Paris to study medicine. But instead she met Isadora's brother, Raymond, who offered to give her lessons ('He had no idea; he told me I was as good as his sister') and soon her latent passion for dancing surfaced in recitals in fashionable salons.

Were these really as weirdly snobbish and decadent as Proust makes out? I asked her. 'They certainly weren't extravagant where the entertainers were concerned. I never dared ask more than 100 francs and I remember one hostess complaining: "But, my dear, you must remember I have my decorator, my confectioner, my florist to pay, not counting the champagne!" Decadent? I really don't know; you'd never believe to what a degree I was ignorant. I was just penetrated at that time by the spirit of dance, that was my only passion.'

The passion took her to Switzerland, on a course with Jaques-Dalcroze, the teacher of Eurythmics – the use of movement to illustrate rhythm. One day 'a tall portly man with black hair' accompanied by 'a very small man with pale complexion, fair sleek hair and light brown eyes slit slightly upward' came to watch a class. It was Diaghilev and Nijinsky, and next day she found herself invited to join the Ballets Russes to help Nijinsky disentangle the rhythms of Stravinsky's *Sacre du Printemps*, which he was beginning to choreograph.

The collaboration left her totally converted to classical ballet (which her admiration for Duncan had taught her to despise), an experienced performer, even if of modest roles, and of course hopelessly in love with Nijinsky. She shed bitter tears when he unexpectedly became engaged to a Hungarian girl on the boat to America; and when Diaghilev jealously fired him after receiving news of his marriage, her career with the Russian ballet came to an end. In September 1914 she shared a crowded Channel steamer with Chaliapin to England.

In London she carried on her recitals and met her future husband, the playwright Ashley Dukes; in 1920 she opened a school, which so prospered that by 1926 her dancers were invited to take part in the revue commemorated in the sculpture. She was fixed in London for life, with a British husband (he died in 1959), a British passport, two daughters and a home from which she has never moved.

Marie Rambert is not so much a talking memoir as a one-woman magazine, vividly illustrated, varied, packed with human interest. In spite of her phenomenal memory for poetry, she admits that she has no sense of history nor even of narrative. 'I've read *War and Peace* six times, but I still don't know the sequence of events.'

She never generalises, is vague about dates and names and looks as puzzled as a child if you ask her a general question or invite her to guess about the future. 'I'm not an observer. I'm terribly unconcerned with philosophies and theories. I'm always completely unaware of what is happening in the world. I just know that I have an instinct for dance to a very high degree. I don't find things change so much. Humanity remains the same, only its follies take a different shape. I don't know any rules for art. I think the only rule is that the artist should give absolutely his very best, that he should dig deep, deep until it hurts, into his soul, into his motives, his life. What shape the result takes, that's God's will.'

Phrases like 'soul' and 'God's will' slide off her tongue, tremulous with instant emotion. She could have made a fine actress in the Comédie Française style; she is well aware how to turn on the pathos, as she sometimes used to do – to the embarrassment of her company – when exhorting the audience to support her impoverished ventures. Her volatile, short-focus temperament still bubbles with enthusiasms and sudden shafts of recollection.

'I've just remembered hearing the French actor Coquelin imitating Diaghilev, putting on a thick Russian accent: "Je tro-o-ouve que le premier repas de la journée doit être copieux." "Et les autres, Monsieur Diaghilev?" "Aussi." She blows out her cheeks to imitate the great impresario.

She does have one theoretical hobby-horse which she is always ready to mount – the idea that dance should break loose from music.

'To say that the art of movement is not independent still makes me horrified. I find that dance is itself a complete means of communication, just the passing from one movement to another. Of course it can use music and a story and scenery and so on – but just as music doesn't always need to have singers and an orchestra and a stage, so it should be able to stand on its own feet, and it can.'

She purses her lips determinedly, in a way her pupils used to dread – she had a caustic tongue in her time, but you feel that she has decided to let the nice things take over. She has always been a great 'admirer' and now she is sadly dismissive of what she doesn't like rather than fiercely denunciatory. At the drop of a hat she falls into plaintive panegyrics over her current company (her rose-tinted view of her own performers is legendary) or an evening at the opera house; she has managed to remain a fan all her life, retaining an awe-inspired capital-letter vision of Art, Artists and even Life.

Twice I try to say goodbye, but each time she detains me with a last reminiscence. 'I can see now that most of the poetry I recall is romantic, but I love Dante too,' she protests as I struggle to leave down the narrow hall. She begins to chant:

*Francesca, I tuoi martiri a lagrimar mi fanno tristo e pio.*
*Ma dimmi: al tempo de' dolci sospiri. . . .*

'Isn't that beautiful? And what about Sappho? "Where is the breath of Poseidon, cool from the sea floor?" Marvellous!'

Outside she sniffs the damp air, watching somebody's children stumping home across the street. 'Isn't it wonderful to be a grandmother?' she declaims to the sky. As she shuts the door I think I hear the lilt of French alexandrines. Whatever did Racine write about kids?

19.2.78

*She has been a fighter all her life, a female David up in arms against the big battalions. Her weapons have been energy, faith in her cause and her colleagues, a shrewd charm and a reasonable dash of guile: her opponents were vulgarity and insensitivity, commercialism, phoniness and waste . . . The witty, wiry, emotional little insomniac who has squeezed so much out of so many is as firm as ever in her beliefs and ideals – the kind of rock on which tradition is built.*

185

## *Mayerling*, The Royal Ballet, Covent Garden

Drugs and sex, murder and suicide, royalty and revolvers, love, politics and the steamy depths of the Vienna woods – the only question about the *Mayerling* story seemed to be whether it would be too strong meat for ballet audiences. Nervous audiences can relax. In his new production at Covent Garden, Kenneth MacMillan has deliberately pitched the horror-story in a low key, easing the highlights by a wealth of additive detail and marginal action. This is a bio-ballet, the dance equivalent of the historical novel. It traces the decline and fall of Prince Rudolf and of Austria-Hungary. He inherited an unstable temperament from his mother's family and his brief career turned into a debacle, combining elements of both Hamlet and Romeo – restless and lonely at court, he ended his unhappy days in a death-pact with a teenage girl.

MacMillan has sternly rejected the option of turning the sad events – they do not quite add up to a tragedy – into a sob-story. He has aimed at setting the individual pressures within the tangled knot of sexual intrigue and political plots which made up the Austrian court in the 1880s. His Rudolf carries the seeds of his destruction in himself; his accomplice, Mary Vetsera, seems merely the instrument of escape, broken in the act of suicide.

It is a tale of doom and hysteria set in the claustrophobia of a Central European palace. This is where its dramatic difficulties lie. To extend the character development convincingly (and to fill out a three-act ballet) means a long run-up to the final climax. We start with a ballroom scene introducing the characters and proceed through a lengthy succession of short episodes – there are eleven scenes, a prologue and an epilogue, not counting those fill-in moments when characters pass or pose in front of the curtain during scene-changes.

MacMillan has clearly enjoyed these twists and turns, each skilfully designed to explore some new corner of the situation. But they are uncomfortably confusing (a close reading of the programme notes is essential) and they often decoy the interest away from the main theme. A hunting episode and a long scene introducing a song could disappear without the least effect on the story and the sub-plot of a Hungarian separatist conspiracy, represented by an odd little quartet of nimble-footed hussars, never gets off the ground. The short and often unconnected scenes seem more appropriate to television or the cinema than to a three-hour ballet, which needs a clear, driving theme to keep the dramatic pulse beating.

The structure recalls his *Manon*. He has kept his big emotions until the last two *pas de deux*; in the middle is a brothel scene, and there is much playing of cards, passing of notes and general standing about. Georgiadis has used an identical russet and gold palette for his ingenious designs and array of superb costumes. The assorted Liszt score is romantic, though sometimes in a too relaxing way.

This is essentially a domestic drama – after the ballroom waltzing there are virtually no ensembles, apart from an inevitable Dance of the Prostitutes. The nub of the choreography lies in the series of *pas de deux*. These follow one another in amazing profusion, inventive and eloquent – always with Rudolf (David Wall) as the male component. The female roles are almost embarrassingly numerous. Lynn Seymour and Merle Park looked ravishing and danced wonderfully as the heroine and her sexy patroness, Countess Larisch; Wendy Ellis was a prettily naïve bride; and Georgina Parkinson managed to look imperial and passionate even when suspended upside down.

But the evening revolved round Rudolf, and Wall rose to the occasion splendidly. In the first acts he is not helped by the choreography to suggest neurosis, and his buttoned-up uniform and beard restrict and conceal his expressiveness; but at the end, when he rejects – rather surprisingly – whiskers and all, he plunges into hysteria with total conviction.

Friday's Rudolf had nothing to lose by comparison. Wayne Eagling's sharp style lent a brilliant edginess to the dancing and his frail physique and sensitive acting gave pathos to his nervous collapse. Lesley Collier was a heedless, headstrong Mary, and Jennifer Penney a seductive Prostitute. Graham Fletcher's Coachman was outstanding on both nights.

This is a handsome achievement, taking its place alongside the choreographer's *Anastasia* and *Manon* and carrying his exploration of the narrative ballet one stage further: it is a brave and often skilful attempt to use the form as a straight, serious psychological drama. Yet it leaves lingering doubts. As a theatrical experience it is a good deal less intense than the material suggests; the agonies seem swamped by the sheer length and richness of the production. Has the genre itself become, like the orchestral symphony, a cumbersome survivor from a more leisurely age, or is it that MacMillan has not got the formula quite right? There are enough incidental pleasures in *Mayerling* to make it an enjoyable subject for diagnosis.

19.2.78

## Interview with Yuri Grigorovitch of The Bolshoi

Sitting on a stool in the lighting-box beside the vast empty stage of the Paris Opéra, Yuri Grigorovitch, the director of the Bolshoi Ballet of the USSR in Moscow, looked like a middle-aged imp. He is fifty; small, slight, tense and quick, with an ascetic medieval face, bright eyes, a thin, sensitive mouth and an overgrown crew-cut, which makes his hair flare up briskly like a terrier's coat after a bath. He is as unlike the stereotype Russian as you could imagine. In his neat grey jacket and flannel trousers you might take him for a professor at the Sorbonne – witty and civilised, but a terror to the students.

He was in Paris last week to mount a ballet for the Opéra's dance company. 'Not the first one,' he explained. 'I put on my *Ivan the Terrible* here last year – but that had been originally created in Moscow. This one is quite new, the first I have ever arranged away from home.' Home to Grigorovitch now means Moscow, where he lives with his wife Natalia Bessmertnova, a top Bolshoi ballerina. Like many of the Bolshoi Ballet's notables, he came originally from Leningrad and its Kirov Ballet: he was appointed director of the Bolshoi in 1964.

'I knew I wanted to be a choreographer when I was only nineteen,' he said. He was twenty-nine before he got his first chance to try his hand; he had a big success the very next year with a new version of an existing three-acter, *The Stone Flower*. He was a capable but not outstanding dancer and he decided to make choreography his career.

For fourteen years he has borne the crushing double burden of company director and chief choreographer. I told him that his predecessor, Leonid Lavrovsky, had said to me one evening during an interval at Covent Garden that to direct the Bolshoi you need 'the strength of a bull and the courage of a lion.' Grigorovitch grinned sadly. 'It's true. Administration takes up so much time when one would like to be thinking about a new ballet.'

His strength is certainly not bull-like, as Lavrovsky's was, but his wiry physical stamina has impressed the French dancers and his courage shows in the ballet he has chosen for Paris – *Romeo and Juliet* to the well-known Prokofiev score. This ballet is already the pride and joy of the Bolshoi in the version arranged by Lavrovsky (and admired in London). He has danced in it repeatedly himself – as a Jester, an attendant and many other roles – and it has been his responsibility to keep it in good trim in Moscow. What is more, there have already been two versions at the Opéra (by Lifar in 1955 and Attilio Labis in 1967), several visiting productions, and by chance the London Festival Ballet has just finished a five-week non-stop season of the Nureyev version of the ballet in the Palais des Sports.

Grigorovitch seemed positively stimulated by the challenge. 'I did find it difficult sometimes to forget the Lavrovsky version – the music kept suggesting the same movements. It is one of the cornerstones of our repertoire, a great production. But I have secretly wanted to do a version of my own ever since I first heard the score. When, after seeing *Ivan*, Rolf Liebermann, the director of the Opéra, suggested I should mount it here, I was taken aback that he had guessed my dream.'

As we talked, Grigorovitch had to keep breaking off to answer a question from one of the stage staff, from his designer Simon Virsaladze, or to greet passing dancers. The first performance was only a few hours off, and some of the Opéra dancers were practising. 'They are an excellent team,' said Grigorovitch, 'and I think the new ballet director, Violette Verdy, will make them even better. They have a good basic classical training which makes it easy for me to work with them, but of course they are French and reflect their own French culture. This led to some difficulties at first with *Ivan*, because the subject is so Russian, but this time it has been much easier.'

Would he have arranged the ballet differently if he had been working with Russian dancers? 'I doubt it.' Would it be mounted later in Moscow? 'Perhaps.' Was this a reciprocal arrangement? Would a French choreographer be invited to work with the Bolshoi? An evasive, hopeful semi-nod.

Grigorovitch's approach is evidently based on ideas formed when he was young, part of a reaction against the nineteenth-century literary ballet tradition. In the West this movement reached a climax quickly in works like Balanchine's abstract ballets. But in Russia it is still evidently working itself out in a modified form. A tendency towards simplification has already appeared in Grigorovitch's earlier works and in other Soviet versions of *Romeo*.

In this production he has applied the theory vigorously. 'I decided to condense the whole action into two one-hour acts, and to prune many of the details of the story, much of the miming. There's no question here of Verona and its ramparts, picturesque street-scenes, local colour or archaeological evocations. There's no point in ballet competing with the cinema. It has its own very effective idiom and that is suited to a semi-abstract treatment of a well-known story which today interests only by its central theme – love and hate.'

It is a perfectly valid approach, even if to our eyes it seems rather out-dated – after a long reign, abstraction is on the way out in the West in all the arts. As *Mayerling* has shown at Covent Garden, the tendency here is in exactly the opposite direction, towards more realism and narrative. Paradoxically Grigorovitch has jumped right back to an older tradition in which the characters were merely symbols – Love, Hate, Envy and so on (much like Massine in his symphonic ballets).

Shakespeare was fundamentally opposed to this idiom and virtually not a trace either of him or his play survives in this experiment. The plot proceeds via a succession of dance numbers and tableaux, framed in a carnival which becomes the setting for the whole action. There is no attempt to relate the principals to their background nor to each other. Everything is generalised and depersonalised in true classical style.

If you forget about Shakespeare, this has its point, but it raises two difficulties. Prokofiev's score was planned in great detail against the play and in spite of much cutting and cobbling, it is not enhanced by the new treatment; and the removal of psychological and narrative interest lays big demands on the actual steps. Grigorovitch has stuck close to the conventional Soviet vocabulary and this does not sustain interest over two hours. The final snag is the designing which sets revue-type fancy-dress-ball costumes against Expressionist black curtains.

Now and then there are some striking showbiz effects and Grigorovitch has got the company moving with tremendous dash and discipline. There is no demand to act, but of the two casts I saw the best all-round dancing came from Jean Guizerix as Tybalt. Bessmertnova (imported for a few performances) as Juliet, Michael Denard as Romeo and Patrick Dupond, a youngster with a jump like Evel Knievel, as Mercutio, were outstanding in an impressively strong and well-rehearsed company.

What was Grigorovitch planning next, I asked him. 'First another classic, a new *Raymonda*. Then something – well, it's not gone far enough yet to discuss.'

26.2.78

# Festival Ballet in New York and New York
# City Ballet in Saratoga Springs

'We are all dance-mad here,' New Yorkers mutter to you with a perplexed, half-apologetic smile. Certainly arriving in this city is a heady experience for a ballet-addict. Even in the doldrums of July and August, queues besiege the box-offices, while dance-studios shake to the thump of rehearsing troupes and the aspiring and perspiring students who steadily fill up the astonishingly overflowing tank of young American dance-talent. But Britishers need not feel unduly mortified at this moment, for the prestigious Metropolitan Opera House has been playing host to the London Festival Ballet. Sold out weeks before the opening (largely due, it must be said, to the appearance of the magic name Nureyev at the top of the posters), the event turned out to be something of a double triumph – a personal one for the star and a corporate one for the company, whose long-delayed visit to what is now unmistakably the dance-capital of the world has proved well timed and shrewdly planned.

To break into this ornate citadel – the vast theatre is flamboyantly festive in scarlet and gold – and capture an audience accustomed to the world's top companies requires a powerful thrust, and Nureyev's *Romeo and Juliet* proved exactly the right choice, an outsize combination of dance, drama and spectacle which broke down resistance like a sumptuous battering-ram. Ezio Frigerio's settings filled the cavernous stage and Nureyev's device of counter-pointing groups in separated pools of lighting, which can become confusing in smaller surroundings, looked splendidly impressive. And the zest of the performers, led on the first night by Nureyev and Patricia Ruanne, kept the temperature fizzing to the end of what was hailed as 'a major ballet by a major choreographer.'

The other programmes have been almost as successful. Mary Skeaping's production of *Giselle* (danced at its premiere here by Nureyev and Evdokimova) was acclaimed by the critics, who were also favourable to the varied charms of the third programme. This included Ronald Hynd's Wildean *Sanguine Fan* and three new roles for Nureyev – in the 1849 Danish charmer *Conservatoire* and in two old Nijinsky ballets *Le Spectre de la Rose* and *Schéhérazade*.

A New York success for Nureyev is nothing new (though *Romeo* was his first venture here as choreographer), but the breakthrough for

191

the Festival Ballet was a milestone. With tributes like 'a world–class ballet company' and 'a troupe loaded with talent on every level', these 'leaping Londoners' can return home with justifiable satisfaction.

To sample the home product necessitated (or offered an excuse for) a trip to the country. Every summer the New York City Ballet mounts a season in Saratoga Springs, a health resort four hours north of New York in the Catskill Mountains. Almost exactly the equivalent of Cheltenham, the little country town was once a fashionable spa (the waters are still bottled), became famous for its racing and gambling, then faded into gentility. It still has its races, but the new prosperity of the town – an enchanting old Main Street lined with Edwardian hotels set among lavish, white clapboard fantasy-mansions in gloriously incongruous styles ranging from Robert Adam to Charles Addams – stems partly from its Arts Festival. The contrast between Manhattan and these shady avenues is startling.

The Arts Centre is sited in the grounds of the old Pump Room and revolves round a vast, modern, semi-open air theatre of a rather unlovely metal austerity. In front of the 5,000-strong audience, mostly seated but partly spread out on sloping lawns, the New York City Ballet nightly displays its dazzling talents. The atmosphere is inevitably rather circusy and stresses the degree to which Balanchine, the company's founder-director-choreographer, has been influenced by American music hall traditions. Works like his modern *Stars and Stripes* are direct tributes, but even an earlier piece like his *Symphony in C* (to Bizet) suddenly reveals a Radio City flavour, which also disastrously dominates the designing and even contributes to the company's dance style. Its blend of athleticism and coyness, the substitution of glitter for radiance and glamour for grandeur, seems a legacy from the nineteenth-century theatre (and sometimes oddly reminiscent of Soviet style).

The three programmes I saw very naturally leaned towards entertainment. Curiously, the most serious offerings were by Jerome Robbins, who is sometimes regarded as the showbiz element in the choreographic team. His *Other Dances pas de deux*, rather steadily performed by Suzanne Farrell and Peter Martins, contrasted with Balanchine's *Stars and Stripes*, while his *Goldberg Variations*, a suite of courtly manœuvres to Bach, are as far removed from sizzle and pop as can be imagined.

This is the day of the male dancer and public applause was reserved almost exclusively for the men's variations – and not without reason. It is the male half of the company which has made the most progress

192

since I last saw it. Fast, springy, virile and musical, they exemplify the style which Balanchine prefers: a battalion of harlequins who dart and skip and soar like swallows. Their number has recently been swelled by Mikhail Baryshnikov, formerly of American Ballet Theatre, who made a single fleeting appearance during my visit (he had earlier appeared in the full-length *Coppelia*, in Robbins' *Faune* and in *Stars and Stripes*).

He took on the old Villella part in the 'Rubies' movement in Balanchine's *Jewels* and showed at once what a mark he will make on the company. It was not so much his virtuosity which impressed; the previous night Robert Weiss had jumped and spun almost as high and fast in the same role. What stood out was that Baryshnikov invested the dancing with a strong personality and a theatrical characterisation.

This interpretative, strong-personality approach, very different from that of the average NYCB dancer, could change the whole direction of the company. Its amazingly sharp-honed uniformity was illustrated by the way another Europe-trained dancer, Peter Martins, stood apart by his legato phrasing and floor-conscious elegance. The noblest of partners, his generous *ports de bras* were a joy to watch, especially among the inexpressive arms and flickery hands which are the weakest weapons in the NYCB's formidable armoury.

Patrica McBride was Baryshnikov's ideal partner – small, warm and vital – and Suzanne Farrell was dancing as beautifully as ever. The array of slimline beauties revealed when the curtain first rose against the Saratoga skyline was a sight for tired British eyes. American girls not only dance amazingly, they look terrific.

30.7.78

## Wuppertal Dance Theatre at the Edinburgh Festival

Even in his wildest moments (if such there be) Peter Diamand would not, I think, claim to have made dance an important element of his reign over the Edinburgh Festivals. A larynx man to the last, his final contribution to ballet lovers was three performances by a single company. Fortunately, the choice of troupe and programme proved both original and rewarding. The Wuppertal Dance Theatre has never appeared in this country before and one of its items was arrestingly successful – none other than an interpretation of Stravinsky's 'Le

193

Sacre du Printemps,' which, for the first time in my experience, came near to the heart of that Everest among ballet scores on whose towering flanks so many choreographers have come to grief.

The company is the creation of thirty-eight-year-old Pina Bausch. Born in Germany and trained partly at the Jooss-orientated school at Essen and partly at the Juilliard School in New York, she was appointed Ballet Director at the Wuppertal Opera House in 1973 and promptly reformed the company to her own taste. It is a modern-dance troupe, but with a style clearly stemming less from the Graham tradition than from Central European roots.

Miss Bausch has apparently created a number of works (I would love to see her *Seven Deadly Sins*), but on this occasion presented only one programme, a triptych of ballets to Stravinsky scores with the overall label 'Spring Offering'. The device seemed a bit strained, as the three works were widely different both musically and choreographically and the link between them, if any, was subliminal. They made more sense as contrasts than as companions.

The opening was done to Stravinsky's 1951 'Cantata,' a tightly organised setting of piercingly lyrical traditional English poems, which he has squeezed into a disciplined format. To this low-toned accompaniment Bausch has arranged a succession of simple, expressive dances built round a girl (Jo-Janne Endicott, very Lynn Seymourish), her husband (?) and her dream-man – they writhe and yearn between frustrating layers of gauze, against a background of companions who seem to act as a Greek chorus.

This was followed by a mime-sketch, a satirical impression of an elderly bourgeois couple's conflicting memories of their early courtship (an echo here, perhaps, of the real-versus-ideal theme of the first ballet). Done to some slight, witty miniatures, the piece holds up through its odd mixture of realism and fantasy. Agreeable but expendable.

In the last item, *Sacre*, we moved into another world. This was a major statement, unexpected and yet long-awaited. The titanic scale of the music and its massive emotional thrust have proved an obstacle to those trying to match it by stage movement. Miss Bausch has come up with a surprising solution. Proceeding in exactly the opposite direction to Glen Tetley, whose beefcake version was presented here last year by American Ballet Theatre, she has concentrated on the female participants. This is more natural – after all, the Sacrifice is a girl – and, by skating over the original themes of the various sections as most post-Nijinsky choreographers have done, the mounting

194

tension is powerfully conveyed. We watch a huddle of frightened and yet excited girls worked up to hysterical anticipation and orgiastic frenzy as one of them is finally chosen as ritual victim and then publicly, in front of the whole tribe, dances herself to death.

The notion of giving the main action to the girls, who start as trembling adolescents and turn into thrashing maenads, is marvellously dramatic. In this ritual the men are merely a collective male presence, with the Priest a guilt-ridden and unwilling delegate. It is the girls, in scanty shifts from which breasts fling loose as the tempo mounts, who dominate, pounding, jerking and sweating as they lose control. Spring is about birth and birth is the business of women; we seem to be watching a fatal parturition rather than a fertility rite.

The final stroke of inspiration is to set the whole action not on a normal hard, echoing wooden stage, but on a thick depth of peat. For once the driving pulse of the music is matched by the dull stamp of bare feet on earth or the dreadful thump of bodies flung, not artfully dropped, against the ground. By the end of the ceremony soil is streaked over the dancers' faces and caked on to their skins. It has taken a woman to restore barbarity to this most basic of celebrations. Let us hope we can one day see it done to a full orchestra and not, as here, to a tape.

3.9.78

# Richard Alston and Dancers at the Riverside Studios

It is easy to bemoan the scarcity of choreographers working interestingly in the classical style, but the situation is not much better in the world of modern dance. Considering the vast number of young dancers having a go in this idiom, very few have made an impact; there are plenty who can be labelled 'promising' or 'talented', but where is the personal British signature which is as instantly recognisable as that of Americans like Cunningham, Taylor, Tetley, Murray Louis, Cohan or Twyla Tharp?

One of our few local exceptions has been Richard Alston, whose little group appeared last week at the Riverside Studios. An acknowledged pupil of Cunningham, he displayed early on a style which looked like developing into something really individual. But recently his pieces have begun to look rather repetitive; the movements have become foreseeable, the range narrow.

195

His six dancers last week were good – stronger and better rehearsed than on his last appearance. *Double-work*, a silent ballet for the whole troupe, seemed different from then, perhaps because better done, and a new piece, *Windhover* – based distantly on courting birds and accompanied by sounds suggestive of babbling water and reed buntings – made a striking duet strikingly danced by Siobhan Davies and Ian Spink. A solo 'blues' number by Alston himself seemed a bit limp, but the final dance, an almost traditional ensemble to a cheerfully kitschy piece by Satie (*Jack-in-the-box*) made an acceptable finale. Still not a strongly individual evening, but the promise and intelligence endure.

8.4.79

## *Coppélia*, Sadler's Wells Royal Ballet, Sadler's Wells

If by a 'classic' you mean a work which can be seen with undiminished interest over and over again (I cannot think of a better definition), then *Coppélia* just misses that category. Few people could fail to succumb to its charms on a first viewing. But the lack of any serious undertones (such as Tchaikovsky gave to the equally beguiling *Nutcracker*) leaves its surface attractions cruelly exposed to the ravages of repetition. For the critic who must watch it again and again it is in constant danger of disappearing with a gurgle down the kitsch-in-synch drainpipe. But of its unpretentious kind it is perhaps the best, needing only the laundering effect of a fresh production to bring up its colourful appeal. Peter Wright's new version, which opened the Sadler's Wells Royal Ballet's season at its home theatre last week, nearly brings this off.

The first act succeeds, in fact, entirely. The designer, Peter Snow, has clearly and cleverly gone to Balkan naïve painting for inspiration, and the cornfield, big sky and doll's house architecture have just the right windblown poetry, while the costumes look both convincing and eye-soothing. Wright has introduced enough rethought detail into the action to keep it alive. The principals, Marion Tait and David Ashmole, danced with splendid precision and style. John Auld and David Bintley made a couple of racy oldsters (as Dr Coppelius and the Burgomaster) to set off the youth of the *corps de ballet*.

The 'doll' act was slightly less successful – though it had some nice new notions about puppetry – mainly because Marion Tait's interpretation, which had leaned in the first act more on termagant vitality than on innocent charm, here became almost unsympathetic. Her bad

196

behaviour had too sharp an edge for comfort. And the last act – a Waterloo in which I have seen many losers and no conquerors – once again failed to provide the properly triumphant happy ending. The costume designs came garishly unstuck; the new choreography was pleasant but unremarkable; and the principals, though they did the famous *pas de deux* very featly, did not come up with the extra lyrical allure on her part and the virtuosity on his to set the scene on fire.

But the company is in good form and it needs little to make this a very acceptable production. Tait could aim at a softer 1870-ish sense of mischief; Ashmole, who has developed a good personality and a sexy plasticity in his small movements, could afford to take more risks in his big ones; and pink satin could be banished from the wardrobe.

The second programme introduced a new short ballet by David Bintley, which proved again that he is a young man with talent as a choreographer, and so with promise, even if his achievement is still small. He is certainly ambitious. Only a madman, a genius or a terminal optimist would think of trying to marry Goya ('particularly his Black paintings') with the chirpy and sophisticated tunefulness of Darius Milhaud. In the event, *Meadow of Proverbs* is best seen as a lively set of snapshot numbers in twentyish style adroitly mirroring the Parisian-Spanish flavour of the score. The tone is nearer to the nightclub than to the nightmare, but carried off with a nicely varied invention which does not stretch the dancers, led again by Marion Tait, too far. It has an odd look of photographs of early de Valois ballets.

It was followed by a loving revival of Andrée Howard's elusive *La Fête Etrange*, with Margaret Barbieri as the remote and beautiful heroine. This is an oddly resilient work whose frail appeal survives apparently tougher ballets. Like *Les Sylphides*, it presents a dream world which needs the most delicate handling. Barbieri caught the mood well, but David Morse lacked the innocent dignity of the Country Boy and Desmond Kelly was, for once, a cipher as the Bridegroom. The snowflake gentleness of Fauré's melodies is a test for any dancer.

29.4.79

197

# Nureyev's Tribute to Diaghilev, Coliseum

Nureyev paid his own tribute to Diaghilev last week at the Coliseum by dancing in no less than three of his most famous and formidable ballets – formidable because they were all created by the legendary Nijinsky. The salute was almost more to the dancer than to the director.

By opening the programme with a dazzingly clear, bold bit of Bournonville in *Conservatoire* and juxtaposing this with the three Diaghilev ballets – *Schéhérazade* (1910); *Spectre de la Rose* (1911) and *L'Après-midi d'un faune* (1912) – it became obvious that an essential ingredient in Nijinksy was a vein of exoticism; dancers who lack this streak are simply debarred from any hope of evoking the feel of his performances.

It was in the blood of the period, emerging most openly in *Schéhérazade*. The part of the Slave in that familiar work turned out to be the least interesting of Nureyev's interpretations. He looked stunning in the costume, leaped and whirled with brio and caressed the beautiful Manola Asensio (very good) with lascivious panache. But the two-dimensional, over-naïf role gives little scope for a personal contribution.

In the other two ballets the intangible bond between Nureyev and his great forebear (perhaps due to their Tartar strain) emerged strikingly. The most electrifying example was in Fokine's *Spectre*. This is the most elusive of all the Nijinsky roles and for years I have believed that the little ballet was dead – a pale, pretty specimen pressed between the leaves of history. Suddenly it came alive again, no longer a pastel reproduction, but a vibrant theatrical experience.

How was the miracle achieved? First by the bold stroke of jettisoning the pink rose-petal rug and baby-cap which Bakst devised as a costume. Its disappearance has the added advantage of removing the museum overtones of the ballet. Secondly, by a new and positive approach to the dancing. The heavy arms curve like petals, the long, strong neck bends and stretches in ecstasy; again and again familiar poses flash before the eye like stills from a film; but they flow from a full-blown, generous movement which has the juice of oil paint. Nureyev has grasped that the essence of the role is not so much in graceful airborne lightness as in a quality which Nijinsky must have had in abundance, what wine experts call 'body'. Only four dancers I have seen have possessed this essential gift: Eglevsky (whom I saw in the role), Babilée and Soloviev (neither of whom, alas, ever danced it), and now Nureyev. The mysterious night-bloom which he conjures up is no faint poetic fantasy but one of those darkly crimson roses, 'blood drops from the burning heart of June', which evoke passion rather than sentiment. Suddenly it became believable that those who saw Nijinsky in this slight and usually trivial ballet remembered it for ever.

Nureyev's impact in Nijinsky's own *L'Après-midi d'un faune* – a far more interesting work than *Spectre* – was more predictable. The part seems custom-built for him and he has several added advantages. In the first place the work was given in the original and very beautiful Bakst setting (from Nureyev's season with the Joffrey Ballet) and the correct costume – tail, covered torso and all. This is the first time it has been seen here since Nijinsky danced the role himself. Nureyev was joined by Margot Fonteyn as Chief Nymph, who brought to the part her special gift of innocence and freshness. It was not only the spell cast by the sight of the famous pair together again which laid a hush on the audience. When it goes right this is a work of hypnotic power; and on this occasion the sense of authoritative command of the chief role was unmistakable.

24.6.79

*Diaghilev had the luck to be born into a period when a drastic change was coming over the art world, and he had the flair to appreciate the new ideas and the courage to exploit them. . . . He made novelty not only smart but culturally de rigueur and in so doing influenced the whole social-cultural pattern of our times.*

## Dance Theatre of Harlem at Sadler's Wells

It is just over ten years since the Dance Theatre of Harlem was born in New York, the brain-child of a black dancer, Arthur Mitchell. Its immediate aim – quickly and brilliantly expanded to cover a wide range of activities – was, roughly, to offer a classical opening to other black dancers, thus rescuing them from the jazz routines to which they were usually confined. With support from Balanchine and Robbins, the company was soon on its feet and in 1974 it scored a big success at Sadler's Wells. It returned in 1976 and now it has been back there again. As before, its performances raised a fascinating variety of questions – none of them yet conclusively answered.

About its vitality and theatrical impact there are no doubts. But the share in its popularity of show-biz appeal and artistic achievement is questionable, and the basis on which the whole enterprise rests still feels insecure. The sense of adventurous experiment gives excitement to the performances and freshness to the dancing. But its corollary is a bumpy unevenness about the programmes and some rough edges among the performers. The carefree exuberance which animates the dancing so delightfully is a rare quality; but it has the alarming radiance of a morning dew which, when it vanishes, may reveal awkward features if they are not smoothed out in time.

The notion that all art is the same at heart – a doctrine preached in at least two of the big production numbers which mingle ethnic and classical dance – is a seductive fallacy. Art is a language and can absorb a few foreign expressions with advantage; but a mixture produces only a dialect. To quote an apposite example, when Picasso at one time drew on African motifs it was only to exploit them in the severe classicism of Cubism: when later artists tried to combine alien idioms with Cubism, the results were second-rate. The same dangers attend the blending of two ways of moving. This was intriguingly illustrated by this company's *Agon*, one of the treats of its last visit. The marriage of musicality and wit in these artists fits the ballet like a glove and their amazing loose, easy movements give it an arresting, flip, New Yorkerish bite. But this time Balanchine's wry allusions to revue-style gestures seemed to be returning dangerously near to their origins, while the classical dancing lacked the sharpness of correctitude.

We know that black dancers can acquire a pure classic style – there are examples in several companies; but in this troupe few look as though they could ever fit into, say, *La Bayadère* comfortably. Turn-out (and turns) for the men and proper placing for the girls' feet would need a lot of attention. These are great dancers, but not great classical dancers; the problem is to find exactly the right idiom in which to exploit their talent. At the moment they are always warm and exciting. In their African-based numbers they are unbeatable. As an extension, Balanchine choreography looks like the best solution so far, particularly his late style with its strong American flavour. But the (vastly attractive) ghost of cabaret is not yet exorcised. The first programme I saw was unconvincing: the highlights were some sensational jumps by the otherwise technically not very strong Ronald Perry in *Le Corsaire*. The second programme was lit up by two Balanchine works, *Allegro Brillante* which showed off the well-drilled *corps de ballet*, and *Agon*, in which Lydia Abarca shook her diamond earrings and danced to ravishing effect. Mel Tomlinson is an inspired comedian.

19.8.79

## *La Sylphide*, Festival Ballet, Festival Hall

August Bournonville shares with Diaghilev (who probably hardly knew his name) the commemorative honours this year. Born in 1805, the Danish dancer-choreographer died exactly 100 years ago. Two of his full-length ballets were presented in London last week – an event which would have seemed impossible a generation ago, when his work was known only to specialists.

The most popular of his ballets is *La Sylphide*, which entered the repertoire of the Festival Ballet at the Royal Festival Hall on Wednesday. It is, as it happens, not typical of Bournonville's wholesome and uncomplicated approach to his art; he borrowed the quintessentially Romantic subject from Paris, where it had been launched in 1832. Bournonville's 1836 version is, paradoxically, more famous (because better preserved) than the original, which starred the famous Marie Taglioni. The first British production was mounted by the Ballet Rambert in 1960. The Scottish Ballet presented a version (to be seen in London this week) in 1973. Both were produced by Danes. Now another Dane, Peter Schaufuss, has arranged his own version for the Festival Ballet – and very enjoyable it is.

There is a basic difficulty about *La Sylphide*. Its naïveté is such that it is impossible to approach it without a faint condescension. It cannot compete with *Giselle*, written nine years later, as a serious piece of theatre, and to maintain the right balance of loving respect for its fragile charm is a delicate operation. Schaufuss has got it just right. He has slightly enlarged it in every way. David Walker's delightful Scottish sets have moved the story up the social scale into the baronial, not to say Balmoralian, belt, bagpipers and all. Missing parts of the – admittedly undistinguished – score have been restored

201

and new dances devised to fill them. In particular the role of the hero, dominant when Bournonville danced it himself, but truncated later to fit nineteenth-century ballerina-mania, has been expanded, with a fine new solo and some psychological subtleties.

Evdokimova is ideally equipped for the Taglioni role of the Sylph, with a fey allure mysteriously linked to an electrifying jump, which gives the effect that she is dancing on an invisible trampoline. If she could only manage the melting and wilting as perfectly as the flitting and floating she would be unbeatable. James, the hero, was Schaufuss himself – and who else? Understandably, after his exertions as producer, he was not on tip-top form on the opening night (his beats were a bit blurry), but his quick travelling jumps were a joy and his clean, not over-romantic style was exactly in the Bournonville vein. The Witch was superbly mimed by Niels Björn Larsen from Copenhagen; Nicholas Johnson was an unusually dapper Gurn; and the whole company showed how it can respond to the right coaching.

26.8.79

# Fernando Bujones in Scottish Ballet's *La Sylphide*, Sadler's Wells

This is, without doubt, the day of the male dancer. Star-gazers train their telescopes less on the ballerinas than on the ballerinos, as they used to be called, watching out avidly for the birth of a new luminary.

For some time the more knowing ones have been talking of a young New Yorker who can already challenge the brightest talent around. His name is Fernando Bujones, and on Thursday London will have a chance to make its own assessment of him when he dances the hero of the Scottish Ballet's production of *La Sylphide* at Sadler's Wells. It will not be his first appearance here. He was one of American Ballet Theatre's team at the Coliseum in 1977; but the company was putting all its money on Baryshnikov that season and Bujones hardly appeared. Last summer he flashed briefly across the stage of the Festival Hall in a *pas de deux* in the Gala Ballet Season; audiences gasped, but it was a mere instant exposure. This time he will be interpreting a full-length role – one with which he is familiar and in which he scored a decided success with the Scottish company in Edinburgh last year.

Bujones, though well known in America, is still a dark horse here.

He has somehow grown up in a shadow. The shadow is easy to identify: its name is Baryshnikov. By ill luck the Russian's jump to the West coincided with the triumphant return of the nineteen-year-old Bujones to New York after winning the coveted Gold Medal at the international ballet competition at Varna. Ever since, he has danced under the handicap of being a home-grown boy competing with Slav glamour.

Bujones is American – and hardly even that. His name (pronounced 'Boo-ho-ness'), and his features, reveal that, though born in Miami, Florida, both his parents were Cuban. He spent his childhood in Cuba and received his first dance training there; and his style is as Latin as his origins. His dancing has a flashing rapier-like speed and sharpness rather than a Russian drive, with a very un-British, almost childlike openness sometimes verging on exhibitionism. His American career began when he was spotted soon after he returned to Miami from Cuba at the age of ten – a leggy boy who was originally intended to be a pianist. He won a scholarship with the School of American Ballet and eventually moved to New York to study there. His very first perform-ance of a dance from *La Sylphide* took place under the eagle eye of Stanley Williams, the Danish head teacher at the School. Bujones was sixteen. Curiously, when he graduated, he did not opt to join the New York City Ballet, the company to which the School is linked. Instead he chose American Ballet Theatre, preferring its European repertory; already he had his eye on being a Prince. He became a soloist at nineteen and has remained with the company ever since, only recently embarking on the international guest circuit. He is married to the daughter of the ex-President of Brazil.

Now twenty-four, he still sometimes betrays a lack of maturity in his work. But his youth gives him an edge over his rivals. The still ubiquitously dominating Nureyev is, dancewise, of a different gener-ation already; our own Anthony Dowell is twelve years older than Bujones, Martins nine, Baryshnikov seven and Schaufuss six.

Technically Bujones is already second to none. There is probably no trick-step which he cannot perform as well as any living dancer, with the addition of a very individual high, quick, deer-like jump. Style is a different matter. Here he has both advantages and handicaps. He is slight and long-legged, with a correct and elegant classical line ending in feet as sensitive as a ballerina's, a physique which puts him into the same rare category as Dowell. Ideal though this build is for many parts, it lacks the tough muscularity for heroic and epic roles; and, even as a conventional balletic lover, Bujones will probably have to work out his own Latin-style approach. The acting side of his profession seems to come less naturally to him than the dancing; but, with the aid of the choreographer Antony Tudor, an early admirer, and experience in the big classics, it is evidently developing.

If the style and stage personality of Bujones is individual, so is his image. Abandoning the customary self-deprecating approach, he has fought his rivals by an assumed Manhattan cockiness which has earned him the reputation of the Mohamed Ali of the ballet. There are strong traces of the arrogant, aggressive posture of the flamenco dancer both in his features and his public stance. It creeps only mildly into his private character, which is quiet and friendly, but businesslike.

26.8.79


## New York City Ballet at Covent Garden

With the possible exception of the Kirov, no dance company in the world can be more sure of a warm welcome from London than the New York City Ballet. Now thirty-one years old, this already legendary organisation has such a clear-cut character that we feel we know it well. In fact it has visited London only twice in the last twenty-seven years. It has the simultaneous charms of recognisability and unfamiliarity. Already its distinctive features have emerged sharply. Any general conclusions about them must wait until the full repertoire has unfolded. For the moment it can only be said that the first two programmes revealed reassuringly that the grip of its founder-director, George Balanchine, is as firm as ever – in fact even a shade more noticeable. The flavour is as sure and sharp as a Manhattan-made vodkatini.

The opening ballet was perfectly chosen – a choreographic marriage between American and classical traditions. *Square Dance* transforms the convention of country dancing into courtly formality to music by Corelli and Vivaldi. As for any community activity, the essential requirements are unanimity of style and expert execution. These were marvellously in evidence, with Merrill Ashley, unobtrusively partnered by Sean Lavery, performing wonders of technique perfectly controlled by style.

Almost since the company's inception Jerome Robbins has contributed to it some strongly contrasted pieces. *Other Dances* is a short, semi-ethnic work to Chopin piano mazurkas and waltzes, originally composed for Makarova and Baryshnikov and danced by them here with American Ballet Theatre two years ago. It is a delightful little piece – not remotely Balanchinian – and Baryshnikov repeated his delightfully intelligent interpretation of it; light, quick and playful but always fluid and musical. This time his partner was Patricia McBride – good to watch but adding little to the give-and-take.

This was followed by the most interesting piece so far, an abstract arrangement by Balanchine to the 'Stravinsky Violin Concerto' marred only by some painfully unbecoming costumes for the ballerinas. It is slightly in the style of his *Agon* – bracing and brisk, original, sharply accented, difficult and altogether absorbing. At its centre are two duets – the first danced by Karin von Aroldingen with a force which rather overshadowed her partner, Bart Cook, the second a more tender affair in which the tall, cool Peter Martins sets off the warmth and liquidity of Kay Mazzo. The swift, clean, athletic style of the company showed at its best in this work.

For a finale we had an old favourite, *Symphony in C*. This is a display piece in which Balanchine's mastery of geometrical intricacies rivals that of Petipa. Bizet's felicities are matched by the exhilarating flow of invention. The three allegro duets were splendidly dynamic; Suzanne Farrell was serenely glamorous in the adagio; and the corps (after a slightly shaky start) filled the stage in true Maryinsky style.

If Balanchine had been the hero of the first programme, Robbins was the winner in the second. His *Dances at a Gathering* (first cousin to *Other Dances*) can stand up to any competition; what was fascinating was to see how this company's interpretation differed from that of the Royal Ballet. The contrast was exactly the opposite of what might be expected from an American troupe. In this work the New York City Ballet is more royal than the Royal, changing the casual countryfied style into a series of distinguished, almost refined variations.

They were superbly danced, with an unrivalled pace and sureness but – apart from Baryshnikov, who performed with the spring and expressive vitality we have learned to expect from him, and a dark little charmer, Judith Fugate – little character. The touches of comedy and lyricism were almost lost. But who could complain when treated to the glorious dancing of Ashley, McBride, Martins and the outstanding young Lavery. Different maybe – but refreshing and equally enjoyable.

Neither of Balanchine's two pieces in this programme showed him at his best. *Kammermusik No 2*, to an abrasive score by Hindemith, was strangely muddled, with some very unflattering movements, uncertainly done, for the ballerinas and awkwardly contrived work for the corps. *Vienna Waltzes* is only for those excessively addicted to three-four time – forty minutes of swirling couples to Strauss (Johann and Richard) and Lehar, all gowns and gloves and gallant hussars. A trite conception carried out with an expertise worthy of better things. *Liebeslieder Walzer* is much to be preferred.

9.9.79

# New York City Ballet at Covent Garden

In its second week at Covent Garden the New York City Ballet continued to set out a banquet of new ballets – some lollipops, some snacks, and some rare, rich concentrations of pure nourishment. It was impossible to sample the whole menu but, in the programmes I saw, the touch of master-cookery was missing in only one ballet (*Mother Goose*) and the dance-ingredients were always of the finest quality. The stickiest lollipop I came across was a little Tchaikovsky *pas de deux* called *Meditation* (surprisingly by Balanchine), and the largest and most sugary was Robbins's *Four Seasons*.

A show-piece for the technical brilliance of the company, *Four Seasons* is arranged to the oom-pah Verdi score familiar here in the versions of MacMillan and Prokovsky. Its pastiche flavour is so subtle that now and then Robbins's tongue seems in danger of slipping out of his cheek altogether; the style varies from pure clown-ing (the opening and Baryshnikov's brilliant Autumn cha-cha acro-batics) to serious lyrical episodes like the Spring and Summer duets, exquisitely danced by Kyra Nichols with Daniel Duell and Stephanie Saland with Bart Cook. The fragile humour really needs a more sophisticated acting style than that to which the company is accus-tomed: the period sense was better sustained when Peter Martins took over the Autumn variation and translated it into perfect Vic-torian-hero classicism. He is an astonishingly versatile dancer, who needs only to develop his acting to the same pitch to hit the roof.

The snacks have been varied and tasty. One of the spiciest was Martins's duet *Calcium Light Night*, a set of epigrammatic solos ending with a duet for the beautifully matched Heather Watts and

Daniel Duell, to music by Charles Ives. This had been preceded by Robbins's lively and at times moving arrangement of Ravel's jazzy Piano Concerto in G Major and was followed by a fine piece of 'chamber dance' by Balanchine, in which Kay Mazzo and Martins explored a mutual relationship to, with and around Stravinsky's fascinating 'Duo Concertant' for violin and piano.

*Sonatine* is virtually a companion piece, another small-scale work with the pianist sitting on stage (playing Ravel's work of that name) while Patricia McBride and Baryshnikov quietly explore the shifting moods of the music. Probably more effective in a smaller theatre, it is consistently interesting and offered Baryshnikov a chance to show his more serious artistry.

But the core of the programmes consisted of ballets like Balanchine's *Four Temperaments* – an early work now in the Royal Ballet repertoire and danced here with a transparent technique which becomes a kind of eloquence, especially by Bart Cook in the Melancholic solo and Merrill Ashley and Daniel Duell in the Sanguinic *pas de deux* – and his *Le Tombeau de Couperin*, a marvellous tapestry of formation dancing, in which two 'quadrille groups' weave and interlace with infinite variety to the bewitching Ravel score. It was finely done and the simple practice costumes here seemed just right, though a slight differentiation between the two teams would greatly help us to follow the patterns.

Another substantial offering was *Jewels*, three totally contrasted ballets united only by their title (and their tasteless costumes). The lyrical 'Emeralds' (to Fauré) did not work too well, due to miscast ballerinas – neither Ashley nor von Aroldingen could muster the necessary gentle poetry – and a general company style which is too energetic for this kind of melting charm. But 'Rubies' (to Stravinsky's 'Capriccio') bubbled with vitality, a salute to burlesque-show glitter crowned by McBride, Wilhelmina Frankfurt with Baryshnikov in puckish Twyla Tharp mood. 'Diamonds' (to parts of Tchaikovsky's Third Symphony) is a straight salute to the choreographers of *The Nutcracker, Swan Lake* and *The Sleeping Beauty*, danced with glittering ease by the whole company, led majestically by Suzanne Farrell and Martins.

16.9.79

# Interview with George Balanchine

In the middle of the smash-hit season of the New York City Ballet, which ended last night, I found myself sitting in the canteen at Covent Garden opposite its founder-director, George Balanchine.

Most celebrities look, when you meet them, smaller or larger than you expect, but Balanchine characteristically fits precisely into his own image. As you might guess from his ballets, he is neat and dapper, with delicate jeweller's hands, alert blue eyes and a gentle Russian accent. At seventy-five, he remains nervous and quick-thinking, with a suggestion of perching, rather than sitting, on his chair. Levitation, you feel, would come easily to him.

It would not surprise his dancers, to whom he ranks only just short of godhead. Not that he himself is at all mystically inclined. He has always maintained that he is just a craftsman. 'As you writers use words,' he explained, 'I use steps and movements. I just start anywhere, according to which dancers are available – sometimes that means doing the finale first. Of course you must have an idea where you're going, maybe a visual idea like clouds or the sea. But waiting for inspiration gets you nowhere.'

I asked him how he felt the season, his first in London for fourteen years, had been going. 'Wonderful. London has changed. When I first came here with Diaghilev, and even when I brought my company from New York in the fifties and sixties, everybody was very smart. I bought a suit from Hawes and Curtis. Now the audience doesn't have to dress up. That makes a difference. They're more open.'

Balanchine nearly settled in London in 1933. After the death of Diaghilev, C. B. Cochran invited him here to work in revues and musicals. According to legend, he would be with us still had the Home Office not refused, in spite of pleas from Maynard Keynes, to grant him a work permit. 'It probably would have been a mistake,' Balanchine has admitted. 'In England you have to be dignified; if you are awake it is already vulgar.' Though technically fastidious, he certainly lacks the regulator of good taste, which is one of Britain's hallmarks. He once choreographed a polka for elephants, asking Stravinsky for a score (and getting it) and he revels in the vitality of chorus-line dancers.

I asked him if the reaction to his ballets here had been different from that in New York. 'Not much. At first the dancers were surprised that there was no applause in the middle of a ballet. I like that. There is more respect for the music. When I began as a boy in the Maryinsky Theatre most of the clapping came from the upper circles, the rest were all officials in gloves. Maybe a few fans cheering from the gallery; we called them "psychopaths".'

He seemed to think that London audiences were rather expert and select. 'Remember that we are here only for three weeks. In New York we have fourteen-week seasons, with eight performances a week. At Covent Garden there is always the problem of sharing with opera.'

I mentioned that this time people had been remarking particularly on the men in his company. 'It's true that at first we had only two male stars – Villella and d'Amboise. A ballet-master must look after the women. The men, with their jumps and their turns and their muscles, they will always look all right. But the women must be presented. Ballet is still about women, but now we have men too.'

Thinking of the foreigners who have worked with him, particularly men, I asked if he had ever been under pressure to make it an all-American company. 'Not a bit. Never. And now our Americans go out and dance in other countries. It is the dancing which counts, not the nationality.'

Following a thought which had often struck me, that Balanchine's *Apollo* was the archetype of Art Deco, perhaps its only masterpiece, I tried out on him a quotation from a book on that period: 'The qualities which distinguish the years around 1930 are precision, luminosity, transparency, immediacy, sensitivity to material, logic and freedom from sentiment and dogma.'

Did he think that described his own approach? Balanchine shook his head. 'I was already formed by then. My first influences were in the twenties and they were German. German cabaret performers, German films with stars like Conrad Veidt – you know, elegant and decadent.'

He left the canteen briskly – for the stage, not for his hotel, as he rarely misses a performance, where he sits watchfully in the wings – leaving me to collect my thoughts about the impact of the season. It has certainly been the most stimulating one for a long time, illustrating a powerfully different approach to ballet from that of our own companies: the lavish, scatter-gun programmes, ranging from the arcane to revue-type romps; the deliberate disregard for whole areas of ballet, particularly the narrative element in which we specialise, as well as Diaghilev's multi-media doctrine; above all the style of the dancing with its stress on speed and clarity at the expense of softness and expressive lyricism.

The company's quality is summed up by its general director, Lincoln Kirstein: 'The New York City dancers epitomise in their quirky legginess, linear accentuation and athleticism a consciously thrown-away, improvisational style which can be read as populist, vulgar, heartless, over-acrobatic, unmannerly or insolent.'

Of course it *could* be accused of that, but the company and repertoire is now so large that there are many individual exceptions to these attributes and in any case the style is designed for a special purpose, the finest execution of a special kind of ballet.

In spite of Balanchine's protestations, his artistic talents do seem firmly rooted in the cool, hard-edged, late-Bauhaus world of around 1930; it is a tragedy that they were never married to the New York school of painting, with which they have such obvious affinities. Unluckily, his art-mentor Kirstein is unsympathetic to abstract art and Balanchine is hardly interested in painting at all.

His work is rooted in music and his name is rightly linked with that of Stravinsky. He could in fact be equally well compared to the French architect Le Corbusier, who defined a house as 'a machine for living'. In the same way Balanchine has created a company which is 'a machine for dancing' (some people would extend the metaphor to his actual dancers). It is a marvellous instrument, whose artefacts are unique, memorable and important.

For the record, the company's last week produced some of the season's best works. Robbins revived his irresistible *Interplay* of 1952 and gave us his new *Opus 19* to Prokofiev's first Violin Concerto, designed as a vehicle for Baryshnikov's dazzlingly mercurial talent with McBride dashingly holding her own. *Union Jack* held too few surprises for us Britishers, but the all-Stravinsky evening was pure joy, introducing three new Balanchine wonders – *Symphony in Three Movements, Monumentum pro Gesualdo* and *Movements for Piano and Orchestra* – with stars like Farrell, Martins and Lavery in top form, some more eye-catching dancers like Sheryl Ware, Bart Cook and Victor Castelli, and orchestral performances which deserve bouquets for the conductor, Robert Irving, and clinch Balanchine's reputation for musicality. A genius? I wouldn't say No.

23.9.79

# Nureyev's *Manfred* for the Ballet de l'Opéra, Paris

How odd that Byron, the epitome of romanticism, has featured so little in our ballet programmes! It took the French and Russians to translate into dance his poem 'The Corsair'; and now it is Nureyev, abetted by Tchaikovsky, who has brought to life for the Paris Opéra company, at the Palais des Sports, another of Byron's poems, 'Manfred'. It was an early work (1817), written during the poet's first exile and it reflects only half of his nature. The wit and irony which lightened his later work are missing. Here we get only the dark side, the reflection of the sense of guilt which was to haunt him all his life. It was this feeling, arising from his relations with his half-sister and with a chorister from Cambridge, which found an answering echo in the homosexual Tchaikovsky and which reverberates through the composer's powerful Manfred Symphony.

Proceeding from the premise that the poem was inspired by Byron's own forbidden loves, Nureyev has woven the poet's life into the poem, which tells of a doomed hero searching for absolution. It is a ballet about torture – the pangs of a conscience twisted ever tighter on the rack. This head-on encounter with the romantic agony is depicted with the violent, restless brush of a Delacroix.

Tchaikovsky's score is so strong that it controls the whole work. His 'programme' was drastically simple – guilt constantly erupting and finally overwhelming everything in an orgasmic climax. Nureyev has fleshed out this theme with real events and characters.

First he sets the tone with Byron/Manfred's youthful dissipations, his over-intimate relationship with his sister, the death of his horrified mother, his brief days of comfort with the consumptive choirboy and his banishment from society. Next we find him in the Alps, happy with Shelley and his friends but haunted by memories. There follows his affair with an Italian contessa, an idyll punctuated by restless dreams of adventure and destroyed by the death of Shelley. Finally we see his disastrous plunge into the squabbles of the Greek patriots who leave him alone and dying.

The symphonic construction of the music – very different from an episodic ballet score – has doubtless dictated the form of the ballet, which takes short recurring themes and knits them together until in the last scene they mingle in a final cataclysm. The growing army of dead, ruined or abandoned loves builds up into a pack which 'slowly hunts him down.

The blend of live characters and ghosts and the often simultaneous visions of reality and illusion make a complex fantasy which must be swallowed whole rather than dissected. The hour-long choreography runs in a single torrent from start to finish, rushing, leaping and spiraling without a single moment of mime. Even the gentle passages give the feel of slow eddies in a gigantic whirlpool. The dreaded ghosts drag like an undercurrent, and the lovers often seem to be rocking on a deep swell. Appropriately, the final apocalypse (rather conventional and poorly executed) shows an all-extinguishing flood.

Inevitably the focus of the whole piece is the Poet. It is a role of truly heroic proportions, with the most striking choreography in the ballet, which starts with a neurotic solo that hints at physical and moral lameness, goes through the whole gamut of romantic *pas de deux* and ends with a desperate but still fighting solo which somehow recalls the sacrificial dance in *Le Sacre du Printemps*.

Dancing it for the first time after a serious injury, Nureyev gave a passionate and perfectly balanced performance which proceeded naturally from *angst* to anguish; but in the big numbers he did not extinguish memories of Jean Guizerix, who has rightly been enjoying a big success in the part. In a strong cast from the Opéra company, Dominique Khalfouni was a delectable Contessa, Florence Clerc a seductive Sister and Jean-Pierre Franchetti the powerful king of the underworld.

There are some rough – but no thin – patches in the ballet. The ever-swirling choreography tends to be too consistently fluid (the music in the mountain scene suggests sparkle rather than ripple) and there are moments of confusion and difficult identification. Some of these could have been avoided by the designers, Radu and Miruna Boruzescu, who have devised an unhelpful rocky setting and costumes which lend a curious 1820s flavour to a work which is actually full of originality and individuality.

23.12.79

# The Eighties

# Fonteyn at sixty

Ballerinas are proverbially long lived; but this generally used to involve years of shadowy retirement. What is new in our own times is a dramatic extension of the active career of a dancer. This has vastly enlarged the influence of an individual star.

Martha Graham, who was over seventy when she retired from dancing, is an obvious example; Alicia Alonso, who will be appearing with her Cuban company at Edinburgh in August aged fifty-eight, is another. But perhaps the most remarkable of all is Margot Fonteyn, whose sixtieth birthday is to be celebrated at Covent Garden on Tuesday. She is not only a legend; she is a permanent ingredient in the character of our national ballet.

This character is rightly held to express a general truth about the British. The admired qualities of the Royal Ballet are those we like (rightly or wrongly) to associate with ourselves. It is unshowy, perfectionist, stylish, lyrical, dependable and firmly grounded. Much of this is due to its founder, Ninette de Valois, and her choreographer associates. But it is becoming increasingly clear that Fonteyn has also left a permanent imprint on the company. Consciously or unconsciously there is hardly a dancer – or indeed a choreographer or teacher – in the company who does not bear the traces of her extraordinary career.

This legacy is pleasantly paradoxical, for she is herself far from a typical Britisher. True, she was born in Reigate, the daughter of a British engineer called Hookham. But her mother is half-Brazilian (her stage name is an adaptation of her maternal family name, Fontes), much of her youth was spent in the Far East, and her early training was mainly from Russian teachers – first in Shanghai and then in Chelsea.

Her looks – jet black hair and huge, dark eyes in a pale oval face – are as foreign as her temperament, which is sharp-edged, quick-witted and decisive, with a Latin liveliness. She does not take kindly to the English climate, likes foreigners, and has never felt completely at home in Britain (she has a flat in London but her home these days is in Panama with her Panamanian husband).

But – and it is a massive reservation – the atmosphere she absorbed, first in her home, then in her long years as a teenage ballerina under the watchful eyes of de Valois and Frederick Ashton at Sadler Wells, visibly coloured her basically volatile and receptive temperament, giving it an almost exaggeratedly British veneer. She emerged cool, unflappable, clear-headed, self-controlled, inclined to deflect a crisis with a joke and to poke fun at emotional pretentiousness.

She carries the always severe self-discipline of a dancer to an unusual extreme; she does not smoke, eats carefully, hardly drinks (not even water) and watches her bedtime. Her only addiction is to travel; she becomes restless quickly and finds relaxation even in a night-flight, from which she will emerge crisp, cheerful and game for a hard day's work or a party.

She rides her world acclaim as easily as she seemed to have won it. Superficially her climb to the pinnacle of her profession appears to have been uncannily simple. The head of a small company in her teens, she rose up as it prospered, unassailable and virtually unassailed. Few dancers can have received such uniformly favourable reviews all their lives (though, oddly, she has an exceptional aversion to critics). Her success looks as effortless as her dancing; but like her dancing it hides courageous efforts.

Though she was born with most of the attributes of a ballerina, she was never a virtuoso and perhaps her greatest feat is to have resisted all temptations to compete in this field and to have built instead on her other assets. The result has been the artist whom all the world admires – quiet, gentle, consistent, musical, inviting attention rather than compelling it, with a distinction which comes from acute attention to phrasing, line, expressive detail and simple elegance.

This approach – born of Fonteyn's particular artistic make-up – was developed and exploited by Ashton in a long series of ballets and came to set the tone for the whole company. When we watch Fonteyn dance with the Royal Ballet we have the feeling that she has no particular individual manner, that her style is the perfect norm from which all others are deviations. It's an illusion, of course, as can be seen when she performs with other companies. What has happened is that the Fonteyn style – or, to be accurate, the Fonteyn-Ashton-de Valois style – has become the hallmark of the Royal Ballet.

This effect has been achieved over a very long period (Fonteyn became the company's top ballerina in 1935) and with exceptional diligence and determination. A clear sense of direction and total commitment towards achieving it lies behind Fonteyn's apparent carefree charm. The deceptively smooth upward curve of her career

216

has in fact had to surmount formidable obstacles: competition, patches of bad form and personal tragedy.

A change came over her relationship with the Royal Ballet when she married a Panamanian diplomat in 1955; she seemed less closely tied to Covent Garden and there were those who thought she was considering retirement. Then, in 1962, the arrival of a new partner from Russia, Nureyev, began a new phase in her career during which the head of a British company was to change imperceptibly into an international star with no particular base.

The shooting affair in 1964 which left her husband paralysed would have stopped any normal performer in her tracks. But she has carried on as usual without for one second neglecting her role as devoted wife. Disclaiming any attribution of unique gifts or special exertion, she implies that she has always just kept doing her best with an awareness of her own problems and advantages, a cork bobbing along on the tide of ballet history.

13.5.80

*After [Fonteyn's] first full-length* Swan Lake, *this paper wrote of her: 'The little pork-pie coronet of the Swan Queen sparkled on her brow as if by right.' To-day, forty years later, she no longer wears the crown: she is the crown.*

## Nureyev's production of *Don Quixote* for the Zurich Ballet

A comparatively unfamiliar visitor is a rarity, and the Zurich Ballet company, which Nureyev introduced into his Festival last week, started out with a welcome which turned out to be well deserved.

Its opening programme was a new production of his *Don Quixote*, the old 1869 Petipa ballet which Nureyev mounted (and filmed) a few years ago with the Australian company. What has preserved this, out of dozens of probably not dissimilar Petipa ballets, is presumably the fame of Cervantes' story, the excellence of some of the solos and *pas de deux*, and the humble, hummable vitality of the Minkus music. Its bright, brisk jollity is, however, a bit much for modern ears. In his cavalier style Petipa pushed the semi-philosophical fable of the Doleful Knight well into the corner to make way for a series of colourful numbers with a plot centred round two young lovers. The result was an extrovert entertainment, which only those with strong Costa Brava sympathies can swallow.

For the Australian production, strikingly designed by Barry Kay, Nureyev retained an overall high-key brilliance, but introduced a moonlit love duet beneath the sails of the windmill. The much-needed addition of a touch of romanticism and seriousness is carried further in the new production, designed this time by Georgiadis. By a daring stroke which succeeds completely, he sets the whole scene in the time of Goya. Without any specific references we become aware of the dark side of Spain lurking behind the merrymaking. With some inspired use of shadowy lighting (the backlit presentation of the famous fandango is stunning), rich and dusky costumes and stormy skies, the whole action acquires a weight and depth which makes the well-known highlights stand out all the more vividly.

The new slant makes slightly different demands on the dancers. The heroine, Kitri, needs not only the blend of stylishness and virtuosity in which Petipa specialised, but a sense of solid characterisation. Of the three ballerinas who have danced the role here, Evdokimova filled out the role most convincingly; with the advantage of a mop of unruly curls she looked like Carmen's first cousin, with the jump of a fire-cracker and, in the set-piece episodes, the elegant line of an El Greco. By contrast, the diminutive Yoko Morishita danced the role with delicious classical clarity and an impeccable control, but she missed the hoydenish streak which gives life to the part. Elise Flagg, the third Kitri, seemed too engrossed in the dancing to bother much about the character.

All three were partnered by Nureyev, to whom the central role of the mischievous Basilio is a gift. It demands above all a sustained outpouring of physical and temperamental energy; as he slips like an eel in and out of the crowds, clowning and teasing, emerging now and then to fire off a salvo of fast, twisting virtuosities, Nureyev conveys, as in few other ballets, the sheer joy of dancing – a zest which turns dramatically in the last Act into a display of *haute école* style.

The Swiss company swung with spirit through his succession of swirling Spanish numbers, with Stephanie Herman, Alain Debrus and Floris Alexander especially noticeable. As might be expected from a Balanchine-based company, the classical Vision Scene showed it at its best; the weakness of the troupe is in its character work. The small but vital mime roles need far stronger definition to make their mark. Exactly where the Petipa choreography ends and Nureyev's

218

inventions begin only a necromancer could discover; between them they have clearly had a lot of fun.

29.6.80

# New York City Ballet, Festival d'Automne, Paris

This year's Festival d'Automne in Paris is saluting Igor Stravinsky, so what other company could launch the International Dance Festival, which forms part of it, than the New York City Ballet?

The company opened the season at the Champs-Elysées theatre (newly taken over by the administration of the Paris Opéra) with a characteristic all-Stravinsky, all-Balanchine evening; but the programme I caught a few nights later was more mixed.

Its core was *Agon*, which had been part of the intended repertoire for the company's recent London visit, but which was eventually jettisoned. It was pure joy to catch up with it. If any single ballet announces Balanchine's claim to the title of genius, *Agon* is it. His instinctive accord with Stravinsky's musical thought, his bold but unforced movement-invention carrying the classical idiom into new territories without losing its basic disciplines, the dance-style which he has imposed on his company, even his ideas on costume and design – all Balanchine's best qualities converge here.

It is a work which has lent itself to several interpretations by different companies, but this is the true original; serious but not solemn, deadpan but not cold, snappy but not jerky, swift, smooth, deft, as perfectly articulated as a Swiss watch. The dancers were by no means automatons nor even very similar. The girls ranged from the coolly voluptuous Suzanne Farrell to the majestic Karin von Aroldingen and the strikingly named Wilhelmina Frankfurt with her bird-like elegance.

The men are equally varied. Peter Martins is a golden giant who moves like a sword; Daniel Duell brings the eloquence of simplicity; Victor Castelli is quick, lithe and accurate as a cat. The severe black and white costumes (which look as 'designed' as the most complicated confections) strike exactly the right note. At both the performances I saw the ballet seemed an indisputable masterpiece.

*Agon* was created in 1957 and looks like new. Jerome Robbins's *The Cage*, which also featured in the programme, is six years older and looks its age. Awkwardly arranged to Stravinsky's Concerto Grosso in D for Strings, it is a melodramatic version of the theme so delicately handled by Gautier and Perrot over 100 years earlier in *Giselle* – the Freudian myth of Woman as man-devourer.

In spite of the title, the females presented here are insects – in fact they used to prowl and clutch beneath a vast spider's web. This seems to have disappeared, but the sinuous, sharp-taloned choreography remains. The heroine is an apprentice whom we see, under the guidance of her Queen, making her first sexual victory and killing.

In its day it was a bit of a shocker-thriller. But it spawned so many successors that today it looks cliché-ridden. Béjart must surely have seen some of those angular, predatory crouching postures, while rapier-slim ladies finishing off their male victims with one stab of their ballet-shoes feature in every second French revue number. Absurdity was kept at bay only by an extraordinary performance by Heather Watts as the necrophiliac novice: she turned herself into a yard and a half of alluring venom.

The two other ballets, presumably planned to lighten the programme, both suffered from the danger attending many such works; they left an uncomfortable doubt as to how much of the comedy was intended. Is the high-kicking, pelvis-thrusting choreography of Balanchine's *Capriccio* (or 'Rubies') meant to be a send-up, of his own style or not? Do Karinska's costumes deliberately imitate circus vulgarity? Are we intended to smile at the ruthless roguishness or – uncomfortable thought – is the cuteness meant to charm? Anyway it was brilliantly danced, particularly by Patricia MacBride and Wilhelmina Frankfurt (as in London) and, at another performance, by Balanchine's latest Danish recruit, Ib Anderson, whose lyrical joyfulness was refreshing among so much athletic high spirits.

The final work was Robbins's *The Four Seasons* to Verdi. This too had been stripped of its setting, which made the pastiche joke almost invisible. This left much of the action (and Santo Loquasto's costumes) dangerously exposed. But once again the dancing conquered all resistance. Heather Watts and Victor Castelli were crisp and clear in Winter; Kyra Nichols and Ib Anderson brought the house down in the charmingly Ashtonian Spring; Stephanie Saland was orientally seductive in Summer and Peter Martins (robbed of his usual partner, Farrell, by injury) a noble Autumn. Not quite a Stravinskian programme, nor an all-Balanchine one; but very much and very agreeably the real face of the New York City Ballet.

21.9.80

# Twenty-first anniversary performance of
## *La Fille Mal Gardée* at Covent Garden

This is without doubt the year of anniversaries. One of the nicest and most genuine was the twenty-first birthday performance on Wednesday of Ashton's *La Fille Mal Gardée*. The evening had all the warmth and gaiety of a real family party, with just the right touch of nostalgia. At the end Ashton himself led on to the stage some of the principals in the original performance: not David Blair, alas (he died in 1976), but Nadia Nerina, Alexander Grant, Stanley Holden and – still in their old roles – John Lanchbery from the orchestra pit and, in his farmer's smock, the irreplaceable Leslie Edwards. A snapshot to be treasured.

The whole ballet is a celebration of happiness, perfectly translated into creative felicity. The only cloud that arises is the charming summer-storm which drives the lovers into each other's arms. Amazingly, this persistent felicity, far from leading to monotony, gives a lift to every passage; even the doltish Alain seems delighted with his own antics. This is surely because it is rooted in human emotions, in personal experience.

Ashton has described it as his tribute to nature, a 'poor man's Pastoral Symphony'. 'There exists in my imagination a life in the country of eternally late spring, a leafy pastorale of perpetual sunshine and the humming of bees – the suspended stillness of a Constable landscape of my beloved Suffolk, luminous and calm.' The scene may ostensibly be eighteenth century France, but every Englishman will recognise the rural dream which floats at the back of our native genius.

The ballet is a perfect blend of what Samuel Butler saw as nature's own mixture of Luck and Cunning – luck in the spontaneous birth of stroke after stroke of invention, cunning in the adaptation of stage devices which Ashton had glimpsed or read of elsewhere. The list of sources quoted in David Vaughan's monograph on Ashton is fascinating. Yet the ballet emerges as personal and fresh as a bunch of country flowers.

1.2.81

221

# Anna Pavlova

Anna Pavlova, who was born 100 years ago last week-end, is an awkward maverick in the ballet star-parade.

She flourished at one of the most exciting moments in dance history, when Diaghilev was breathing new life into a faded art; yet she took virtually no part in the renaissance and, indeed, opposed it. Pitching herself single-handed against the vast, genius-impelled, millionaire-fuelled bandwagon of the Ballets Russes, she not only survived – she throve. She ruled out all chances of approval by right-minded progressive critics. To admire her art was difficult; yet not to admire her performances was impossible. How does the dilemma look today?

She will perhaps always remain an enigma. Even her origins are obscure. Her St Petersburg parents were ostensibly a simple soldier and his laundress wife. But her father may well have been a rich Jew (the name of Poliakoff has been put forward); her dark, exotically aristocratic features certainly suggest it. As a student at the Maryinsky School she was exceptional; at a time when her friends were trying to emulate the current technically brilliant Italian ballerinas, she was casting her sights back to the romantic Taglioni. Delicacy, lightness and speed were her ideals. *Giselle* seemed cut out for her and she had a big success when she danced it for the first time at the age of twenty-two.

She was soon given all the big classical roles – *The Sleeping Beauty, Swan Lake, La Bayadère, Paquita, La Fille Mal Gardée* (in the Petipa version) and the Snow Queen in *The Nutcracker*. Petipa was a huge admirer (which vouches for her classical technique), and her mysteriously dramatic and lyrical qualities appealed strongly to her young partner, Mikhail Fokine, who in 1907 composed two dances for her: the *Dying Swan* solo, which was to remain a lifelong personal success, and a *pas de deux* to a Chopin waltz which was to become the core of *Les Sylphildes* – the ballet which, above all others, most conveys her peculiar quality.

Inevitably, when Fokine joined Diaghilev's breakaway company in Paris, Pavlova was its first ballerina. Inevitably, too, she did not stay with it long. She quickly realised that she was going to play second fiddle to Diaghilev's favourite, Nijinsky, and, ostensibly after turning down the lead in *The Firebird*, she left. Unlike today, there were few, if any, alternative options. She took up a tempting commercial offer to set up a troupe of her own.

She was right to do so. There would have been no place for her in the later developments of the Ballets Russes, and her temperament, conventional, egocentric and dominating, would never have harmonised with Diaghilev's. What is open to doubt is whether she might not have been happier if she had returned to Russia, which was to remain – as can be seen in Soviet ballet even today – sympathetic to her approach. In the event her move gave her the chance to develop to the full her personal style and to make her fullest contribution to the history of ballet. We cannot regret it.

What was that contribution? It was based, consciously or unconsciously, on a clear choice. Diaghilev saw the future of ballet as a multi-media art, in which dance, music and design would be equal partners. Pavlova put dance first and last. What she offered was dance carried (in her own person) to its limit as an expressive medium. A very respectable team – she had some top-class Russian soloists and a *corps de ballet* probably not much inferior to Diaghilev's in his later years – acted as back-up. Scenery was kept to a minimum, for reasons both of cost and easy transportation, but she employed good designers for her costumes, including Bakst, Bilibin, Soudeikin, Korovin, Anisfeld and Georges Barbier.

This was exactly the recipe adopted later by Balanchine. But in two vital ways he was to have the edge over her. He had a first-rate choreographer (himself) and he used first-rate music, whereas Pavlova relied more and more on the third-rate Ivan Clustine, who – encouraged by her commercially minded manager/companion (possibly husband) Victor Dandré – turned out sugary trifles and potted classics. And she used trivial scores. For her the dance was so dominant that music was unimportant; she even talked of dancing without it.

The result was that, by the end of her career, Pavlova had restricted herself to a diet of trifles. Many of these were probably adapted or rehashed versions of variations lifted from the classics of her youth; the rest were numbers designed to display her specialities without unduly taxing her waning technique (she was touching fifty when she died in full career).

But any idea that she served up a diet of trash is nonsense. In a new, fascinating illustrated record of her repertoire (*Pavlova*, by John and Roberta Lazzarini) more than 190 roles and divertissements are listed, including 45 by Petipa and 20 by Fokine. In 1916 she mounted and danced in a short version of *Sleeping Beauty* (designed by Bakst) in New York for twelve weeks, while at Covent Garden, as late as 1925, she was offering *Giselle*, one-act versions of *Coppélia* and *The Nutcracker* and a two-act *Don Quixote*.

Today such productions would be acclaimed as 'classics' (what would we not give to see her in the once-derided *La Bayadère?*). But meanwhile smart audiences were flocking to the Coliseum to see the Ballets Russes in *Les Biches* and *Le Tricorne*. Pavlova was out of fashion. She was carrying the torch for tradition – and for dance.

We can see now that in her way she was a non-conformist just as much as Diaghilev (she had joined in a dancers' strike at the Maryinsky) and just as much a pioneer. If Diaghilev had invented the roving company, it was Pavlova who carried ballet out of his basically élitist circuit and made it what it is today, an international art. The record of her non-stop tours and performances is almost unbelievable; the dynamo which carried her round the world without once considering relaxing her standards must have fired her every performance, producing that mixture of gaiety and sadness, fire, elegance, speed and wispy soulfulness which bowled over everyone who saw her.

In her uncontrollable rage to express herself through dancing she hacked out a path down which others have followed. Without subsidies or snobbish backers, with no organisation, no State support, no base, not even a regular partner, she reminded us that in art a single personality can contribute as much as a team – and often more. We need the big battalions to carry on the history of dance; but in the long run it is individuals who make it worth reading. Pavlova was one of these, a passionate outsider who made the grade.

8.2.81

*[Pavlova] was concerned only with The Dance. Nor was she interested in good taste or originality; they would only cloud the clear stream of inspiration which poured through her. It is most unlikely, in fact, were she performing today, that she would be drawing anything from the Arts Council. A sobering thought.*

# Isadora Duncan

Writing recently about Pavlova, I remarked how curious it was that her simple and conventional art had triumphantly survived all the thrilling innovations of Diaghilev.

More curious still, a near contemporary of hers, born 6,000 miles away and fiercely opposed to her doctrines, acted out the same simplistic role in a more extreme form and also passed into the history of dance – Isadora Duncan. The lesson – and Isadora, with her puritan Californian background, was a great one for lessons – is clear. No degree of expertise can compete with the force which stems from furious personal commitment.

Isadora's beliefs were muddled and her life was a mess but somewhere inside her was an instinct fixed on a single target as inexorably as the needle of a magnet. It gave her the push to get started, the courage to go on and the wild momentum which spun off more and more into silliness and excess. Without doubt it also fuelled the confidence and drive which mesmerised her audiences – a child-like conviction that she was 'special', completely satisfactory as she was, outside grown-up rules and conventions and not in need of any extra help or training. Her strength was as the strength of ten because her art was, in its way, pure.

She seems to have been endowed with a sense of mission from birth. Born in San Francisco in 1877 (four years before Pavlova), she was brought up in a tight family atmosphere. Her father had disappeared, after trouble with the police, and her mother – a lady of artistic bent – supported the four children by giving piano lessons. This led to dancing, first in the home and then in other people's homes. These blissful childish scamperings and posings, to the strains of Mendelssohn played by her mother, were to become the foundation of Isadora's whole career.

She never really grew up either artistically or emotionally; her loves were adolescent crushes, her ideals remained those of high-minded Victorian tracts filled with references to Art and Life and the Soul, her performances were ecstatic schoolroom improvisations writ large. But – and it is a big but – she managed to develop and exploit the innocence which gives child-art both its charm and its importance; she retained, through thick and thin, the free flow

225

between feeling and action, which for most people becomes clogged by experience or mental conditioning. 'Movement is lyrical and emotional expression,' she wrote. Her dancing began and ended there.

What raised Isadora to the stature of a star was vitality, dedication, a radiant personality and a streak of rebelliousness in her character which turned her into a natural revolutionary. Her life and her art were a continuing protest against authority. Discipline – even self-discipline – was a dirty word for her. A brief session at a local ballet-school produced only a deep antipathy to the formal rigours of classical ballet; a spell with a pantomime troupe in New York disgusted her with its silliness.

She persisted with her simple barefoot solos. 'This sort of thing is no good for a theatre; it's more for a church,' an impresario advised her mother shrewdly; and in fact this liberation of dance from the artifices of the theatre – a gesture widely repeated by many modern-dance exponents today – was to be as influential as her more widely publicised bare legs and revealing costumes.

Isadora never did dance in a church; she started in the salons of rich hostesses in New York, then London and Paris. She danced in studios and lecture halls, among ancient ruins, on the street, in many bedrooms: she would dance to anybody who would look. But she turned each venue into a kind of pagan shrine. And she did end up in some of the grandest theatres in the world.

'I saw her dancing in the biggest theatre and on the biggest stage in New York – a figure dancing all alone on this immense stage,' wrote the painter Jack Yeats in 1908 to his poet brother in Ireland, 'and once again you felt the charm of the self-contained woman.' She had no need of colleagues or costumes or the tricks of the theatre. Like an overgrown Alice, she carried her Wonderland within her, and revealed it ecstatically to her audiences.

This total devotion to self-expression was, of course, an extreme example of the Romantic Revolution and was linked to the current back-to-nature fashion, which led to such manifestations as vegetarianism and the garden-city. Isadora was not the first amateur to charm the super-sophisticated (one thinks of Emma Hamilton posturing in Regency salons) and even in the dance world she was not unique; while she was aping ancient Greece in costume and life-style (she and her brother Raymond astonished the guests by parading in the Hotel d'Angleterre in Athens in chiton and sandals), her compatriot Ruth St Denis was cavorting in Egyptian robes in New Jersey. But her doctrine was perfectly timed, indeed necessary. Conventions were stifling society, and ballet, particularly in America, had reached an all-time nadir of commercial sterility. A liberal revolution was in the air.

Like a pink-cheeked prophetess, Isadora Duncan strode through Europe in her sandals and home-made robe, preaching freedom and practising simplicity (with a dash of champagne afterwards). Believing that her art came from within, she worked hard at the development of her own personality, visiting museums, reading poetry and philosophy ('I would sit far into the night in my white tunic, with a glass of milk beside me, poring over the pages of Kant's *Critique of Pure Reason*').

She seems never to have indulged in any practice or exercises, but relied on her inner strength: 'Before I go on the stage I must put a motor in my soul' was how she phrased it. But she evidently possessed a genuine feeling for harmonious and expressive movement and a musicality which was equal to the high-quality scores on which she insisted – in itself a vitally important innovation. Whatever her physical limitations as a performer, the fact remains that she not only impressed a whole gamut of experienced viewers, from Stanislavsky to Diaghilev and Fokine, but that she actually influenced them.

It seems evident that her personality, performing integrity, theatrical instinct and physical style fused to produce that vital result – the power to convince. After one of her recitals in 1904 (she was then twenty-seven) Craig wrote: 'What is it she is saying? No one would ever be able to report truly . . . yet no one present had a moment's doubt. Only this can we say – that she was telling to the air the very things we longed to hear, and until she came we had never dreamed we should hear; and now we heard them.'

With such a personal approach Isadora's work and her private life became inextricably entangled. Famous throughout Europe and America, her sensational loves and tragedies were front-page news. A series of lovers ranged from casual pick-ups to celebrities – Gordon Craig, the sewing-machine millionaire Paris Singer, the young curly-haired Russian poet Essenin, idol of her middle age whom she actually married. She saw him as the reincarnation of the little boy she lost, together with his tiny sister, when a car plunged into the Seine (the boy's father was Singer, the girl's was Craig).

'There are some sorrows that kill,' she wrote later, and her private life was irreparably shattered by this cruel blow. Her maternal instinct was stronger even than her sexual drive (pathetically, she dreamed of running a vast school, started one, and even performed with a little band of youngsters all imitating herself) and after this

227

loss, and the instant death of another baby, by an unidentified father, born a year later, she kept going through drink and sheer guts as her body and her finances fell apart.

Obstinately she clung to that vision glimpsed as she performed childish pirouettes in San Francisco. Like the painter Henri Rousseau, Isadora turned her naïvety into an art-form. Like him, she was inimitable, an inspiration rather than a founder. Like him, she left no pupil, no child; her heir was her own legend. When (again like Pavlova) she died at fifty – accidentally strangled by her scarf caught in the wheel of a car – it was born and it lives on still in bands of earnest improvisers dedicated to the Spirit of the Dance.

26.4.81

## *Isadora*, The Royal Ballet, Covent Garden

Nobody could accuse Kenneth MacMillan of lack of courage. He has already contrived two full-length ballets recounting real-life histories, both set in the first quarter of this century and now, in his new *Isadora*, launched at Covent Garden last week, he offers us a third.

As heroine he has chosen a highly individual dancer with a style manifestly linked to her own physique – and given it to a dancer of diametrically opposite build and style. Finally, he has borrowed the lecture-demonstration technique which Duncan – with characteristic late-Victorian missionary zeal – often employed, and used it throughout the evening. An actress tells the story by reciting passages from Duncan's autobiography, while Merle Park dances it out. An old-fashioned formula remote enough to be a novelty.

Alas, courage is not always rewarded and something has gone seriously wrong this time. The introduction of spoken 'captions' seemed a fatal handicap to start with. The whole basis of Duncan's art was a kind of spiritual elevation, a mixture of rapture and blinding tragedy which she somehow maintained both in her art and in her life. But every time our spirits begin to take wing, the action stops, Mary Miller steps forward with her text (the ultra-naïve prose, touching in the original with its Californian ring, takes on arch English overtones here) and the dramatic tension sags. We are left with a series of lurid snapshots which never build up into a dramatic or narrative climax, interspersed with imitations of

228

Isadora's little solos. We see dead children, hysteria, drunkenness, and sex in many variations: yet the evening drags depressingly.

The problem of sustaining the note of high Duncan lyricism and melodrama throughout a whole evening was clearly difficult, and MacMillan has tried to solve it by injecting comic relief in the form of caricatures of Duncan's surroundings. But this also proves destructive. We get off to an awkward start with some painfully corny send-ups of Empire-style ballet: a Ken Russell-ish scene where Isadora tries to seduce her accompanist under the piano and some frequent jazz-romps serve only to hold up any emotional development.

These last are very reminiscent of MacMillan's own *Elite Syncopations*; he has drawn freely on his earlier ballets, even introducing a replay of the funeral scene in *Mayerling*, umbrellas and all. One inadvertent touch of comedy is provided by a party of cavorting Eton boys at Victoria Station, which – like the St Petersburg platform – also serves as a setting for some nimbly prancing porters.

In such a long and complex ballet it is inevitable that some moments will work better – particularly at a first performance – than others; but in fact the ballet is not markedly experimental or imaginative. There are no big spectacle-numbers, no daring effects such as the last act of *Anastasia* provided, no surprises. Barry Kay has stripped the stage back to simulated brick walls, suggesting the scenes only by a few props. His costumes are the most completely successful element of the evening, though inevitably they too carry period echoes of previous MacMillan works. The determination not to indulge in lush Art Nouveau romanticism has its rewards – but this was, after all, the undulating backbone of Duncan's whole art, and the stage sometimes felt rather empty.

Richard Rodney Bennett was probably right to go for an eclectic style in his specially composed score. It works well enough as an accompaniment; but the contrast between the deliberately innocuous piano pastiches to which Isadora dances and the passages which reflect her raging emotional life is thin; her duet with young Gordon Craig calls for the full-blown rapture of Isolde.

The fact that this and other characteristic erotic-acrobatic *pas de deux* make less effect than usual may be due to inadequate musical passion. Perhaps even more use could have been made of Duncan's vivid imagination – such as her (fictional) glimpse of massacred revolutionaries in 1905; one of the best passages is a set of visions of her ex-lovers.

In a big array of characters, few have the chance to establish themselves. Julian Hosking as Craig, Derek Rencher as the millionaire Paris Singer, Ross MacGibbon, Derek Deane and Stephen Jefferies as the Russian poet Esenin do their bit as lovers, but the burden rests on Park and Mary Miller as Duncan the dancer and Duncan the talker. Park is more a Pavlova than an Isadora and the dances she has been given are not very gripping; she lacks the statuesque sense of stillness and inner power of which we read. But she acted strongly and was flung aloft with great aplomb, while Mary Miller did her revolutionary number very well.

3.5.81

## Dame Ninette de Valois, a jubilee celebration

As part of this year's Royal Ballet jubilee hullabaloo, a royal gala took place recently at Sadler's Wells. While the audience, eyes turned to the dress circle, waited for Princess Margaret to arrive, a little grey-haired lady appeared at the top of the gangway and instantly everybody rose to their feet and started clapping. She stumbled down hurriedly to her place, looking over her shoulder. 'I nearly fell. I thought the Princess must be right behind me,' she remarked afterwards. Typical de Valois reaction. For it was Dame Ninette herself whom the audience was applauding, a thought which simply had not occurred to her.

Not that she is inhumanly immune to flattery: her face still lights up like a child's at a compliment to her dress or her hair. But when a reference is made to her work as dancer, choreographer or director her expression changes. The feminine aspect of her character disappears; what emerges is totally professional, serious, knowledgeable, well-balanced and above all far-seeing with a legendary energy and indomitable courage. Meeting her, her achievements seem both natural and foreseeable. She is a supreme example of a very unusual species. Creative artists are rare enough; but creative administrators such as she can be numbered almost on one hand.

After fifty years of intense and dedicated service to ballet, her interest and indeed her practising routine is as lively as ever. She will be eighty-three next month, but her commitments and her activities are enough to tax a thirty-year-old.

A normal day might find her catching the Underground from her home on the river at Barnes to take a rehearsal at Covent Garden, where she has just mounted a revised production of *The Sleeping Beauty*; then, after a canteen lunch spent in technical discussions, off by Underground to Baron's Court for a session with the Director of the School or a meeting of the ballet benevolent fund; afterwards, a bit of shopping in Hammersmith before catching the bus home, with often a lecture or an evening at the Opera House to wind up her day.

Her husband, a retired doctor, has had to learn to amuse himself for long periods. When the company goes to America next month, de Valois will accompany it during the whole tour to attend first nights and gala occasions, lecture, appear on television and in general help it on its way as she always has done. Her official position has dwindled, but her presence persists and always will, for the company was moulded in her fashion.

This style was British, but not at all English (Ashton was to provide that element). De Valois is of Protestant Anglo-Irish stock, born in the shadow of the Wicklow hills into a Somerville-and-Ross-type family. When her father, a retired army officer, went hunting he rode in his pink coat out of the lodge of a large mansion with a walled garden, stables, servants and a nanny (later a succession of governesses) for the four children. Her blend of practicality and patriotic idealism, her officer-class leadership qualities, her homely autocracy and confident disciplinarianism seem to carry traces of this origin; while the streak of irrational – sometimes unfair – eccentricity which runs like a bright thread through her character suggests a Celtic mysticism of which she is proud; she frequently asserts that there is a temperamental link between the Irish and the Russians.

She started to take classes in 'fancy dancing' at the age of eleven after the family moved to London, and at twelve her mother launched her on her career by entering her into a school for professionals; it was her mother who, after little Edris Stannus (de Valois's real name) had served her apprenticeship touring with 'The Wonder Children', suggested the exotic stage pseudonym, harking back to a reputed family connection.

Under this name de Valois joined Diaghilev's famous Ballets Russes in 1923, and her two years with the great man formed her tastes, taught her many lessons and set firm her resolve to start a company in Britain. The story of how she achieved this – her establishment of a tiny school, her meeting with Lilian Baylis of the Old Vic and the eventual creation of a regular company in the rebuilt Sadler's Wells – is part of ballet history.

231

The first vital years called for an exceptional combination of talents: she acted not only as administrator and talent-spotter, but also as teacher, choreographer and even, at first, as a principal dancer. Of the first twenty-two ballets mounted by the company seventeen were by de Valois herself and she continued to contribute as a choreographer until 1950, her work including the legendary *Job, The Rake's Progress* and *Checkmate*. In 1963 she handed over the directorship of the company to her long-time collaborator Ashton – as rich a legacy as anybody could desire.

What is remarkable is the clarity of her aims and her far-sighted consistency in carrying them through. She set them out for all to read in a book, *Invitation to the Ballet*, published in 1937, only six years after she had set up her company. In it she analysed almost every problem faced by the organisation today. For instance, she became aware that Diaghilev's freedom to experiment (in ways of which she did not always approve) arose from the sound tradition and classical training of his dancers.

He fortified her faith in ballet as a theatre-art blending several ingredients, rather than as a display of technical tricks. She learned the proper mix of works to form a good repertoire and the number of dancers needed to perform them. And she analysed the different types of artist, from the purely classical *danseur noble* with his 'lethargy and lyrical musicality', through the brilliantly speedy and precise virtuoso *demi-caractère* dancer to the specialist in character and mime.

Severe about the proper use of these, she was equally firm about the behaviour of the audience, with a special horror of applause and flowers: dancers, for her, were just members of a dedicated team serving their art. Her favourite date with the Ballets Russes was Cologne, where such demonstrations were forbidden; though impressed by intellect (her chapters carry *envois* by Nietzsche, Charles Lamb, Samuel Johnson and Matthew Arnold), she found it inessential to a performer; and she became acutely aware of the dangers of undisciplined temperament.

In fact her attitudes were based on the Victorian Protestant ethic and these suited exactly the function of a national troupe as she saw it. For, in spite of the regal glamour of her company today and of her theatrical pseudonym, she is deeply democratic by instinct. A 'people's theatre' is where she began and where she feels happiest. Galas and grandees are accepted as part of the job, but backstage is where she belongs.

There what she calls her 'practical idealism' – a formula which

232

permits ruthless principles riddled with exceptions – her obstinate grit (she has hardly passed a day for years without pain) and her totally unassuming and accessible humanity find their best outlet. There 'Madam', as she is universally nicknamed, still reigns, even if she no longer rules. She has no need of applause or flowers; perhaps her mother's choice of a royal pseudonym was right after all, for there is a touch of majesty in her achievement.

17.5.81

## Jiri Kylian and Nederlands Dans Theater in Paris

Choreographers are the rarest of all creative artists; even a minor dance-arranger is a precious commodity and major talents are so few that only one or two appear in the whole world of dance in every generation. A three-day visit to Paris last week confirmed that we have a new one among us. He is thirty-four years old, born in Czechoslovakia, and currently directing the Nederlands Dans Theater, which is appearing at the Théâtre de la Ville. His name is Jiri Kylian.

The company used to be a regular visitor to London and Kylian himself is not entirely unknown here. After initial training in his home town of Prague, he spent a year as a student at the Royal Ballet School. John Cranko spotted him there and invited him to Stuttgart, where he soon began to show promise as a choreographer. In 1973 he became joint artistic director of the modern Dutch company and in 1978 he took over sole charge.

London has seen samples of his work danced by other companies – the Stuttgart Ballet will present two during its forthcoming season at the Coliseum – and for his own troupe he has arranged over a dozen ballets. The programmes in Paris consist entirely of his choreography. Both there and in New York, where he had a triumphant season last year, the company has both packed the theatre and delighted the critics. Kylian seems to be a genuinely original talent who immediately appeals to the public.

It is easy to see why. He is not avant garde in the sense of demanding a new set of judgement values to appreciate his work as, say, Merce Cunningham did when he first appeared. Nor is he revolutionary in his approach to ballet, rejecting its theatrical conventions and apparatus as some contemporary troupes do. Even his

233

movement-language is mostly familiar, compared with that of experiments by some of his predecessors in Holland.

Kylian's training in Prague gave him a belief in art as a human communication and a deep grounding in folk dance. He fell in love with the music of his compatriots, Bartok and Janacek – both deeply imbued with popular idioms. Then, in London and Stuttgart, he absorbed the rich vocabulary of classical ballet. His ballets – to judge by those I have seen – are musical, plastic and theatrical in the accepted sense. Yet they strike an immediately recognisable note of individuality and invention.

His approach is broad-based but sharp-tipped; he demands a special instrument for its expression. The team he directs consists of thirty-two dancers, but they are really two alternating teams. They are of many nationalities from many schools and vary widely in shape and size. Yet their way of moving is so special and uniform that they suggest a flock of birds of the same species. Amazingly, they have at present no ballet-master, nor even a regular teacher. It is evidently Kylian himself who imposes his demands.

The style is unmistakably shaped to fit Kylian's own choreography – fleet, finely balanced and strong, athletic but not showy, quick but not jerky, expressive but never sentimental. Of the six ballets shown in Paris, one is an outright masterpiece, *Symphony of Psalms*. Set to Stravinsky's magisterial score, with a brilliant setting (simply curtains of old carpets and a few chairs) by William Katz, it was shown by BBC television last autumn as one of the ballets chosen by Nureyev for his 'Invitation to the Dance' series. In the theatre its effect is overpowering.

Kylian has matched the score's driving but serious rhythms with dynamic patterns of fast, vigorous leaps and runs alternated with instant stops, quiet walking, small, simple gestures of foot or hand or head, and moments of solemn stillness. There is no trace of religion, yet a strong ritual reigns; there is no obvious invention, yet each combination is arrestingly new and unforgettable.

It is matched by a totally different work *Kinderspelen* (*Children's Games*). Set to an improbable combination of taped sounds and two of Mahler's 'Songs for Dead Children', this draws on the rich theatrical tradition which has produced modern Polish directors such as Grabowski. Strange, illogical and dreamlike, it shows a Bosch-like fantasy in which children in rag-bag nightshirts and underwear seem to act out the follies and tragedies of their parents. Dance and drama, music and poetic vision, are miraculously fused.

The other ballets range from near-classical variations of Balan-chinesque ingenuity to irresistible proto-folk numbers, from virtuoso pyrotechnics to show off his company to a hyper-dramatic war piece to Martinu's impressive Field Mass. Kylián seems to offer a valid European alternative to the once invaluable, but now increasingly arid influence of contemporary American choreographers. The sooner London sees his ballets danced by his company the better; he might well provide a language more in tune with our own national temperament.

24.5.81

## Nureyev, twenty years on

This year certainly gets top marks for celebrations. Yet another was clocked up last Wednesday, the twentieth anniversary of Nureyev's somewhat abrupt decision to make his career in the West.

It is still too soon to estimate the full effect. Tartar invasions are notoriously uncomfortable and the descent of this visibly dangerous cat among the peaceful pigeons of Western ballet caused flutters which still set up vibrations. As always, they tend to camouflage the more purely technical side of his contribution which, by a lucky chance, can be assessed at first-hand in his performances at the Coliseum, where his sixth festival has just opened with a week of *Giselle* with the Festival Ballet.

No ballet could be better to study his approach. The role of the 'hero' Albrecht is one he has been dancing right through his career. It was one of the first he performed in Russia, as a precocious twenty-one-year-old, opposite the Kirov ballerina Dudinskaya and it was also the ballet in which he made his Covent Garden debut with Margot Fonteyn. Watching him in it last week, this time with Evdokimova, it was fascinating to compare and learn, to observe the similarities with those early performances and mark the differences today.

The visionary second act has remained virtually the same, but wonderfully refined and intensified. Nureyev has been lucky enough to have preserved his classical line, and his *arabesque* today is virtually identical with that shown in photographs taken in his youth in Leningrad. Nor has he lost his romantic aura, which can raise pathos almost to tragedy. But he has developed even further his concept of an acting style which should be an extension of the dance idiom – I can recall him explaining that the 'mad scene' was basically just another variation – and one can feel now that every tiny detail is the result of reflection. A striking example is his entrance with flowers for Giselle's grave. Often a rather perfunctory bit of business, this is now a sustained and modulated cantilena which could be the subject of a whole thesis on the romantic style.

21.6.81

## The Twyla Tharp Dance Foundation at Sadler's Wells

The American Dance Season at Sadler's Wells moved into its second phase last week with the arrival of the most vigorously transatlantic of all companies, the Twyla Tharp Dance Foundation. Its flavour is pure Manhattan – that mixture of wry wit and treacly nostalgia, cuteness, energy and calculated sloppiness, slick showbiz *chutzpah* and alert intellectual rigour which makes up the Broadway cocktail. This tangy bouquet hit the London dance world seven years ago, when Tharp brought her first little band of finely honed hoofers to the Roundhouse. Seen in retrospect, its arrival was not so strange. It formed part of the surge of American parking-lot culture which swept over Europe on the tide of Pop Art. It was an exhilarating and healthy experience. It still is, though now it inevitably looms less large as it falls into historical perspective. Tharp's style, based on negro dance as handed down in music-hall routines – fast, dazzlingly deft and acrobatic, with an underlying self-mockery – is familiar from modern New York musicals. And the use of popular art forms in a sophisticated way is an idiom exploited in many fields.

Tharp remains a master of this craft; her new pieces show the same virtuosity of invention as the older ones – works like the *Eight Jelly Rolls* and *Rags Suite* – which shone so new and bright when we first saw them; and the troupe she has assembled is as lively, skilled and well-rehearsed as before. What is now clearer is the outline of her talent, which is definite but narrow. When she strays outside it towards emotion or narrative, or even conventional revue routine, symptoms of triteness and fussy repetition begin to show.

The result is a diminishing return. The opening six or seven minutes of the season was dazzling – a solo performed with

236

breathtaking dash and ease by William Whitener. It emerged that this single number conveyed just about the whole of Tharp's message (though the solos danced by Jennifer Way and Shelley Washington ran it close). I suspect that her devotion to old-time jazz restricts her, it certainly contributes to the monotony which steals over the programmes (particularly when relayed over a fearsome loudspeaker system). The variations in style from one short ballet to the next are like changes of stitch in a tapestry: the overall effect is unchanged. If you like the idiom, you will enjoy yourself from the start; but don't look for variety or surprises.

28.6.81

*With her wit, nostalgic love of show-biz and polished artifice, Twyla Tharp seems a symbol both of New York today and of the Paris of yesterday. Her tone is a close parallel to that of the French musicians known as Les Six. It will be interesting to see what she can do when she takes her tongue out of her cheek and puts some heart into her chic.*

## Nureyev in *Swan Lake* at Covent Garden

Some kind of time warp seemed to hit Covent Garden last weekend. The curtain rose on the familiar setting of the current *Swan Lake* and in no time a familiar figure came running on, bright-eyed, ardent, boyishly slim, as keen to get on with the show as we all were – Rudolf Nureyev. Six years had slipped away as if by magic.

It turned out to be the start of a masterly contrived evening. Rejecting the youthful arrogance which at one time he injected into the role, together with the defiant panache with which he used to stop the show in the big Act III solo, he concentrated instead on a seamlessly consistent interpretation of the whole role in which every detail of acting and dancing was integrated both with the character of the Prince and with the rest of the company. Curiously, he looked more intimately a member of the company than ever before. The breathtaking virtuosities which used to hold up the show were missing. There was no forcing, but instead a model of perfectly paced and stylish dancing, with his own very individual way of moving and subtle variations of speed and dynamics which brought life to the smallest incidents; the contrast between the moody Prince and the ecstatically transported lover was clearly but unostentatiously emphasised. To put it briefly, he looked happily at home.

His Odette/Odile was Lesley Collier, never a cut-out model for a romantic ballerina; but she is an artist of such dramatic gifts, spirit and impressive technique that she can carry conviction to every role. She and Nureyev seemed to strike an immediate rapport, and their *pas de deux* were both secure and touching. The company, always at its best in the classics, was in top form, with the *corps de ballet* unmatched in gentle unity and some fine individual performances. The *pas de trois* in Act I was a beautifully matched trio – Fiona Chadwick, Deirdre Eyden and Phillip Broomhead; Gerd Larsen and Leslie Edwards entered the new spirit with quiet authority and the Act I waltz went as smooth as silk.

The sure overall grasp of the ballet's stature and style threw into uncomfortable relief some patches which still mar it: let us hope that we shall see jettisoned once and for all the botched-up costumes that have been compiled from previous Leslie Hurry versions; that Ashton will rethink the cheerfully perky but incongruous solos in his otherwise splendid *pas de quatre*; and that some traces of the charming original choreography will be restored to Wayne Sleep's manic whirligig Tarantella.

21.2.82

## *La Bayadère*, The Royal Ballet, Covent Garden

There is probably no finer example of the way in which a single stroke of genius can summon up what sometimes takes a mountain of scenery, lighting, dry ice, gauze and fancy costumes to convey than Petipa's extraordinary and – in its day revolutionary – choreography for the Dream Sequence in *La Bayadère*, which returned to Covent Garden on Thursday. That now celebrated slow cascade of girls undulating down out of the darkness as they emerge into the imprisoned Solor's imagination has the hypnotic effect of a Warhol film repeated over and over until reality and illusion merge. The ballet's ingredients are in fact very subtle; intricate floor-patterns; an important, indeed vital, role for the *corps de ballet*; some of the most 'exposed', demanding and musically satisfying of all Petipa's variations for the soloists; and, for the stars, the role of holding absolute domination of the stage in some exquisite *pas de deux*.

The virtuoso solo for the hero is a later interpolation from an early scene – necessarily so, because in the full story this whole episode passes through his mind as he sleeps. On Thursday, Nureyev seemed, in fact, almost as much a vision as the rest of the cast. Could that really be him again stalking the stage, proud and aloof beneath his osprey head-dress as he used to nineteen years ago? It was; and we must be grateful for all the elements which have restored to us this whole visionary Garden Of Delights.

The ballet was a triumph for the company on that first night, and the audience's obvious welcome last week proved it so again. Maybe the *corps* has not yet completely recaptured the original softly swaying rhythm like corn in the wind – but it was already a joy to watch and will undoubtedly get even better. The three soloists (traditionally always the most rewarding roles) were Bryony Brind, Ravenna Tucker and Fiona Chadwick – with Tucker's perhaps the most perfectly phrased dancing on this occasion. As for the principals, Merle Park contributed exactly the right mixture of brilliance and classical poise, while Nureyev remains the undisputed king of this particular jungle. He is more of a lion now than a panther – but nobody can better display the structure, timing and emphasis of a step or of a whole variation; and above all he brings what the company needs most of all, a sense of style which is more than just skin deep.

28.2.82

# Index

242

244

247